The Outport People

Claire Mowat

KEY PORTER BOOKS

Library and Archives Canada Cataloguing in Publication

Mowat, Claire
        The outport people / Claire Mowat.

ISBN 1-55263-647-X

1. Mowat, Claire. 2. Mowat, Farley, 1921–.
3. Newfoundland and Labrador—Social life and customs—Fiction.
4. Fishing villages—Newfoundland and Labrador—Fiction.
I. Title.

PS8576.O985Z47 2005   C813'.54   C2004-906694-3

THE CANADA COUNCIL   LE CONSEIL DES ARTS
FOR THE ARTS   DU CANADA
SINCE 1957   DEPUIS 1957

ONTARIO ARTS COUNCIL
CONSEIL DES ARTS DE L'ONTARIO

The publisher gratefully acknowledges the support of the Canada Council for the Arts
and the Ontario Arts Council for its publishing program. We acknowledge the support
of the Government of Ontario through the Ontario Media Development Corporation's
Ontario Book Initiative.

We acknowledge the financial support of the Government of Canada through the Book
Publishing Industry Development Program (BPIDP) for our publishing activities.

Key Porter Books Limited
Six Adelaide Street East, Tenth Floor
Toronto, Ontario
Canada M5C 1H6

www.keyporter.com

Text design: Peter Maher
Electronic formatting: Beth Crane, Heidy Lawrance Associates

Printed and bound in Canada

05 06 07 08 09 6 5 4 3 2

To Farley,
who encouraged me

Author's Note

BALEENA CANNOT BE FOUND ON THE MAP, but there are dozens of places very much like it—harsh and beautiful and home to thousands of people who struggle to make their livelihood from the sea and the small portion of arable land that was left behind after the glaciers retreated.

I spent several years living among them and this book is a fictional memoir of those years. The people I knew retain their anonymity. Apart from my husband and myself and a few public figures, all other characters in this book are fictitious. If I have used anyone's real name, it is accidental and occurred because I have selected Christian names and family names that are indigenous to Newfoundland.

My thanks to Lily Miller for her invaluable editorial advice. I'm also grateful to Robin Long, who provided me with a place to work. My deepest gratitude, of course, goes to the people of Newfoundland among whom I lived.

Preface to the New Edition

THIS BOOK IS HISTORY NOW. First published in 1983, it chronicles the life my husband and I lived in a Newfoundland outport from 1962 to 1967. I knew then that the lives of the outport people would inevitably change but I could never have imagined by how much.

There were no telephones when we arrived there by sea in our little schooner. There was no road leading out of nor into the community. Television had yet to arrive and, apart from the men who left to work seasonally elsewhere, most residents' view of the wider world was limited to the grainy films shown in the parish hall and to the few books and magazines available in the tiny village library, which was open only six hours a week. This isolation had its advantages but it also brought some hardships, such as the absence of dentistry, except for a technician who arrived on the coast boat, once a year, to fit dentures to replace teeth that had been painfully extracted by a nurse in the cottage hospital.

Our outport had full employment, with a large fish freezing plant, a fleet of draggers and the assorted jobs that accompanied an active fishery—even if it was cold, harsh work and poorly paid. Family life was fundamental and reliable. In those days before birth control information, it was not unusual for a couple to have a dozen children. In the 1960s, Newfoundland had the highest birth rate in

Canada. Today, Newfoundland and Labrador (as the province is now officially called) has the lowest birth rate in the country.

Cod, the economic base of this seabound land since the fifteenth century, were dwindling in numbers even forty years ago, but no one in government or business was prepared to heed the warnings. The rape of the ocean continued unabated to its inevitable end.

Now most of the fish plants are closed and the draggers have been scrapped. Young people have moved away by the thousands and their much smaller families are being born in Ontario or Alberta or even as far away as Norway or Hong Kong. Legions of Newfoundland grandparents travel great distances to visit grandchildren who, in that bygone era, usually lived just down the road.

In recent years tourists have discovered the generous nature of the people and the scenic grandeur of a land which, when I lived there, barely existed in the consciousness of most Canadians. Happily, that has changed now that a generation of talented homegrown writers, painters, actors and musicians are telling the stories of "The Rock" to the rest of the world.

As for me, I wouldn't have missed my Newfoundland years for anything. Part of me will belong there always.

CLAIRE MOWAT
Port Hope, Ontario
January 2005

*The
Outport
People*

One

MAPS ARE SEDUCTIVE. And I'm not the first person to fall in love with one. It hung on the back wall of our windowless office in Simpsons-Sears Store Planning Department. One of our draughtsmen had brought it back with him after a three-month stint supervising the construction of our new store in St. John's, Newfoundland. He used to amuse us with funny stories about that odd province, the dialect of the workmen he hired, the ferocious weather, the terrible food in the restaurants, the exasperating shortages of everything. He told us about the time he had to phone head office and tell them there were absolutely no finishing nails to be bought anywhere in the entire city; and no one had believed him. But it was the truth, there weren't any. And the nearest big city—Halifax, Nova Scotia—was nine hundred miles away. They had to delay the store opening for two weeks—the time it took to get a supply of nails from Toronto to St. John's through the blizzards of February and the insouciance of the local freight handlers.

Head office was not amused. But I was. We opened a lot of new Simpsons-Sears stores during the four years I worked there—but the draughtsmen's stories from Burnaby or Rouyn or Galt were never so amusing as the ones we heard about building stores in Newfoundland. Often when I came back from my lunch hour, fresh from the squalor of Dundas Street, the sulphuric smell of the Toronto air and the heat of a July noon, I used to stare at the Newfoundland map, entranced by the icon of that distant island of cool winds surrounded by the blue Atlantic. In time I almost memorized the map. I could feel the salt spray on my face and hear the foghorns bleating in the distance, along with church bells on quiet Sunday mornings. What kind of place was it where people named their towns Heart's Content or Witless Bay or Joe Batt's Arm, apparently with a straight face? Who were these people who didn't give a damn about finishing nails or schedules that came from Toronto? Or Canada itself, for that matter, because a decade earlier only half of them had voted to join us. I only knew it was a place that had to be totally unlike Toronto. I didn't know then how I was going to do it, but I knew that someday I would find my way there.

The sky over Port-aux-Basques was as grey as pewter. It was an afternoon late in October, three years after Newfoundland had first caught my imagination. The wind quickened my progress up the gangway of the *Baccalieu*, a sturdy Glasgow-built ship which was going to take us along the coast of the windblown island of my dreams. That weekly ship, and her sisters, the *Burgeo*, *Bar Haven* and *Bonavista*, provided the link between forty isolated coastal communities and the rest of the world. Each Saturday one of the ships sailed eastbound and one westbound along a rockbound shore which was without roads, railroads or airports.

A long blast from the ship's horn announced our impending departure. My husband put his arm around me as we stood by the rail shivering in the wind and watched the unlovely terminal town gradually disappear behind us.

Ahead of us lay our new home in the outport village of Baleena.

I had married an author—a man who could pack up his typewriter and make his living anyplace in the world within reach of a post office. And by one of those flukes of fate that make you wonder if someone up there is looking after you, he shared my infatuation with that windswept rock; and so we decided, irrationally and passionately, to live there. Of course we had a number of logical reasons for doing so. It was going to be so much cheaper to live in an outport where houses were half the price they were in Ontario, and without roads we wouldn't need a car. We planned to eat a lot of fresh fish and wild berries. I would make my own bread and my own clothes. We would be as far away as possible from the vexations of the urban, managed world. There were a lot of sound reasons but they had little to do with our decision. The truth was that we were in love with the idea of the place. We would have gone there no matter what the cost or the difficulties. The sixteen hours of choppy seas that lay between Port-aux-Basques and Baleena were as nothing to us that cold Saturday. The ship plunged and rolled in a heavy swell as she sailed east through a moonless night. We lay snug in our bunks filled with optimistic dreams.

The government wharf at Baleena was far from crowded at breakfast time on Sunday morning as the *Baccalieu* approached the dock. A few men wearing heavy jackets and peaked caps huddled by the freight shed, out of the wind. A family carrying suitcases was struggling along a gravel road towards the wharf. A clutch of boys watched attentively as the mooring lines were thrown from the deck of the ship. Two men caught the lines and made them fast to the bollards on the wharf with considerable difficulty because of a fierce east wind pushing the ship away.

Two old trucks were parked nearby. One looked as if it was in the final stages of its life. The other was a slightly more recent model but it had two fenders missing. The only motor vehicles on the entire coast were a few trucks like these. Although it was 1962—the year of the Corvette, the Fairlane and the Grand Prix—there wasn't a single passenger car for two hundred miles. Nor was there a foot of pavement.

Baleena appeared to be a haphazard scattering of small tidy houses connected by pathways and bumpy trails. Houses seemed to grow together in clusters in those places where massive boulders and rocks did not. Spindly fences and stunted spruce trees outlined and dotted the scene. There wasn't a tree anywhere that was taller than a man. Only two structures stood high above the rocks and the houses—the steeples of the two churches, Anglican and United. Close to nine hundred people lived in this place in which the major technological trinkets of this century had yet to arrive. Most of them had never seen a car except in the movies. Wherever people went, it was on foot or by boat. I was going to become one of them and, since my idea of Heaven is a place without cars, I couldn't believe my good luck.

"Figured you to be on this steamer," said a short man with a hawk nose as he approached Farley. "Seein' as how your freight come on the last boat. And mail and parcels. You and yer missus can ride to the cove with me. Dan Quayle's me name," he added as an afterthought. "Dan

16

Quayle Junior they calls me since me father got the same name as I. Me dory's alongside here."

We were about to become Dan Quayle Junior's next-door neighbours. He was a shopkeeper and so we waited on the wharf until his dory was piled high with cartons and sacks for his shop, and then finally with our own luggage. We climbed cautiously down a ladder at the side of the wharf, and found a space to sit in the crowded boat. Dan followed us down, and so did a small boy who hadn't been in evidence before. He was Dan's son, a thin lad of eight or so, who looked long and hard at us but said nothing.

"That's Jackie. He's the shy one," said Dan.

He spun the flywheel and the single-cylinder engine coughed into life. Loaded to the gunwales we chugged along at a slow, steady pace through a waterway that led past several small coves and inlets, past coveys of dories quietly at anchor in front of unawakened houses. Under a sky that foretold rain before long, we saw occasional meandering dogs but few people. Dan steered a sure course in the lee of a string of bald uninhabited islands and through a chain of partly submerged reefs. Though these looked menacing, they protected us from the ocean's swells. Dan didn't know where all the rocks were, he told us later on, but he knew where they weren't.

Baleena, a mere dot on any map, was officially one community but in fact it was really five. At the western-most end towards which we were heading was Dog Cove, our home-to-be. At the government wharf we had been in Round Harbour. Between these two and presided over by a gothic wooden church was Muddy Hole. Over on the north side, near the fish plant, was The Gut. And at the eastern end was Hann's Island. Dan, who explained all this to us, didn't seem to know where Baleena itself was. "P'r'aps down around the post office," he speculated. There was only one post office, a single bureaucratic designation for everyone.

We rounded a small island of grey granite topped with a pelt of tawny grass, and suddenly there it was, lonely as a lighthouse, the house we had impulsively bought a few months earlier during a brief summer visit to Baleena. I had had a lot of reservations about it afterwards, wondering just what we'd done. Were we crazy—buying a house in an isolated place like this where we had no friends, no relatives, no past and only a questionable future? How would I feel about the impulsive act of a summer vacation when the reality of winter came upon us? Well, I would soon find out.

Our new home stood apart from its neighbours, its clapboard walls painted a pristine white in contrast to the turquoise, yellow and green of the other houses. Behind it was a steep rocky slope, with a marsh below, and beyond that only the cold and stormy North Atlantic.

About a dozen children and two grey-haired men were waiting on Dan Quayle Junior's stage as the dory sputtered to a stop. A boy quickly tied the dory's line to a post and we clambered out.

"Hello," I said tentatively to the group in general. The children stared back in silence, and the two older men merely nodded. Nevertheless, all hands pitched in to help haul our luggage out of the dory. When it was all ashore, one of the men finally spoke to Farley.

"I'm Dan Quayle," he said in a shy but cordial tone. "Dan Quayle Senior, they calls me, since me son here got the same name as I. Reckon you're the first strangers iver we had come live here in Dog Cove, you and yer woman," he concluded, casting a sidelong glance at me.

"Well, I hope we won't be strangers long," Farley offered hopefully. There were no reassuring words in reply. A flurry of activity developed as the children vied with each other to help carry our luggage up to our new house. The ones who lost out got to carry the more mundane cartons and crates up to Dan Quayle Junior's house. I could see no sign of a shop. It was there, nonetheless, in a room at the back of the house behind an unmarked wooden storm door. There were no signs and no advertisements since everyone who shopped there *knew* where it was.

We led the parade towards our small bungalow. The back door was ajar and I stepped warily inside, unsure how I would react. But the kitchen was warm and welcoming. Dan Junior had fired the oil range into action the night before. Children strode in purposefully with our suitcases and garment bags and portable typewriters. For a while they wandered in and out, then most of them drifted back down to the dory to finish unloading the merchandise for the shop. Finally we were left with only Dan Quayle Senior and a little girl of seven or eight who was his youngest daughter. The girl had something in a brown paper bag which she held out to us.

"Me missus sent this fer you," Dan said. It was a loaf of homemade bread, a gift more welcome than roses since it was Sunday and the shops were closed, there were no restaurants, and there wasn't a morsel of food in our new house.

"And that's me house there," Dan said, pointing through our window to a rooftop about two hundred yards away.

"If iver you've a mind to, you come over. Bein' strangers, 'twill be lonesome. I bides home every night 'cept Mondays when I goes to town council meeting."

We felt doubly blessed that our two nearest neighbours, father and son, were so concerned about us.

As we stood there chatting, I began to look around our house, my very first home as a bride. The furniture we had ordered from the mail-order catalogues—which had seemed like a mammoth purchase at the time—had all arrived. There was a refrigerator, a table and four chairs, a rug, a couch, a bed and a chest of drawers. But it wasn't nearly enough to fill the five rooms. And everywhere I looked I saw things that needed fixing or finishing.

This six-year-old house had never, in fact, been finished. The kitchen was by far the biggest room, and the other rooms branched out from there. There was a tiny parlour—a room intended for ceremonial use such as weddings or funerals or visits from the clergyman. The two bedrooms were also small and neither of them had a door in the frame. There was a minuscule room which was intended to become a bathroom, though it contained no running water or fixtures. Although the kitchen floor was covered in salmon pink and turquoise blue checkered vinyl tiles, the other rooms had only rough subflooring. There was still a lot to be done to finish the place, and some of it had to be converted into office space so Farley would have a place to write.

"You don't happen to be a carpenter, do you, Mr. Quayle?" I asked.

"No, missus, I works down to the plant," he said with considerable pride. "I'm foreman in the packing room. Got twenty-six women as works fer me. Fish is plentiful just now. So is the work. Yes, Mr. Drake hired me on back in 1952. Been there iver since. But I b'lieve I knows where I can find you a carpenter if you wants one. A man come round looking fer to work a fortnight back. Not one of we people. Man from down the coast—belongs to Wilfred's Harbour."

"Send him over to see us," Farley said. "We're going to need all the help we can find."

Frank Oxford arrived early the next day. He had just finished a job for the doctor's wife, helping to build a stable. Now that it was getting too cold for outdoor work, he was delighted at the chance to find a few more weeks' employment indoors. He came up the coast to look for work from time to time. Most of the men from Wilfred's Harbour—a small outport thirty miles or so east of us—went away to work. Some went to the Great Lakes, where they worked aboard ships during the season that ran from April till early December. Frank hadn't wanted to do that, he explained, because his only son, who was five, had been born blind and Frank didn't like to be away from the child for too long a time. All too soon the boy would have to go away himself to a special school in Nova Scotia.

Short and slight of build, Frank was a soft-spoken man with kindly brown eyes. In Baleena he lived in the tiny forepeak of his trap boat, which he had rigged out with a narrow bunk and a small coal stove. When we discovered he had nowhere to eat except aboard his cramped boat and had been existing mainly on cold tinned food for several weeks, I insisted he eat with us.

I hope Frank never realized it, but he thus became almost a guinea pig in a one-woman cooking festival. Liberated from having to go out to work, I at last had my own kitchen and some time to spare, so I was bent on trying out all the recipes I'd been collecting for years. No more hurry-up meals of canned soup or bacon and eggs—the sort of food I had eaten when I lived alone. I was particularly determined to learn how to cook fish now that I was in a place where it was so readily available. And this I did, with Frank and Farley as my test subjects. Although fish was the staple food of Newfoundland, I'm sure Frank had never before eaten Dover Sole Bonne Femme, Bouillabaisse or Scallops St. Jacques; and though he approached these dishes with some hesitancy, he ate them all. He politely ate my first sad efforts at homemade bread too, with a dent in the centre that looked like one of the craters on the moon.

After dinner we would sit around and chat over a cup of coffee, and Frank gradually overcame his shyness and talked freely to us. He was much worried about the future of Wilfred's Harbour. There were too many old people there, and not enough children. He wondered who was going to keep things going in a few years' time. A lot of those young men who went away to the Lakes to work didn't come back. At least not to stay. The three of us pondered the problem, but we newcomers had no solutions to offer.

All three of us worked on the house. I painted walls and cupboards while Frank and Farley hammered away at doors and floors and baseboards. They installed bathroom fixtures and in order to get running water they ran an intake pipe to a shallow well they dug in the muskeg behind the house. It was only six feet deep but the rain kept it full. The water was the colour of clear tea but it was pure and we soon got used to the colour. They also dug a sewer line and installed a pipe that led downhill into the sea a hundred yards away. No one objected to this simplistic sewer system on either sanitary or ecological grounds. In a land that was both too marshy and too rocky for septic tanks, the standard practice of all our neighbours had always been to empty the night bucket over the side of the wharf every morning.

Little by little the house began to look as if it was really ours. Frank boarded up the foundation, which had previously stood open to the wind, and built a large bright office there for Farley. It had two windows—one that looked east to the sea and another that faced north to a gigantic boulder covered with lichens. However, the house couldn't be finished that year because we began to run out of money and Frank began to run short of time. The weather was steadily getting worse as pelting rain and gale-force winds assaulted us. It was becoming too risky to travel the coast in a small boat.

As the stormy blasts became more frequent, Frank began to look for a "civil" day when he could dash for home. Then one day the wind died, the sea grew calm under a pale November sun and Frank, like a migratory bird, was gone. We didn't see him again until the following year.

Two

SHORTLY AFTER FRANK'S DEPARTURE, I was startled one afternoon to find three little girls sitting on the daybed in our kitchen. I had been typing and hadn't heard them come in.

"Hello there," I said brightly. One of them smiled tentatively but the other two didn't. I commiserated with them about the bad weather that day, but there was no reply, just guarded glances. Trying to establish some friendly contact, I decided to ask them their names. They looked at the floor, at the ceiling, and at each other, but made no answer. I concluded that they were shy; very, very shy. I tried harder to draw them out of their shells. I asked them where they lived, if they went to school yet, and if they had brothers or sisters. They giggled a bit, but still no one responded. Their silence was disconcerting and I felt flustered.

Since I was in the kitchen anyway, I decided to make a cup of tea. I put some cookies on a plate and offered them to the children. The youngest girl gingerly took one, but the other two silently declined. Obviously they had not come expecting a snack. Why then, I wondered, were they here at all? I continued to chatter inanely, smiling a fixed smile at the children as I drank my cup of tea. After about fifteen minutes they suddenly got up and left, without explanation and without apology, leaving me very confused.

As the days passed, several other children came to call, including older ones who came after school or on Saturdays or Sundays. But despite the relative maturity of the older ones, they behaved in much the same manner as the smaller children had. They had almost nothing to volunteer, nor were they willing to answer any questions. They just sat there in silence, watching every move I made as if I were some strange specimen in a zoo. Eventually, in utter frustration, I gave up trying to be a bright conversationalist, and whenever my solemn young visitors came calling I merely greeted them, and, after a few words about the weather, continued doing whatever I had been doing.

And that, it took me a long time to realize, was precisely what I was supposed to do. The role of visiting children, as well as that of many adults, was simply to *be* there. They did not feel obliged to do or say anything, nor did they expect me to alter my daily routine for them. All the while that I had persisted with my prying questions and silly remarks, they felt the same squirming embarrassment that I might have experienced if some stranger in, say, a bus station kept probing me with personal questions.

Gradually I realized that our kitchen, along with every kitchen in every outport, was public space. Any time of day, from breakfast to bedtime, might bring unannounced visitors who simply came in and sat down. Farley and I quickly learned not to wander into the kitchen in our underwear. Our visitors were almost always men or children. The neighbouring women rarely ventured into our kitchen, alone or in company.

Having been brought up in the city where doorbells and locks guarded one's privacy, it took me a while to come to terms with this new concept. But I began to enjoy the parade of young visitors who came as an audience, not as actors. As time passed they did begin to talk a little but they were as hushed as they might have been in church. Outdoors they ran and shouted and shoved and chased each other with abandon, yet when they entered our kitchen, or any kitchen, a self-imposed quiet descended. No raised voices, no attention-getting trickery, no little games. They were an Observers' Corps, content to watch and listen with an intensity that may have been flattering but which could also be embarrassing to someone like myself who was by no means sure of the role I was expected to fulfil.

Two girls who came more frequently than the rest—as if they had singled me out in some special way—were eleven-year-old Dorothy, and Ruth, who was twelve. They were inseparable best friends in the way little girls can be. Both of them bore the last name of Quayle, and both had brown hair and brown eyes, but they were not sisters. Ruth was Dan Quayle Senior's daughter, while Dorothy was Dan Quayle Junior's. They were aunt and niece. Ruth, a year older than her niece, had a round dimpled face but seldom smiled. Dorothy had an angular face with a finely boned nose and a tendency to break into a grin whenever she spoke to me.

In due course, as other children told me their names, we realized that we were surrounded by a large flock of people bearing the surname Quayle, the name of a bird which, ironically, had never been seen in Newfoundland. There were the assorted offspring of Dan Quayle Senior, and of his sons Dan Junior and Clarence and Charlie Quayle. "I'se Charlie's bye," or "Dan Senior's girl," they would explain patiently. It took me a long time to sort out the tangle of sisters and brothers and cousins and aunts.

All of the Quayles in Dog Cove were descended from John and Etta Quayle. Both in their eighties, they lived in a tidy wooden house in what was known as the "bottom" of Dog Cove, a grassy area that was further inland from the sea. Of the nine children born to John and Etta half a century earlier, only one remained here. The others had either died in infancy or emigrated to the "Boston" states, as the New England states were known, as soon as they were old enough to work. Their one stay-at-home son was Daniel Quayle Senior, our amicable neighbour, then aged fifty-eight. He and his wife, Lizzie, were the parents of sixteen children. And of those sixteen, eight were married and raising families hereabouts.

John and Etta Quayle had no cause to worry about a lonely old age. They had at least thirty-five direct descendants living within walking distance. Another sixty or so lived in Massachusetts, but these they had never seen.

I had barely sorted out all the Quayles when another, less numerous group of children came calling. Their surname was "Pointing" and it was obvious that they were of a different breed. Thin children with pale faces and unkempt hair, they lacked the bright-eyed alertness of the Quayles. Their clothes were shabby and, often as not, dirty, and on the coldest days they went without overshoes, mitts and caps. They seemed to consort with no one other than their own brothers and sisters. Unlike the Quayle children, who mostly refused the cookies I passed around, the Pointing children hungrily took everything. And they soon started to ask for things—pencils, old clothes, books, orange juice for a sick brother—the list was long. They gladly took away our old magazines—*Chatelaine* and the *Star Weekly*—and I naively hoped that their mother might heed the sound domestic advice and the nutritious recipes.

Their house was a weathered, unpainted building badly in need of repairs. It was isolated at the very end of a pathway, standing apart like an outcast. Unlike the housebound wives of the brothers Quayle, Rosie Pointing seemed to be "on the go" a lot. I used to see her puffing up the hill, a plump woman with a well-proportioned face who couldn't have been more than thirty but was already the mother of six children, with a seventh on the way.

Once, after a day devoted to mastering the art of baking cakes, I gave Edith and Maizie Pointing a lemon sponge to take home to their family. Covered with fluffy lemon icing, it was a masterpiece, I modestly believed, which I wanted to share. I only asked the girls to bring me back the plate.

They were back within the hour, with the plate and a note from their mother.

"Please Mrs. Mote my birthday is Tuesday would you make me a cake like one you give Edith ony choclate and I will send up cake mix and icing sugar and I will pay you let me no from Mrs. Garland Pointing."

I read this note twice. Had my neighbourly gesture been misread as a promotion for a bakery service? I wondered. I was a little miffed that there had been no thanks offered, but even more so that Rosie thought I had used a cake mix.

"I'm sorry, Edith," I said after studying the note again, "tell your mother that I have to do some typing on Tuesday and I won't be doing any more baking this week."

Edith accepted this rebuff without any visible reaction. At the age of twelve she seemed worn out by an uncaring world.

"Pointings? I got no time for 'em," Dan Quayle Junior said flatly when I cautiously asked him about them. "Hard racket, that crowd. Humph. That Garland just goes off gunnin' whenever suits he. Sells a bit of wild meat different times. 'Tis all he's good for. And that woman of his. Humph. Always on the road. Them youngsters niver get a meal—just candy bars and chips from the shop." Dan shook his head in disapproval.

I told him about the cake I had given the girls and the note from Rosie. He smiled wryly.

"Don't you pay her no heed. Her birthday's not till the middle of summer. Don't do no good to give 'em nothing. Beat it down before your back is turned. I give 'em Susie's old coat what was too small for her, like new 'twas. Last week I seen it lying out in the mud with all the buttons tore off and a big rip into it. Not fit for nothin'. Best leave that lot be, missus."

I listened to his advice but I couldn't be heedless of the obvious plight of the Pointing children. Despite Dan's admonition, I did give them things—scarves or gloves or whatever I could find that might be of use to them for as long as they could keep track of it.

Only the youngest Pointings went to school with any regularity. I did not often see the oldest three—Edith, Harold and Maizie—joining the morning procession for the mile-long trek to school. Whatever cleaning and washing got done in their house was done by Edith and Maizie. Eleven-year-old Harold preferred to go gunning in the country with his father. He was the one who went stealthily from house to house after dark delivering parcels of out-of-season moose, caribou, ptarmigan, sea ducks or hares. The money from the sale of this illicit meat was added to their basic cash income—the Family Allowance cheques for the children, and an Old Age pension for Garland's mother, who lived with them.

Rosie doled out the money to the children when they were hungry, and then they headed for Dan Quayle's shop, where they spent it on childish choices that defied the dictums of nutritionists. When the money ran out, as it frequently did, Rosie did the rounds of the more prosperous homes of Baleena. They all knew her. People saved things for the Pointings.

It was little wonder that the several Quayle families, whose women baked bread every day, served a "cooked" dinner every noon, scoured their houses every Saturday, and whose laundry lines snapped and flapped with crisp clothes, had nothing but scorn for this slothful family.

But I shared something with Rosie Pointing, for I too liked to leave my house and walk around. While most families sent their children to do the shopping, one or two items at a time, I did the shopping myself. I bought everything that I could from our neighbourly Dan Quayle Junior, and what I couldn't find there I looked for in the larger shops that were located in Round Harbour or The Gut.

Dan's shop was a marvel of organization. In a room no bigger than the average living room, he ran a general store which stocked everything from rubber boots to tinned peas. Pots and pans dangled from ropes on the ceiling. Children's clothes were in cardboard boxes stacked unsteadily one upon the other. Potatoes, turnips, cabbages and carrots were stored in sacks in a cellar under the floor, while scribblers and pencils and Dodd's Kidney Pills were piled on shelves behind the counter. A barrel of salt beef stood in one corner, under a shelf full of fishing gear. Dan and Melita Quayle ran the shop themselves, assisted by the oldest of their four children—eleven-year-old Dorothy. The three of them knew exactly where everything was.

I love long walks, even in bad weather, and so I decided that the weekly trip to the post office to retrieve the mail, a mile away at Round Harbour, should be my chore rather than Farley's. The neighbouring women might think of me as a solitary, gung-ho athlete, but I knew I couldn't bear to stay indoors as much as they did.

A brave but faded metal sign bearing the Canadian coat of arms was the only visible indication that an unprepossessing doorway led to the post office, a rough-hewn addition built onto the side of the postmaster's house. Into it, and to a nearby building which housed the telegraph office, came almost all of the communications from the rest of the world. The so-called "lobby" was as gloomy within as it was outside. There was not a scrap of furniture, and in one corner was a large stack of empty mail bags that were peed on by visiting dogs. The only decorations were the framed portrait of the Queen and the notices that the federal government broadcast across the land; a torn reminder to mail your parcels early for Christmas, a faded poster extolling the virtues of a career in the Royal Canadian Mounted Police, and above them an official cardboard sign proclaiming "This Settlement Is Called ...." where, above the dotted line, someone had printed BALEENA. Not a village. Not a town. Only a settlement. Yet people had lived there for centuries and were long past the era of "settling." The sign had been there for so long no one noticed it anymore.

If the coast boat arrived on schedule on Sunday, the mail was ready by Monday afternoon (though in winter the ship could be anywhere from one to six days late). I learned to listen for the sound of her horn, day or night. That way I could calculate when to go and get the mail.

On my first trip to the post office I joined a group of people, mostly children, who stood in the lobby, staring at a dingy wall where a closed wicket and a closed door seemed to be staring back. The door opened and the postmaster's head appeared. Percy Hoddinott was the postmaster, and he and his wife and son sorted the mail.

"Hello, Mrs. Mowat, come right in please," he beckoned.

I was embarrassed by this preferential treatment and protested that I would wait in line with the others. He wouldn't hear of it. So, right in front of them, a group who didn't seem to see anything unusual about this invitation, I was ushered grandly into the inner sanctum beyond the wicket.

Whether I liked it or not, I was beginning to understand that I was living in a place with a tightly structured class system. That we were outsiders from the affluent "mainland," able to move in and buy a house and furnishings right away, put us a notch above the rank and file. There were undoubtedly other considerations in the general evaluation of where we fitted into the scheme of things which we did not yet know about. Whatever they were, Mr. Hoddinott had already decided to treat us with respect.

"We're almost finished," he said cheerily. "I've got your mail right over there." He pointed to a large stack of letters, magazines and parcels.

The interior of the post office was not much larger than my kitchen and I stood with my back against the door so I wouldn't be in anyone's way. The room was a wonder of organization, equal to Dan Quayle Junior's shop. There were parcels in stacks and mounds everywhere. The people of Baleena did most of their shopping through Eaton's and Simpsons-Sears mail-order catalogues, and it added up to an avalanche of parcels once a week. The rafters across the ceiling were loaded with parcels; one corner of the room was knee-deep in them. Even the tiny alcove for the chemical toilet had parcels in it.

"Your husband's quite a writer, I hear, Mrs. Mowat," Mr. Hoddinott said, deftly tucking government cheques into their allotted pigeon holes. "I'm something of a writer myself. Yes, I've got some stories to tell . . ." he chuckled as he kept on sorting. "Early days in the post office down Fortune Bay . . . I was all on my own those times. Had to run the telegraph as well as the post office and oftentimes I had to be the policeman, the welfare officer, even the minister. Used to read the burial service if we couldn't get anyone else. I could tell some stories. Oh my, yes."

I couldn't tell if Mr. Hoddinott had any talent for writing, but when he opened the wicket a few minutes later he displayed the most amazing talent for remembering names and faces. He knew every man, woman and child in Baleena. They had only to stand before him and he reached up or down or across or under and retrieved their mail. It was a system known only to himself, I'm sure, but it was fast and he never made a mistake. He had been a postmaster for thirty-four years.

The bulk and weight of our weekly mail turned out to be more than I had reckoned on. Mr. Hoddinott had to reserve a canvas mail bag just for us. The letters, the books and magazines plus the small items I ordered from the catalogues added up to a mighty load for the long walk home. I was almost exhausted by the time I got back, especially as winter had arrived and an icy northwest wind resisted every step I took.

Monday night when I returned with the mail bag was a mini-Christmas. Farley would meet me at the door with a hug and a drink and then together we would sit down and pore over the contents of the sack—our umbilical cord with the outside world. First we devoured the letters from relatives and friends. Then we read the newspapers, which were one or two weeks old when we got them, and then the magazines. Although we did hear the news on the radio, we felt blissfully detached from the problems of the rest of the world, which seemed as far away as Mars.

Rain turned to snow and back to rain again and at night the glass in our bedroom window rattled ominously. Almost every week a gale blew with such ferocity that in the more populous places of this world it would have made headline news. Winds of fifty, sixty and seventy knots were commonplace, and gusts reaching a hundred knots were not infrequent. At the railway terminal at Port-aux-Basques, empty freight cars were blown right off the track at least once every winter.

Fortunately these hurricane winds didn't come without warning. We watched the southern sky gradually turn from dove grey to slate. We bolted our doors against it and waited. It was known locally as a "blow"—surely one of the greatest understatements in the English language. The chimney whistled and the windows rattled as our small house vibrated on its foundations. Tremors could be seen on the water in the toilet bowl.

The first time it happened, I expected we would hear terrible tales of damage and destruction. But no one's roof blew off. Even windows and doors remained firmly intact. The single power line stayed in place atop poles that had been implanted in rock-filled cribs. Boats were moored with extra rope when a blow was expected. And small children were kept home from school. No one went outside unless it was an emergency. The coastal steamer took refuge in the nearest port and stayed until the storm had moved on. You didn't flaunt a man-made schedule in the face of this kind of weather.

Everything, including the trees, had adapted to the force of the wind. Where the stunted spruce trees grew, they huddled together like children waiting for a bus on a cold day. Their branches were so intertwined that they couldn't break off and smash into houses and power lines the way those of large deciduous trees do. A tall tree, like a maple or an elm, wouldn't have survived even one season.

Outport houses were built with only a slight slope to the roof. To have a peaked roof would have been to invite losing it to the wind. There was only one really tall building in all of Baleena and that was the Anglican church. Just after it was completed in 1907—an ambitious attempt to recreate an English cathedral in wood—a gale took off most of the roof. When the persevering parishioners got the second roof on, they wired it down with heavy steel cables attached to iron bolts embedded in the surrounding granite.

Wind was the chief peril of winter and not, surprisingly, the cold. The temperature hovered around the freezing point most of the time. "Glitter storms," which I had known by the less lyrical name of "freezing rain," were frequent and as enchanting as a Christmas window. Everything sparkled and glittered like a Russian fairy tale—houses, boats, wharves, clotheslines and the single power line. It was not so enchanting to try and walk anywhere when the pathways and rocks were glazed like petit fours.

Whatever kind of weather we got, it didn't last very long. Mingled with those tempestuous winter days when not even a bird could move, we had plenty of "civil" days. They dawned sunny and unexpectedly serene and mocked the calendar that told us it was December.

Three

IT WAS IN DECEMBER that year that Freeman and Barbara Drake migrated from Massachusetts back to Baleena. They owned the one and only industry in Baleena—the fish plant, a series of plain wooden buildings that sprawled along the shore of the deep harbour of The Gut. This was where the inshore fishermen sold their catches, and where the three large fishing draggers—which were also owned by the Drake family—disgorged their cargoes. A sizable work force of fish cutters and packers worked inside the plant to process the fish, which once every seventeen days was loaded aboard a refrigerated vessel and transported to the United States.

Freeman Drake owned and operated several more plants like this one in other places in eastern Canada. He and Barbara were, by anyone's yardstick, the wealthiest, most influential and stylish family anywhere on the coast. They lived in a large, lavish house in Baleena for about half the year, and spent the rest of the time in what was reported to be an equally luxurious house in Massachusetts. They were like some minor duke and duchess presiding over a private principality. Owning a gold mine might have been more financially rewarding, but owning Baleena Fish Products, and a number of others like it, was no bad second. They had three small daughters and employed two full-time servants to help look after them. They also owned two cabins "back in the country" which they used for hunting and fishing. And in Baleena they kept a sleek power cruiser called the *Sir Francis Drake*.

Since they also owned the *Bosco*, the refrigerated ship which transported the tons of frozen fillets to the Boston markets, they made use of her several times a year to move the family's entourage of children, servants, dogs, cats and a mountain of luggage from one place to the other. Unlike the rest of us, they didn't have to rely on the uncertain schedule nor endure the crowding of the Canadian National Railway's coastal vessels.

At first glance the life of the Drake family seemed to have all the ingredients of a romantic nineteenth-century novel— brave men who went down to the sea, trusted servants in grandiose houses, and beautiful, tempestuous women who were always standing at the top of a cliff with the wind blowing their hair.

In reality, as I was to discover, the life of the Drakes was not nearly so romantic, though it was not without its drama. The mystery was why a couple who kept an impressive wine cellar, and read magazines like *Gourmet* and *Vogue* and filled their idle afternoons with games like chess and bridge, should choose to live in this uttermost corner of their empire. Both Barbara Renouf Drake and Freeman Drake were descended from families which had made adequate fortunes in the fish business. But by the 1960s people of this class no longer lived in remote outports as they once had. Most lived in the capital city of St. John's, where they huddled together in a world that was far removed from the smell of fish meal.

The Drakes differed somewhat from the rest of the merchant class because a decade earlier Freeman had divorced his first wife and then married Barbara. In a province where it took an act of the provincial parliament in order to get a divorce at all, his second marriage was approved by few. The family was sacrosanct to Newfoundlanders, and most of them were churchgoers, almost equally divided in their numbers between Protestants and Roman Catholics. It thus made matters worse that Freeman was a Protestant and Barbara a Catholic.

The saga of the Drakes' romance and marriage was a local legend; stories about them had accumulated with the years. I used to think it was a shame that Farley didn't write romantic fiction. I'm not sure what I expected to find in outport life, but I certainly had not expected anyone like the Drakes. They seemed like characters in *The Forsyte Saga*, combined with *Brideshead Revisited*.

Having inherited her family's business in Jersey Island after her mother died, Barbara, who was thirty-two when I first met her, seemed to have everything, and it was hard not to envy her. Not only did she have money and power, a handsome husband and three pretty little daughters, she was beautiful besides. Small-boned and auburn-haired, she had the kind of eyes that X-rayed everything around her. She wore elegant clothes, real jewellery, and looked as regally unlike the other women in Baleena as a swan among geese.

Freeman, who was a few years older than his wife, was tall and handsome with just enough grey in his hair to make him look interesting. He wore tweed jackets and grey flannels and silk cravats and most of the time looked like one of those distinguished men you see in advertisements for expensive Scotch. And he liked expensive Scotch too.

Freeman was less sociable a person than Barbara. She was the one who encouraged the constant stream of visitors from "away." He wasn't entirely comfortable during the months he spent in Baleena. He was a St. John's man and he remained ill at ease among outport people. After a few weeks he grew fidgety. The only time he seemed content was when he was hunting or fishing back in the country. The opportunity to hunt and fish in the vast unpopulated regions which surrounded us in Baleena made him the envy of his associates and friends from the city. Many of them came to visit, flying in in chartered sea planes and then travelling to the salmon rivers, trout streams and moose and caribou hunting grounds aboard the *Sir Francis Drake*.

The Drakes' house was a hub of activity not only for their sporting visitors but for a number of local people too. It was in their house that we first got to know the small band of individuals who had come from somewhere else to live in Baleena—the doctor, the nurse, the Mountie, the clergyman and the fish plant management. From the first, the Drakes welcomed us warmly. The arrival of a new pair of faces was an event within this small group of strangers. We gathered in their spacious living room, where the big windows overlooked the waters of The Gut and the hills beyond it. The fire was always warm, the chairs comfy, the talk convivial and the drinks generous. And the food was delicious since Barbara was an excellent cook. It was, I must confess, a welcome change from the hard-backed chairs and restrained politeness that greeted me in the kitchens of my Dog Cove neighbours who, for all their kindness, never seemed able to relax when Farley and I were in their houses.

One cold evening a little boy came to our door with a note. I had never seen him before, but he strode in confidently and sat down on our daybed to wait for a reply. The note was from Freeman to Farley, inviting him to spend a few days aboard the *Sir Francis Drake* hunting for turrs— small, stubby-winged sea birds which are known everywhere else as murres or guillemots and taste like a cross between a fish and a duck. Farley doesn't like hunting, but this invitation seemed like an opportunity to see some of the coast. Also, he had just begun work on a new book and was suffering the prenatal fidgets. He reasoned that a few days away might help to put the whole thing into perspective and help his story to jell.

A short wiry man dressed in heavy clothing came by the next morning at 7:30. This was Noah Joseph, the guide on Freeman's hunting and fishing expeditions. He lived in nearby Muddy Hole and had stopped by so he could walk down to The Gut with Farley. Noah was the Laird's ghillie—or the Newfoundland equivalent of it. In his thirties, with a prematurely weathered face, he was descended from the "country" men, as they were called, who had lived most of the time in the interior. However, during the previous two or three generations they had married into the settled coastal communities, although the men had never fully accepted the role of fishermen. They still tended to make their living from hunting and trapping and odd jobs like cutting firewood, smoking fish or, if they could get a provincial licence, by working as guides to the few "sports" who came down the coast. For Noah there was fairly steady work with Mr. Drake.

Farley put on his warmest clothes and packed a haversack with a bottle of his favourite rum, and the two of them set off.

Light snow was swirling and the wind whistled around the windows. I tried to settle down to the chore of writing cards and letters. I had lots of news to tell our faraway friends and the last westbound coast boat before Christmas was just one week away. But I found it hard to concentrate. The wind was getting stronger. I began to wonder about the seaworthiness of the brass and mahogany *Sir Francis Drake*, a vessel that had been designed for a quieter ocean and was still registered in the Bahamas. I wished, as the snow thickened, that she had stayed there. I didn't have the legendary fatalism of the wives of those men who conduct their business upon the biblical Great Waters.

"My dear, you surely be some feared to stay all by yourself?" Melita Quayle asked me solicitously when I visited the shop to buy groceries. Melita would have been a pretty woman if it hadn't been for her one missing front tooth and the fact that she was about a hundred pounds overweight. She had long, wavy, dark hair and beautiful violet eyes with dark lashes. Melita was shy and spoke in a low voice. In Newfoundland, being shy was an acceptable personality trait that no one tried to change.

I assured her it didn't bother me to stay alone in our house, but she continued to regard me with concern. A woman who slept alone in a house was an oddity—brave perhaps, but of strange inclinations. Melita would have gladly "loaned" me Dorothy or Susie to keep me company, or if I preferred I would have been welcome to come over to their house to sleep—in the same bed with her two daughters—to assuage the terror of my solitary nights. This same neighbourliness would have been available from any of the Dog Cove families. I couldn't imagine what these women were afraid of in this, the most crime-free place I'd ever been. Help, if I happened to need it, was as near as the nearest house. Yet for women who had shared a bed with their sisters until they married and had always lived in houses spilling over with grandmothers or aunts, spending a night alone was a frightening experience.

The Dog Cove children saw to it that I wasn't alone during the day, at least. I had more visitors than ever before. They came during their lunch hour from school. They came after school, and they came after supper. I could hardly find an interval in which to eat my meals when I wasn't being watched by a sharp-eyed posse.

It was something of a relief when I got a note from Iris Finley, the Scottish nurse in charge of the hospital, inviting me to come down and have dinner with her. There was an eighteen-bed "cottage" hospital in Baleena—a legacy from the former British Commission Government which had administered Newfoundland during the 1930s and '40s, after it had lapsed into a form of political and economic receivership. Long before socialized medicine had become a way of life in the rest of Canada, Newfoundland already provided free hospitals and salaried doctors and nurses for its outport people. As new "outporters" in 1962, Farley and I paid a flat ten dollars a year, a fee which covered *all* our medical expenses, including the cost of travelling to any other hospital in the world, if necessary, for treatment that wasn't available locally.

Iris Finley was of that stalwart breed of nurses, produced in Britain, with a sterling sense of duty and a love of adventure. Very few Canadian nurses and doctors wanted to work in places as isolated as Baleena. Attracting qualified staff was, and still is, the major problem in operating these hospitals.

If anyone could have been lonely in Baleena, it should have been Iris. She was almost the only single woman in a place that revolved around family life. She was in her late thirties, with a pleasant face and a fulsome figure, and was one of those cheerful self-sacrificing people dedicated to helping others. Trained in the spartan atmosphere of post-war Scotland, she had replied to an advertisement in a British nurses' journal for a posting in outport Newfoundland. She knew next to nothing about the place before she came, but once she arrived she loved it. In her seven years of nursing on this coast—first in Jersey Island and then in Baleena—she had not once been back home even for a visit.

While I may have imagined that her life in Baleena was a solitary and arduous existence, it was nothing compared to her previous nursing experiences in Jersey Island. About fifteen miles directly out to sea from Baleena, Jersey Island was the outport where Barbara Drake's family had been the merchants for three generations. There were about eight hundred people on Jersey, and it was our closest community of any size. It was even more isolated than we were, since the island was not a very big one. We at least could take a walk back into the country if we wanted a change of scene. But unless the sea was reasonably calm, the Jersey Islanders, in their small boats, could go nowhere.

Yet Iris loved to talk about the place as if it was some distant, fascinating paradise. She told me long stories about life there, stories full of the kind of adventures found in magazines for girls. She was the first person I'd actually met who had done things like going out in the middle of the night in a boat on a stormy sea to deliver a baby. She had been the sole dispenser of medical assistance in Jersey Island.

"Och, I was aye busy there. Not a moment's peace," she said in a Scots burr that sounded oddly out of place amid the ancient English words and phrases that characterized our local dialect. She always insisted that Jersey Island people were different from the Baleena people, and she spoke of them with a longing to return. I couldn't fathom what she had found so remarkable about them. To me they were indistinguishable from their cousins elsewhere along the coast. And the village itself was a flat, wind-swept place, even balder and bleaker than ours. She did not tell me then why she had left this remembered paradise to come and work in the Baleena hospital.

There were supposed to be two registered nurses in Baleena, but the odds against enticing even one to any outport meant that Iris was usually on her own. There were also supposed to be two doctors, one resident in the community and another who was based there but travelled along the coast to serve the many small settlements within fifty miles of us. A forty-foot medical boat was stationed in Baleena but it was usually tied up at the wharf waiting hopefully for a doctor willing to fill this role.

Iris Finley had trained several local girls to be nurses' aides. It was the only career opportunity there for a young woman finished with school who hadn't yet married. It offered more prestige, and more pay, than packing fish at the plant. Iris also taught a first-aid class to all who were interested, and she initiated a prenatal class, which had not been a success. Women stopped coming when she showed them pictures of the unborn foetus. And they had not wanted to hear about the merits of breast feeding. This was considered old-fashioned now, something their poor grand-mothers had had to endure. In these modern times the young mothers fed their babies on canned milk.

In her spare time Iris was often over at the Drakes' house, where she devoted herself to their three little girls, Megan, Nancy and Elizabeth. She taught them how to sew and bake cookies. I suspect Freeman and Barbara regarded her as some kind of family retainer—but it gave her a function within their family, something she evidently needed.

As time went by, I saw more of Iris and enjoyed her company, but I never knew her well. I never understood her almost fanatical sense of duty to other people, with so little left over for herself.

Four

ONLY ONE OTHER PERSON IN BALEENA even mildly rivalled the Drakes in wealth and social position. He was the resident doctor—Roger Billings. Roger was an employee of the provincial health service. Like Iris, he had come from Britain, that longtime source of Newfoundland's medical personnel; but unlike Iris, he and his wife lived as lavishly as she did frugally. While Iris contented herself with two rooms in the hospital staff quarters, and owned only a meagre assortment of clothes and books, Roger and his wife, Jane, lived in a vast house belonging to the Department of Health.

The house had been built in 1909 by a local merchant family, the LeDrews, who, after amassing a fortune over several generations, had retired back to the Channel Islands, whence they came. They were the last of their kind— Jerseymen who had dominated the trade on the coast for two centuries—and after their departure the government bought their Edwardian mansion for a doctor's residence. No local family could have afforded it or would have felt comfortable in it. It did have charm, though. It was situated majestically at the top of a hill with a fine view of the ocean. The ground floor had twelve-foot ceilings and every room had superbly crafted door frames, window sills and baseboards.

It contained a curious mixture of furnishings—an odd blend of English Manor House and Canadian Hunting Lodge. An overstuffed sofa was draped with a caribou hide that left stiff, short hairs on the clothing of everyone who sat on it. Two wing chairs were losing their stuffing to the assaults of a pair of Siamese cats. There was a mahogany Queen Anne coffee table that was always submerged under a pile of medical advertising—that tidal wave of glossy paper which flows into the mailbox of every doctor. Once I had been ambitious to design just such prestigious brochures—a pinnacle for graphic designers. Roger seemed unmoved by this showcase of talent which so intrigued me, and eventually they ended up in the fireplace.

It was the fireplace, and the surrounding fluted wooden mantelpiece, that was the focal point of this eclectic living room. Jane always intended to get rid of the Ionic mantel and replace it with a fieldstone chimney which she would build herself. Jane's father had been an architect and she felt that this qualified her for a whole range of endeavours. She was an unusual woman, tall and thin, with a loping walk and long black hair which she usually wore in a single braid. She was given to great bursts of energy for a never-ending variety of projects. When I first met her, she talked a lot about being her own carpenter. One year she built kitchen cupboards. The next summer she built a hen house. The following year the hens disappeared and she built a kennel and raised whippet hounds—skinny, shorthaired dogs who shivered in the Atlantic winters and had to wear little coats to keep warm. Another year she painted the whole interior of their house in a peculiar shade of mustard yellow which she mixed herself.

Jane did not seem interested in her own appearance. Her clothes, I'm sure, were the ones she had brought from England in 1951—an assortment of "woollies" and "macks" and the riding breeches which she often wore. She had a passion for horses.

Perhaps the cheeriest room in their house was the kitchen, the domain of their two servant girls, who slept in a room above it and spent their days cooking, cleaning and keeping an eye on five-year-old Stephen, the Billings' only child. As well as the girls, there was one other full-time servant, a man named Jacob, who looked after the stable (which Jane had designed) and the two riding horses and a pony.

Roger had almost as many pursuits as his wife. A partly finished short-wave radio which he was assembling stood on a card table in the living room. He was something of a wine connoisseur and ordered it by the case from St. John's. Once, when Farley went down to the cellar with him to help carry some of it upstairs, he saw more of Roger's whims. There was a half-finished kayak which Roger was building during the winter months. There was a scuba-diving suit still in the carton. There were skis and boots—oddly useless in this land of rock and horizontal snowfalls.

Roger and Jane considered Newfoundland still a British appendage, and they seemed to have little interest in Canada as such. They had chosen to come to Newfoundland, rather than another position Roger had been offered in Africa, because the pay was better. They apparently had no intention of ever becoming Canadians. When their son, Stephen, reached the age of ten, they intended to send him "home" to attend a suitable school.

Stephen was a robust little boy who spoke with a Newfoundland dialect—the result of spending most of his time with a passing parade of servant girls, as well as in the kitchens of his many playmates. He belonged to the outport as much as he did to his parents. Either by accident or design, he'd been given a lot of latitude. I never knew if his parents adhered to the theory of permissiveness in child-rearing, or whether, as exiled Brits of a particular class, they simply left the task to a paid servant.

We had gravitated towards the Billings at first, thinking that our shared status as aliens in that place would unite us in some way. But it didn't, because their attitudes were as foreign to us as ours were to the local people. While the outporters continued to treat us with neighbourly accord, and were helpful in any way that they could be, they still maintained a psychic distance. The Dog Cove women, in particular, almost seemed afraid of me. When I dropped in to their kitchens, they immediately stopped talking and stared at me in apprehensive silence. The men, who were more accustomed to talking to strangers, were more relaxed with Farley. They quipped and joked with him, and engaged in light-hearted banter about the weather or the fishing. But it was clear it would take years before any of them, men or women, would feel entirely comfortable with people as radically different in background and experience. If we were to find any intimate friends at all, they would probably have to be from among those people who had come from some other place—strangers like ourselves.

We had better luck with the McEacherns than with the Billings. Doug McEachern was an RCMP corporal and the solitary police presence for ninety miles of coast and about four thousand people. He and his wife, Marjorie, both in their late twenties, lived in the police detachment—which was down the road and around a corner from the Billings' house. Doug—who stood six feet four and had red hair and freckles—came from a small town on Vancouver Island and at the time he joined the Force had never been further east than Vancouver. It was during his first posting, to Fortune, a Newfoundland community somewhat like Baleena only bigger and connected to the rest of the province by a road, that he had met and married Marjorie.

They were a comfortable couple, not driven by ambitions or pretensions. Marjorie—who was also tall—was robust and easy-going. She was always ready to sit down and talk, to put the kettle on, to tempt you with something she had baked. Doug was the exception to that song about the policeman's lot not being a happy one. He liked his work (though there wasn't much of it); he liked Newfoundland, and he even liked living in Baleena, which most of his predecessors had not. The low crime rate suited him. "Sixty, maybe seventy complaints a year. Can't beat that," he said with satisfaction.

The interior of the police detachment was just the opposite from the doctor's house. The architecture was stark and institutional—a reminder that it belonged to an arm of the federal government. It was a long, one-storey structure with two front doors and a flagpole in the yard. Doug and Marjorie lived in one half of the building in a space the size of a large two-bedroom apartment. The other half housed the police office, a spare room for an additional policeman if he was needed and, at the far end of the hall, a prison cell.

They had done everything they could to soften the regimental ambience of their quarters. There were flowered curtains, cosy furniture, crocheted pillow covers and lots of family photographs. There were plants on the window sills, magazines on the coffee table and a pile of records stacked beside the hi-fi. And the first time we ever visited them, there were Christmas cards covering every available space.

"Well, next week the invasion starts, girl," said Marjorie. "Are you ready?"

"Ah, yes. Mummers."

For weeks Dorothy and Ruth Quayle had been telling Farley and me about mummers. All the Dog Cove children had been telling us—warning us, in the way of children trying to scare each other with tales of bogeymen. I'd never heard about mummery until that winter, though Farley had read about it somewhere in connection with the customs of England in earlier times. As he understood it, mummers were originally wandering bands of musicians and actors who performed during the Christmas season, but who had vanished from the English scene as long ago as the early eighteenth century. But this ancient custom had somehow managed to survive in Newfoundland.

I had heard, or read about, the Christmas customs of a wide range of people, including Australians who went to the beach in sweltering heat, French-Canadians who went to midnight Mass and then held a huge all-night party afterwards, and Ukrainians who celebrated Christmas two weeks after everyone else and wore embroidered shirts. I knew all about tannenbaums and wassail bowls, but nothing about mummers. Perhaps it was because very few outsiders travelled to remote outports in mid-winter and also in those days no one in Newfoundland wanted to talk publicly about things the rest of Canada might consider old-fashioned or even laughable.

December 26, the second day of Christmas, was a day of light, powdery snow which fell all day, and by night was sculpted into drifts by a strong north wind. It was a perfect night to sit by the fire with a good book, which was just what we were doing when our peace was shattered by a loud banging on the storm door. Only the girl who delivered telegrams knocked on doors, for hers was an official mission. Virtually everyone else just walked in and sat down.

I padded into the kitchen in my stocking feet, switched on the light and pushed the door open against the gale. In front of me stood a solitary grotesque figure—I couldn't tell what age or sex—asking me in a hoarse, contorted voice if he, or she, could come in. This ghostly apparition had its face covered with a length of white cloth, secured by a fisherman's rubber sou'wester. An enormous oilskin jacket covered a padded bosom the size of Aunt Jemima's. Overly long sleeves hung down over hands that were covered by pink lace gloves.

I've wondered since what my reaction would have been if someone hadn't forewarned me about mummery. Would I have ordered this masked invader to go away, or would I have burst out laughing? Once I got over my initial surprise, I managed to say "Come in."

The mummer clumped in awkwardly and stood against the kitchen wall, not sitting down on the daybed until I issued an invitation to do so. From this hesitation, I guessed that whoever it was had not been inside our house before. Farley, by then as curious as I was, had come into the kitchen and exchanged some commonplace remarks with the mummer about the weather. But once that was done, there was a long silence. We didn't know what we should do next, and this mummer wasn't giving us any clues. Simple conversation was difficult because the mummer, to disguise his voice, could only gasp a strained "yes" or "no" to our remarks.

We started guessing who it might be, and this turned out to be a game like Twenty Questions. No, it wasn't a Quayle. No, it didn't live here in Dog Cove. No, it wasn't a Pointing. Then we were stuck because we could only identify our nearby neighbours with any certainty. The stalemate lasted for ten or fifteen minutes until, perhaps in desperation, the mummer pulled a small harmonica from a pocket, shoved it up under the white curtain mask, and played a few bars of some indiscernible tune. After that he, or maybe she, for I'll never know, got to his or her feet and marched out of the house and headed briskly down the path into the black and blustery night.

Amused, if somewhat baffled, we went back to our books and our fire, but were soon interrupted by another loud bang on the storm door. This time Farley answered it. Instead of one mummer, there were four—two small ones and two big ones. And they could hardly contain their giggles as they asked the ritual question in raspy voices, "Any mummers 'lowed in?"

They shuffled clumsily across the kitchen like a pack of lobsters, wearing rubber boots that must have belonged to their fathers since they were far too big. They all wore comical assortments of other people's clothes. The two larger ones had head scarves over their curtained faces; one had a big pillowy bosom and one had a big padded bottom. The two small mummers wore Halloween masks. I had noticed a clutch of these hanging on a nail over in Dan Quayle Junior's shop and had assumed, wrongly, that they had been left over from Halloween. These shops must have been the only places in the world where Halloween masks were sold at Christmastime.

Unlike our previous uncommunicative mummer, this group never stopped talking, though always in strained voices. I felt sure I knew them, for they acted as if they were on familiar ground.

"Yiss," they replied when I asked them if they were from Dog Cove, and yes, they were Quayles. All of them. I started guessing the names of their potential fathers. Charlie? Clarence? Dan Junior? Dan Senior? They turned out to be a mixture of the offspring of the two Dans. I knew then who the smaller ones must be.

"It's Dorothy and Ruth, isn't it?" I said, delighted at my success in playing this game.

Immediately these two threw back their masks and grinned at us, their faces glowing from the heat and the excitement. However, the other two kept their faces covered and we had to continue to guess who they were. I presumed that they were some of Ruth's older brothers and sisters; but since Ruth was the fourteenth of sixteen children, there was still a lot of guessing to do. We finally deduced that it must be Muriel and Aubrey, Ruth's next-oldest sister and brother. They threw back their veils in the climactic moment, just like one of those game shows on television when the mystery guest is finally identified.

Muriel and Aubrey, both in their middle teens, were still relative strangers to us then. So once they had unveiled, they didn't say another word. In disguise they had been quite bold. We would see this transformation again and again. People who were shy to the point of repression turned into clowns, dancers, actors and singers when they went out mummering. That evening only Dorothy and Ruth continued to talk to us, though they reverted to their polite, everyday tone of voice.

As newcomers, we became the target for more mummers than visited most houses. It was an opportunity to look us over in anonymity. Once the word got around that we accepted mummers—which was important because not every family let them in—they came in droves. Our proficiency at guessing mummers grew by leaps and bounds.

They continued to come every night of the Twelve Days of Christmas, with the exception of Sundays. I was grateful for those Sundays, for it was exhausting to have so many visitors every night. We had the option of refusing them, of course, but such refusals were traditionally acceptable only from families where someone was ill or where there were very small children who might be frightened by the sight of masked strangers invading their home. People who refused mummers when none of these conditions prevailed were generally regarded as spoilsports.

Doug and Marjorie McEachern couldn't allow mummers into their home because even in that peaceable community a policeman had to know precisely who was entering the bastion of law enforcement. However, they came up to our house a couple of times to watch the fun. Although Marjorie had been born and lived her entire life in Newfoundland, she had never seen a mummer. The custom had disappeared in Fortune many years earlier with the arrival of the road and automobiles.

Five

THE BOY WHO BROUGHT THE NOTE to our door was no more than six or seven years of age. But with the solemnity of an archbishop, he handed me an envelope.

> Farly you and Clara want to go mummers
> with us to-night come by 8 oclock
> > Noah

Here was a chance to see the fun from the other side of the veil. I hesitated at first, uncertain whether I would be able to handle the situation, but Farley persuaded me. So we sent our acceptance note back with Noah's son, who had been sitting on the daybed pretending not to listen to our discussion.

I was swept up in a carnival mood for the rest of the afternoon, delighted with the prospect of stepping out of my everyday identity as Mrs. Mowat and dressing up as someone else. I think the desire to masquerade is in us all. The problem was to find something to wear. I searched through our closets and dresser for odd bits of clothing. We had to be careful not to be too theatrical or we would be easily identified. Our aim was to look as much like the mummers we had already seen in our kitchen and as little like ourselves as possible.

I chose an old windbreaker Farley had worn when painting the house, and that, along with his paint-spattered green work pants, plus his best rubber boots and sou'wester, seemed like an appropriate costume. With several sweaters underneath, I reasoned I would look deceptively heavier than I was. Extra pairs of socks filled the spaces in the too-large boots.

Farley decided to wear one of my long flannelette nightgowns, a garment which was roomy enough so that he could wear lots of warm clothes underneath. He had a new woollen toque to cover his head and a pair of old and tattered rubber boots. Most important was the face covering, and luckily I had several yards of white nylon net. It made ideal masks, for it gave us some hazy visibility without revealing our faces. I had to devise a special tucked-in veil for Farley in order to hide his beard. He was the only man in Baleena who wore a beard—a fashion which was at once too old and too new to be popular there then. We both selected unfamiliar gloves and mittens and I took off my wedding ring in case anyone did catch a glimpse of my hands. Hands reveal your sex and often your identity.

Thus attired, we set out at a brisk pace down the path, over the Dog Cove bridge and along the road towards Muddy Hole. We were giggling like a pair of children at the absurdity of our costumes. Indeed, the people who passed us on the road that night must have thought we were a pair of overgrown children.

At Noah's house we found an atmosphere of high excitement. Noah was wearing a frothy white wedding dress. The frayed edges of an old sweater bulged atop the sweetheart neckline and at the wrists. The toes of his rubber boots protruded incongruously beneath the ruffled hem. He was fumbling with his headgear when we came in—a complicated arrangement of a bride's veil pinned backwards on top of a woollen cap. His daughter, Mary, who was about fourteen, was standing on a chair with a pincushion in her hand trying to help him. The other four children, all boys, sat around the kitchen table tittering at the sight of their father dressed as a woman.

I had come with my preconceived image of Noah as a steely-eyed hunter who plodded through the barrens and the woods undaunted by harsh weather or wild beasts. Now here he was encased in white lace, his lined, tanned face peering absurdly at me from beneath the frilly millinery that Mary finally pinned into place. His leathery hands, protruding from the bridal dress, were busy with papers and tobacco, rolling a cigarette.

"Be wit' yas right soon, Farley bye. Sit down here, missus," he said to me, pointing to a kitchen chair.

In a few minutes Minnie Joseph appeared from the bedroom. I was glad to see that she was wearing much the same kind of disguise I was—an assortment of her husband's working clothes. It reassured me that, as a newcomer, I had come to the party wearing the right thing. Minnie, like her husband, was short but she was heavier around the middle. Her face was as round as his was angular and lean. A relaxed woman, she was at ease with strangers and our presence did not ruffle her, the way it so often did with the shy wives of the Quayle family.

Unlike most of the other Baleena women, Minnie had had some experience with the ways of the world. Although she had never been in any community except this one, she had often gone along as cook when Noah was the guide on hunting expeditions. So she had shared close quarters with a variety of men—Americans, Canadians and Newfoundlanders who were often doctors and lawyers and merchants. Around many a campfire she must have concluded that underneath our various façades we all share the same needs. She made me feel comfortable in that unfamiliar situation.

A third couple arrived to join us for the evening's adventure—Minnie's brother, Gus Barnes, and his wife, Dot. Both were dressed in fishermen's rubber clothes with old lace curtains to cover their faces. Dot was a thin-faced woman, and very shy. She didn't say a word to us. Gus, a more outgoing man, was short and heavy-set like his sister. He was the night watchman at the fish plant. When he took off his mitts to light a cigarette, I noticed that four fingers were missing from his right hand. It had been caught in a winch aboard a fishing dragger five years earlier, and the loss was a genuine handicap in a place where a man's strength and agility were so vital to his livelihood.

As we left the house, Noah slung a small accordion across the front of the wedding dress, a garment which, on close inspection, had a characteristic which is rare in wedding gowns—it was shabby and well-worn. It must have been the veteran of decades of mummery.

Our first call was at a house on the opposite side of Muddy Hole, a hundred yards across the water from the Joseph house by dory; but on foot in winter, a half-mile trek over ice and rocks. I was relieved when we finally got there, for despite the heavy socks, blisters were forming on my heels as my feet slid around inside my husband's boots. We stood on some steep steps as Noah rapped.

"Any mummers 'lowed in?" he asked in his sucked-in voice.

We were admitted into the house of a large family. The kitchen was overflowing with children of various ages and a couple of grandmothers as well. A woman whom I took to be the lady of the house was putting dishes away in a pantry. Two small children in pyjamas kept popping around a corner to watch us. Everyone eyed us with keen interest.

"Some foine mummers we got here," said the man of the house, who sat in a rocking chair smoking his pipe.

"I t'inks I knows 'em," said a teen-aged boy who was inspecting us carefully.

"Milly and Donny, you git off to bed!" scolded one of the grandmothers.

"I b'lieve I knows this one," said the lady of the house, poking Noah in the ribs. "You belongs to Hann's Island, now, tell me t'truth!"

Noah shook his veil in denial.

"Well, who'd be this pretty lady then," she asked, pinching Farley's bottom. "I knows you, don't I? Looks like one of them Hatchers to me. You be Archie Hatcher? Or is it Mabel Hatcher? Tell t'truth now."

Farley shook his veil in denial.

The children giggled a lot and the adults continued to eye us carefully, but not one of our hosting family was coming close to guessing who we were. They ran through a roster of names I had never heard, and they kept trying to peek under our veils.

"'Tis a poor crowd of mummers what don't dance," said the other grandmother.

"C'mon, mummers, you dance and you'll git a drop," said the man of the house, coming out of the pantry with a bottle in his hand.

Noah began to play his accordion, wheezing out a rapid jig. Gus and Dot straightaway started to dance, and despite their rubber boots, they performed with surprising agility. The music brought out a new dimension in this quiet couple. The whole room vibrated as they shuffled and stamped. The audience was rapt, but still kept guessing the wrong names. After a minute or two, Minnie Joseph joined in the dance too, though she wasn't as agile as her brother and his wife. The men were usually the champion dancers in the outports and it was rare for a woman to excel.

I watched their feet for a while and then joined in too. It was easy to risk making a fool of myself when I had a veil over my face. Noah kept on pumping out his tune, a melody which he claimed didn't have a name. "I knows how it goes" was all he had to say of this and the one other lively number which constituted his repertoire.

With the kitchen range roaring, this fierce activity was making me unbearably hot, bundled up in so many layers of clothing. I wondered if mummers ever fainted.

I was relieved beyond words when Noah, still playing the nameless jig, led the way out the door, down the steps and into the blessedly cold night. We stumbled along the icy road until we were out of sight of the house, and then we threw back our veils. After catching our breath, we gathered our strength for the next visit. The sheer physical effort of this kind of socializing was proving to be as much as Farley and I could endure, but it didn't seem to bother the others.

The next house also had a large kitchen but there were fewer people in it; a husband and wife, evidence of some small children who had apparently been put to bed, and one school-aged girl sitting on the daybed beside an older man wearing his coat and cap, who looked as if he had just dropped in. They eyed us with moderate interest, but didn't say anything. Our two "ladies," Noah and Farley, sat down on the daybed beside the girl and the old fellow, while us four "men" stood up against the wall.

We stood there in silence for what seemed like a very long time. The little girl grinned at us, the mother continued to fold a pile of clean diapers while her husband, a man with the same weather-worn complexion as Noah, just stood and looked at us. Finally he started to guess names. He must have had an inkling who we were, for Noah and Minnie were soon identified. After that it was an easy matter to uncover Gus and Dot. But who were we—the fifth and sixth members of the group?

They guessed and guessed, and we shook our heads in mute denial. Though they poked and pinched us, they still couldn't guess who we were. While the other four sat there smirking, we remained veiled and mysterious to the end.

Though we visited half a dozen more houses that evening, not once did anyone guess who Farley and I were. Towards the end of the evening Farley decided he wanted our roving band to call on someone *we* knew. He suggested we make a surprise visit to Iris Finley. The others were apprehensive—an invasion of the nurses' private living quarters was not something they would have ever undertaken on their own. The upstairs of the hospital was a sanctum sanctorum that wasn't entered by anyone except the staff.

Nevertheless, the six of us entered the hospital through the unlocked back door and sneaked stealthily through the spotless, deserted kitchen. An institutional wall clock told us it was five minutes to eleven.

The staff quarters were almost as antiseptic as the hospital itself. On tiptoe, leaving pools of melting snow on the polished floor, we headed for the door of the nurses' lounge. Farley knocked.

Iris opened the door briskly and suddenly we were facing not just Iris but Freeman and Barbara Drake, Victor Moss, the genial manager of the fish plant, and a small Oriental who was our second doctor, newly arrived from Hong Kong. They were as startled to see us as we were to see them, for an invasion of mummers in those hallowed precincts was unprecedented. But Iris rose to the occasion and, though she must have wondered who would be so bold, she waved us in.

It was a subdued band of mummers who sat meekly on the floor while Iris passed around her homemade fruit cake.

We had stumbled into a perfunctory visit that Freeman and Barbara made every Christmas to Iris's personal quarters. This was the season of duty visits for them, and that night they were killing two birds with one stone by visiting Iris and making the acquaintance of the new doctor as well. And, I guessed, it was an evening out for Victor Moss, who rarely went anywhere.

They looked us over.

"All right then, mummers," commanded Barbara. "You're supposed to entertain us, so get on with it."

Even in disguise, Noah couldn't refuse a command performance. With his gloves still hiding his hands, he pumped out one of his two tunes, while the rest of us climbed wearily to our feet to step-dance one more time. By then the spring had gone out of my step, and I could see that Minnie was slowing down too. Farley was hardly making the effort, yet Gus and Dot were still as nimble as the Bolshoi corps de ballet. We persevered and our heavy boots ground muddy patterns into the beige carpet.

Dr. Yip Lee watched this performance with polite astonishment. Having only been in Canada for three weeks and in Newfoundland for three days, he must have been more than a little surprised at the antics of the natives in his new home. Iris kept talking in his ear over the sound of the accordion as she tried to explain who we were and what we were doing. It would have been tricky to explain the phenomenon to anyone, let alone a doctor from China.

There was no doubt that our audience enjoyed us. Our unexpected intrusion had brightened an otherwise dull evening. No one was making any great effort to guess who we were. They were prepared to let us continue to amuse them.

Finally Farley, hot and exhausted, called the game. He flopped down on the rug and yanked off his cap and veil. With a sigh of relief, I joined him. The other four somewhat reluctantly shed their veils.

"My, oh my," laughed Iris, "would you look who it is!"

"That takes the cake," said Victor.

"I'll be damned," said Freeman, who, feeling he'd been caught off guard, straightened his tie and pulled himself up more squarely in his chair. No one quite knew what to do at this point. The fun was suddenly over. Freeman was likely not overjoyed to find that some kind of off-duty camaraderie existed between Noah Joseph and the ever-unpredictable Farley Mowat. Gus Barnes, who was due to start work in half an hour, was face to face with the boss. Both of them looked uncomfortable. Even Noah was stripped of his usual self-assurance. Minnie and Dot were as mute as rabbits.

Iris now insisted that we all have some sherry. The men each took a long-stemmed glass from the silver tray, then gulped their drinks with the haste of movie gunslingers. Noah and Gus and their wives were obviously in a hurry to get out of there; so without further attempts at socializing, we thanked our hostess, gathered our mitts, hats and veils, and departed into the night.

The last day for mummers was "Old Christmas Day," as it was known locally, on January the sixth. That afternoon was reserved for children who weren't old enough to go out at night. All afternoon they trooped in and out of our kitchen, platoons of tiny ghosts with masked faces wearing each other's clothes. They crowded onto the daybed and squirmed and giggled and whispered, impatiently hoping to be recognized at once. I urged them to entertain me, and asked for a song, a poem or a dance before I passed around the dwindling supply of cookies. I didn't want to see this children's day turn into a feast of greed like mainland Halloween.

A few of them volunteered to sing. They sang songs about picking cotton, songs about going to jail, songs about being "way down yonder in the pawpaw patch." They were songs about life in the American South, the origin of the country music they heard every day from Marystown radio—our nearest privately owned station, which specialized in country music, albeit from another country. Only a few professional singers were learning the folk songs of Newfoundland in those days, and not the Island's children.

Leroy Quayle's ecstasy was almost visible through his mask—a grizzly Halloween number that looked like a long-toothed dog. He was only four and was swathed in his mother's bulky yellow sweater, which hung down to his boots. His big sister Dorothy was doing the rounds with him. She wasn't dressed in mummers' clothes since she was almost twelve and far too grown up to be taking part in the small children's afternoon celebration.

Overcome with the excitement of the day and the warmth of our kitchen, Leroy finally fell asleep on the daybed. Dorothy came over to the sink to help me wash and dry the lunch dishes. After we had done that, she got out the mop and set about eradicating the trail of muddy footprints that charted the route from the back door to the daybed.

In a rare introspective mood, she started to talk about herself. Someday, she thought, she would like to go away and study to be a nurse. Maybe a doctor even. She liked to take care of people, she said, her words weaving dreams. In her imagination, she was far away from the confines of the shop, from little brothers and sisters, from neighbours and homework. When she wasn't either at school or minding Leroy, she was expected to help out in the shop. And when she became old enough to legally leave school, her father expected her full-time assistance. Going away to study nursing was indeed a fanciful daydream.

"But what I likes best of all," Dorothy confided in a hushed voice, "is I likes to write poems. Songs too, sometimes. I writes 'em in me head nighttime when I'm in bed. Then when I gits a spare minute down the shop, I writes 'em off in me scribbler."

"I didn't know that, Dorothy," I said, surprised to learn that she was interested in poetry, and pleased she wanted to share this secret with me. "Why don't you bring your scribbler over here sometime and read your poems to us?"

She blushed and looked at the floor, caught in a moment of illusion, fearful that I might make fun of her.

"Honestly," I insisted, "I would like to hear your poems and songs. And I know Farley would too. He wrote poems once, a long time ago when he was your age."

"P'r'aps I might sometime," she said. Then she shook Leroy awake. "Bitter get along now," she said, looking into his face as he blinked. And then she hustled him out the door and they waved at me as they crossed the frozen marsh, while she doubtless wondered if she might have given away too much of herself to someone she wasn't sure she could really trust.

Six

SOMETHING I LEAST EXPECTED in mid-winter was a spate of weddings. I had never thought of winter as the season of marriages. For me weddings had always been synonymous with marquees in the garden when the peonies were in bloom, with bridesmaids being photographed against a background of flowering shrubs. The few people I had known who married in the winter (in lush white velvet and their bridesmaids in cranberry red) were those who could afford a honeymoon in the Caribbean.

But in Baleena honeymoons and flowers were not factors in the choice of one's wedding day. In the winter the young men who went away to work on the Great Lakes ships were home, and they accounted for most of the grooms. And in wintertime there was less work than in other seasons, and lots of time for celebrations.

As soon as the frenzy of mummery died down, wedding invitations began to pour in, delivered by eager younger sisters or cousins of the bride or groom. These winter weddings had to be crammed into the weeks between the end of Christmas and the beginning of Lent, the precise date for each being determined by the availability of the tightly scheduled parish hall, where all receptions were held.

Mr. and Mrs. Albert Green
request the honour of your presence
at the marriage of their daughter
Effie
to
Mr. Obed. Kendal
Tuesday, February 12th, at 4 pm
St. Peter's Church, Baleena
Reception at the Parish Hall

The invitation was neatly written on a piece of plain white notepaper, in the same words that are used almost universally in the English-speaking world. Every household received one. To omit anyone—even the poorest or least-liked families, or people like us who did not even know the bride or groom—would have been a grave oversight.

"Nate Young and Annie Ingram got married and they snuck off like thieves in the night. Went away to Corner-brook and done it," Ruth Quayle told me gravely one day.

I considered the improbability of anyone managing to "sneak" off to Cornerbrook, a journey which took two days and a night, by ship and then by train. But practical considerations didn't deter the girls from carrying this scandalous story from house to house. To marry in such an unsociable manner was a gaffe that would not be forgiven or forgotten. Any family which failed to provide the whole community with a lavish evening of food and drink and dancing was looked down on for their meagre and ungenerous ways.

On the other hand, the one thing which was quite unforgivable where I grew up—a pregnant bride—was of small consequence here. Babies were regarded as the inevitable outcome of romance, and the concept of family planning was as alien as the notion of planning your life at all. There were few choices either way.

A young man appeared in our kitchen one morning and lingered uneasily by the door. He didn't sit down on the daybed as most of our visitors did. He just stood around, looking down at the pointed toes of his shoes. Strands of a ducktail haircut fell over his forehead. He seemed reluctant to talk to me and finally, after some inconsequential chit-chat, he asked if Mr. Mowat was at home. I summoned Farley from his office and then diplomatically left the room. I could hear him mumbling something and addressing Farley as "sir" from time to time.

In a few minutes Farley went to the closet in the back bedroom where we kept our supply of liquor and came out with two bottles in a paper bag. He dispatched the visitor on his way with a hearty "Good luck now!"

"What was that all about?"

"Poor devil wanted to buy a bottle of rum. He's getting married tomorrow and the booze he ordered didn't show up on the coast boat yesterday. It might get here a week from now, but that's no use for the wedding."

"So you sold him a bottle?"

"Hell, no, I don't want to become the local bootlegger. I gave him a bottle of rum. And I gave him a special wedding extra—a bottle of crème de menthe."

"Terrific idea!" I said, and we both laughed.

We had inadvertently become the owners of three bottles of crème de menthe a few weeks earlier. Neither of us liked it and we'd been wondering what to do with it. We had to order our liquor from the mail-order division of the

Newfoundland Liquor Commission in St. John's, as everyone in the outports did, whether they wanted one bottle or a hundred bottles. We mailed our order with a money order that included the shipping costs, and it was eventually shipped to us—first by train and then by coast boat. The procedure took about three weeks. The system was slow, but it worked except for one quirk. If a brand was out of stock, rather than delay the order the liquor commission clerk substituted a bottle of his own choice at the same price. It was no hardship getting, say, a different brand of vodka or rum. But in the wide-ranging category of *wine*—which included such diverse drinks as Burgundy, Drambuie, Leibfraumilch, Cherry Heering, sparkling rosé and, yes, crème de menthe—the substitutions were made solely by price. Consequently, we had ordered three bottles of Beaujolais at $4.85, and had received instead three bottles of crème de menthe at $4.85. One of them was now on its way to a wedding.

"Nice fellow. I liked him. Kept urging us to come to his wedding," Farley said.

"What's his name?"

"Mmmm. Obi . . . something. Candle—Kendal maybe?"

I sifted through the wedding invitations on the kitchen counter.

"Here it is," I said. "Obed. Kendal. And he's getting married to Effie Green tomorrow afternoon. Just as he said. Oh, I'd love to go!"

I confess that I love weddings. I'm overcome with emotion whenever I witness a ceremony in which two people promise to spend their lives together, come what may. I know it doesn't often work out that way but that knowledge hasn't lessened my illogical pleasure in it.

So I went eagerly to my first Baleena wedding, dragging my unenthusiastic husband with me, for he could think of many other ways to spend his afternoon. We entered the cold and cavernous Anglican church at a quarter to four and sat down in a pew near the back. A crowd of women, girls and small children had already assembled at the front. One by one, and then in twos and threes, they turned around to look at us.

In a place where any stranger is newsworthy, our unexpected appearance in the church that day was spectacularly so. People continued to turn and watch us at frequent intervals, no doubt wondering what on earth we were doing there. I soon began to wonder too. Four o'clock came and went as we sat there shivering in the tomb-like chill. There was no sign of the clergyman or the wedding party. An eerie silence, interrupted only by the children shuffling and sniffing, dragged on and on.

Our fellow sufferers were almost all female, and a lot of them had curlers in their hair. None wore the kind of clothes I associated with weddings. On this chill February day they were clad in quilted nylon jackets and warm slacks. I wished I had been wearing the same, as my nylon-stockinged legs turned blue. It dawned on me why everyone was sitting at the front of the church. It was to be near the stove, a black monster with a roaring fire inside it that was stationed right in the middle of the apse.

Farley's eyes were fixed on the ceiling. He was engrossed in studying the architecture of the sixty-year-old building.

"Built just like a ship, only upside down," he whispered.

I stared overhead at the massive wooden ribs which supported the vaulted arch of the ceiling, marvelling at the craftsmanship that had gone into building this church. Soon several children began to follow our gaze. They were curious to see whatever it was we had seen up under the roof. Having thoroughly studied the techniques of church architecture circa 1905, we sat back and continued waiting—still the object of curious stares. By then I had to consciously resist an urge to run—to disappear from a place where I felt I had intruded, invited yet uninvited.

At long last we heard the church vestibule door bang open and the sound of someone stomping snow from their boots. Reverend Way, his face red with the cold, and a parka over his soutane, strode up the aisle towards the vestry. He had just returned from Jersey Island, where he had presided at two weddings.

He was deceptively bookish-looking, with a ponderous gaze behind horn-rimmed glasses. There was a boyish energy about him. He walked as if he were on the verge of running. God knows he needed a lot of energy to do his job, since he tended the three Anglican parishes of Baleena, Jersey Island and Enragée River—none of which could be reached except by sea.

A few moments later he appeared in front of our frozen assembly wearing his surplice, and then someone unseen started to play the wedding march, the one from Lohengrin—tum, tum tetum. The hackneyed old tune was painstakingly picked out on a pump organ. We got to our feet as a nonchalant bridal party ambled up the central aisle, making no attempt to keep time with the music.

The bride and her father—the "father giver," as he was known—headed the procession, and that was the reverse of all the weddings I'd previously seen. They were followed by the bridesmaids and the "bridesboys," walking arm in arm. Effie, the bride, was tall and slender like her father. I guessed she was nineteen or twenty, and she had a strong face and straight light-brown hair. She wore a long white dress and a shoulder-length veil, cascades of lace and frills which someday might make the rounds upon an irreverent mummer. She must have been frozen in the church that day, but she moved with surprising composure towards her waiting groom. Her father, a grey-haired man in his sixties, looked confident and dapper in a snug, navy-blue suit. He had six daughters and two sons, and since Effie was the youngest of the girls, he had obviously been over this route before.

The bridesmaids wore long fluffy dresses—one pink, one yellow and one pale green, like a brick of Neapolitan ice cream. Over these confections each girl wore a white Orlon cardigan. The bridesboys, the groom and the best man all wore dark, new-looking suits, and each sported a plastic carnation in his buttonhole.

All the wedding flowers were glossy, bright plastic, the bridal bouquet included. Carnations and roses didn't grow on this coast, I reminded myself, so what was there to adorn a wedding in February? There were spruce boughs, alive and green in the dead of winter, but they were never used. The sight of them couldn't evoke that vision of a warmer land which lurks in the psyche of northern people.

Reverend Way, standing directly in front of the coal stove, faced the bride and groom and began to read the words of the marriage ceremony in his strong voice.

"Obediah," he addressed the groom by his full Old Testament name, which no one, not even his mother, ever used, "wilt thou have this woman to have and to hold from this day forward, for better or worse, for richer for poorer, in sickness and in health and forsaking all others keep thee only unto her as long as thou dost live?"

Then he imposed the same stringent conditions upon Effie—whose name didn't have a longer form. Effie and Obi must have replied, but we couldn't hear a word from them. We had to take it on faith that they had agreed to take one another for better or worse.

It was a long ceremony. There was a prayer and then a lengthy hymn, followed by an even longer prayer and a longer hymn. I wasn't familiar with the hymns and there were no hymn books in the racks. We were expected to bring our own, I discovered. Very few people sang. Reverend Way was almost singing solo in his wobbly tenor.

By the time it was all over, my hands and feet were numb. I couldn't wait to get outside where I could stamp my feet and restore the circulation. As we filed slowly out of the church, we saw a huddled group of men standing on the pile of snow by the church gate. As soon as Obi and Effie appeared at the door, this group pointed a small forest of rifles and shotguns up into the air and fired them at the sky. The noise could be heard by everyone in Baleena. No one could fail to know that Effie and Obi were now man and wife.

The poorly attended church service turned out to be only a preliminary to the real celebration, which didn't begin until nighttime. Then the curlers were banished from the coiffed heads and the ski pants gave way to festive taffeta and rhinestones and high heels. The men put on their dark suits, starched shirts and neckties. Everyone headed for the parish hall. Second only to the church itself, the parish hall was the biggest enclosed space in Baleena. About seventy feet long, it was a wooden building devoid of any architectural frills. For weddings it was transformed by bright crepe paper streamers that were tacked in cheerful twists from rafter to rafter. They were garlanded over a trestle table which had been set up on the platform at the front of the hall. Behind this table the bride and groom sat side by side, unwrapping a mountain of gifts. Obi appeared to be slightly bored and vaguely drunk, a condition to which Effie, with wifely realism, seemed resigned.

It was just past 9:30 by the time we arrived, yet no one was doing much of anything. A lot of people—mostly women and children—were sitting on the backless benches that lined the perimeter of the hall, as if waiting for something to happen. Off one end of the hall was a smaller room where a team of women were energetically assembling the wedding feast. Two long tables were piled high with platters of sandwiches, all made with pristine white bread with the crusts removed and filled with luncheon meat, processed cheese, canned salmon or the new, popular filling—canned asparagus with mayonnaise. There were plates of beautiful homemade cookies—each one crowned with a candied cherry or half an almond or those tiny sugar beads that look like silver gunshot. But surpassing both of those were the *squares*. This was the ultimate culinary treat for special occasions—compressed collages of marshmallow and chocolate chips, rice krispies and butterscotch, coconut and crumbled wafers and corn syrup, all melding in sickly sweet striations. It was a poor wedding that didn't offer at least a dozen varieties of these gooey creations.

"Have a drop of wine, dear?" asked a lady in a flowered dress, sweat standing on her brow from her labours. We were seated at one of the tables with about twenty others, for at that point there didn't seem much else to do but eat. I smiled at the woman and took one of the tiny gold-rimmed glasses from the tray. This was "Cassie" wine, a drink primarily intended for women. It varied a bit from one outport to another but basically it was made from raspberry syrup (which every shop sold in quart-size bottles) and pure grain alcohol—which was smuggled from St. Pierre et Miquelon. These two totally undrinkable substances produced, in combination, an even worse one.

St. Pierre et Miquelon, France's last colony in North America, was only about fifty sea miles away. Before Newfoundland's entry into the Canadian confederation in 1949 and the subsequent arrival of the Canada Customs Act and its enforcement by the RCMP, an unofficial barter system had existed between the people on the south coast of Newfoundland and the people of St. Pierre. Moose, caribou and lumber were traded to the barren French islands for liquor, sugar and several other products which were, due to a stroke of French colonial benevolence, tax-free. A sweet wine, flavoured with cassia, had once been a popular import in the outports and had become the traditional wedding drink for ladies.

However no one risked the ocean voyage to Miquelon for wine anymore. Smugglers were heavily fined if the police caught them, and they risked having their boats confiscated as well. Now the only cargo worth the risk was 97 per cent pure alcohol. This liquid dynamite was diluted with any available fluid, such as hot sugared water (which was popular with the men), or the sticky red syrup which was now sitting in front of me.

Along with the "wine," the wedding cake was passed around, each piece wrapped in a paper doily so you could take it home. A widow made all the cakes for all the weddings. She was an artist with icing sugar and well she knew it. Her three-tiered, rose-budded masterpieces were the object of unanimous admiration. It seemed like an act of destruction to see them cut apart. The passing of the cake and the wine marked the end of the nuptial meal. Then those at the table, like communicants at an altar, were expected to leave to make room for those still waiting.

Out in the main hall again, we found seats on one of the benches alongside Mr. Hoddinott, the postmaster. He was accompanied by his son Sidney, sitting very close to a pretty girl with red hair and a green dress. She was the grade two school teacher and had come to Baleena that year from Pass Island, a smaller outport noted for its production of school teachers. Few Pass Islanders, it seemed, stayed home to fish. Young men and women alike mostly went away to become teachers all over the province.

"Sidney's courting," muttered Mr. Hoddinott as he sidled along to make room for us, nodding towards his uncommunicative son. He seemed glad to see us. He was a garrulous man who loved to talk, and loved to go out in the evenings. Weddings, movies, "times," as parties were called —whatever was going on, he would be there. Although his wife was a shy woman who rarely went anywhere beyond the post office, he revolved in a social whirl that would have exhausted a diplomat. He had seen two movies the week before, he told me. Fine movies too, though he couldn't remember their names. One had been about soldiers fighting in a war, and the other about cowboys.

Movies were shown twice a week in a building which had once housed the now-defunct Orange Lodge, but they were unadvertised. Trying to find out the name of the film in advance simply wasn't done. It would have been like asking your hostess what she was having for dinner before you went. The films were usually old ones and the sound track so indecipherable that it didn't much matter what you saw. Few people, save the articulate Mr. Hoddinott, ever ventured an opinion as to whether or not they enjoyed this dubious entertainment.

Our convivial postmaster was just starting to tell me about the "time" he had attended at the United Church Hall the previous evening (he attended everything, with ecumenical impartiality) when we were interrupted by the sound of an accordion. A man with the russet face of those who spend their lives outdoors had seated himself on a wooden chair at the front of the hall. His long legs angled out below the accordion on his lap. It squawked as he hoisted the leather straps over his shoulders. A group of people, young and old, straggled unceremoniously to the centre of the room where they stood in a loose semi-circle. Bride and groom inched their way down from the platform and joined the group, followed by both pairs of parents. The accordionist tapped his foot and began to play.

Sixteen people started dancing. They didn't have a caller, nor did they need one. All of them, even the youngest —a girl no more than twelve—knew exactly what they were doing. It was a complicated and lengthy dance and I watched closely, trying to sort out the patterns. The accompanying music was a repetitive, almost hypnotic reel, a legacy of music that had crossed the ocean centuries before and changed little with successive generations.

"Altogether different down Fortune Bay," Mr. Hoddinott shouted in my ear during the final surge of furious twirling.

"Is that so?"

"Oh my, yes. Down Henderson's Cove, now that's where I belong, they go round in a circle *four* times before they join up in pairs. Then over in Terrenceville . . . that's where I first started out in the post office . . . well, over there they twirl first, then they break away, then . . ."

His explanations were lost amid the laughing and clapping that followed the end of this epic dance. The dancers dispersed from the centre of the floor, but within a few minutes another sixteen had formed a circle and the whole thing was repeated until most of the people had participated in this reel. After that the fiddler took a well-earned rest.

I had noticed that men past their mid-teens or younger than sixty were in short supply. That didn't daunt the women who wanted to dance. After the reel was over, recorded popular music was played and women cheerfully danced with each other, with the youngsters or with a man if they could find one.

Close to midnight, as Farley and I were preparing to leave, the back door of the hall burst open and a whole crowd of men stumbled in. Some of them were obviously drunk, and most were noisy. Everyone turned to look, including the women from the kitchen, who peered around the doorway to see what was going on. One of these arrivals was Garland Pointing. Feckless Garland, who usually appeared and disappeared into the hills like an erstwhile ghost, was a changed man. Instead of that haunted face set grimly against the wind, tonight he was prancing and laughing, a laugh so broad we could see all the gaps where his teeth were missing.

Garland and some of his cohorts broke into an energetic step dance, or rather they tried to. Mostly they stumbled and lurched all over, driving everyone else off the dance floor. But nobody was annoyed. There were indulgent smiles from the audience, and the children squealed and giggled behind their hands.

"Been down to Kendals', I see," Mr. Hoddinott chuckled.

It was at Kendals'—the groom's family's house—that most of the men had gathered to celebrate the wedding with something other than Cassie wine. This was where our bottle of rum and our bottle of crème de menthe had gone, along with whatever other alcoholic beverages could be rounded up in a community that was six hundred miles from a liquor store. Finally, fortified and uninhibited, the men headed for the parish hall, to dance, to play the fool or chase the girls.

Garland lurched forward and grabbed a stout woman with an apron over her dress who had just finished passing the last pieces of wedding cake. He whirled her round and round in a clumsy mockery of the reel that had been danced earlier. She laughed and protested as her apron flew.

"Come on, auntie," he roared. "I'm an awful fella fer the women!"

Another merry-maker strode towards me. Even though I was wearing my coat and snow boots, he grabbed me and whirled me around, stomping on my toes a couple of times and nearly plunging us into the crowd. The fun was infectious and I could see that it was gathering momentum. This party was clearly destined to go on all night. It would spill over to the groom's house or into any other accommodating household.

But not for us. An author can't write books, with all the self-discipline the job requires, and stay out all night whooping it up. Winter was the season when Farley did most of his work, which meant that again we were out of synchronization with those around us. For them winter was a season of festivities.

Mr. and Mrs. Obediah Kendal didn't go away for a honeymoon. As was the custom, they simply moved in with whichever set of parents had room for them. Later, when their first child would be born, or possibly their second, they would get a small piece of ground and then, with some help from his friends and relatives, Obi would build their home.

Obi came to visit us a week after the wedding. No longer the bridegroom in his wedding finery, he wore a yellow satin windbreaker and his old Dacron trousers. He was, however, still wearing his shoes with pointed toes. He thanked Farley again for the rum (he didn't mention how they had liked the crème de menthe) but mostly he had come over because he wanted to chat with somebody who, like himself, had been "away," who knew about the rest of the world. He didn't bring Effie with him. Now that they were married, their social lives beyond the family would be lived separately in most cases.

He wanted to talk about his future. He was fine for the moment, he said. There was Unemployment Insurance that would last until spring. But what about after that? He didn't want to go back to working on the Great Lakes aboard an ore carrier now that he was married. It was an unsettled life and four years of it had been enough. He didn't have the education to be a teacher and he didn't have any connections that might lead to a government job. Nor did he want to return to the fish plant, where he had worked as a fish cutter when he was only sixteen.

"No, sir, no future workin' fer the plant, and that's the God's truth," he said once he had relaxed a bit. We had to coax him into our sitting room. He was reluctant to leave the familiar setting of the kitchen.

"People here're crazy puttin' up with it. Don't pay them nothin'. You works when they wants you and bides home and be damned when they don't. And they don't pay the fishermen what their fish is worth."

"What you need is some kind of organization. A union," Farley suggested.

"And that's fer sure," Obi agreed. "I'll tell you, Freeman Drake would be in fer some surprises if they iver gits a union. They tried it one time, sure. Reason things is like they is. Six years back and I remember it finest kind. My brother Sim was into the thick of it. Him and a dozen others that got no jobs today."

Obi named the men who had dared to form a union. All of them had been blacklisted after their attempt failed. We only knew one of them, Charlie Quayle of Dog Cove.

"Trouble was," Obi went on with anger mounting in his voice, "they didn't get no support. People said it wouldn't do no good to have a strike because Mr. Drake would just send all the draggers over to the plant at Jersey Island. That's the big trouble we got. Mr. Drake and his missus own so many plants. If they got trouble in one, they just sends the fish to a different one fer to git it cut and packed and froze.

"Me brother Sim always says Mr. Drake got someone what tells him things, cause he sure got wind quick of what was goin' on. How a strike was comin'. So what he done was he got aboard the *Sir Francis Drake* and got talkin' on the ship-to-shore radio, like he was talkin' to his plant manager. He knew how everybody would hear if it was on the ship-to-shore, seein' as all the skippers are tuned in.

And he says, over and over, 'Get ready to close the plant and lock the door! We'll have to abandon the whole business. Close it up and move away.'

"Well, it don't take no time fer that kind of news to git around. Faster 'n a sou'east gale. And folks believed him. Specially all the old fellas, could remember the hard times when people had to try and live on the dole of six cents a day. Everybody got right scared and then they didn't want no part of no union. They're still scared he'll pull out. And don't you think he don't know it too," Obi concluded with exasperation.

"That's a shame. Plant workers ought to support each other in labour disputes—in all the outports," I said.

Obi looked at me indulgently. He knew, even if I didn't, that loyalty was not extended to strangers in an outport. Real alliances existed only among related families and a handful of trusted friends. Many Jersey Island people had never even been to Baleena. Why should they join the strike and risk their livelihood for a lot of people they'd never met?

"Just the same, you keep a lookout to Jersey Island," Obi confided. "They're up to something on their own. That's what I hear. Used to be, over there, people were right feared of the Renoufs. Ran the place lock, stock and barrel for a hundred years. But that crowd's all gone now. I'd guess Jersey Island people has had enough."

Seven

THE BEGINNING OF LENT marked the end of the weddings and of most other events such as "times" and card games. Yet for those of us whose routines didn't follow the local pattern, the endless weeks of late winter drew us together more often than before. Our visits to one another's homes were usually unplanned and informal, and though we tended to see the same group of people over and over, getting together brightened a lot of drizzly evenings.

But Barbara Drake did things differently. When she gave a party, it was an occasion and not a last-minute idea. She was a very well-organized woman. She had to be—with three small children, two or three servants, a clutch of dogs and cats, and God knows how many house guests at various times. They all had to be fed. It was, admittedly, a little easier for her to buy food than for the rest of us. Baleena Fish Products also owned a large general store, and Barbara ordered her food there at wholesale prices. She was a masterful chef and, servants notwithstanding, she did the cooking herself.

She dressed in svelte clothes for her swish little dinner parties, and the rest of us tried to follow suit. It wasn't such a bad idea. There's the illusion, at least, that you're celebrating when you get dressed up in something other than your everyday clothes.

At her parties we would sit in a semi-circle of big chairs in front of a cheery fire. Barbara, who always looked as serene as her surroundings, usually sat in a love seat with her feet tucked underneath her like a cat. From this ceremonial seat, she would pontificate on the local scene.

"What people around here need is television. Then they could *see* the way other people live. That way they would improve their standard of living. Learn to be part of the modern world."

"But, Barbara," I argued, "they've been listening to the radio for thirty years. Do you think that has altered the way they live for the better?"

"Radio's not the same thing at all," she snapped. "If people could constantly see a better way of life—see homes with, you know, things like good furnishings, modern kitchens, plumbing, flush toilets—that sort of thing. Things they ought to have."

"But will they make enlightened choices?" I asked. "How will they know where to begin?"

"And just where," Farley interjected, "are they going to get the money to pay for all these things?"

"Money," snorted Freeman. "My son, you wouldn't believe how much money people have around here. Every family has all kinds of money saved. Tucked away in a cookie jar somewhere. You just notice when someone really has to get something—say, if someone dies and the family has to pay out a couple of hundred dollars for a casket. There's never a family that hasn't got the cash."

"Yes. Quite," added Dr. Roger Billings, puffing on his pipe. "And something I've noticed is how they lavish things on babies, always new clothes, new blankets."

"They've pots of money, you see," added Jane Billings in her imperious voice. "Just too bloody tight to spend it."

"Now stop and think," said Farley. "Suppose every family does have money tucked away. A few hundred, maybe a thousand dollars. If they go out and buy a television and instal a bathroom, that's more than a thousand right there. Then what's going to happen when the television needs a new tube? And what happens when they do have to buy a coffin?"

"The plant has often advanced money for an emergency," Freeman said. "And we've been trying for ages to get the Bank of Nova Scotia to come in here and set up a branch. Then people could easily get loans to cover all kinds of things."

"And then be perpetually in debt," Farley concluded.

"Well, at least they'd be living well," said Barbara with impatience rising in her voice.

There had never been a bank in Baleena. The postmaster or the merchants cashed all the cheques.

"Odd, you know," said Roger, "how people here seem reluctant to go into debt."

"I should bloody well think so," Farley shot back. "After all those years of being born and dying in debt to the merchant! They're not likely to want to hurry back into it."

"Freeman, do get me another drink," Barbara said urgently. "Claire? Jane? Victor? Iris?" Her eyes darted around the circle. "We all need our drinks freshened."

Freeman hastened to the bar in the pantry, as eager as his wife was to change the subject. After some vigorous rattling of ice cubes, he returned with a second round of paralyzing drinks. Freeman and Barbara did not care to discuss the past deeds of the merchants from whom both of them were descended. They rarely talked of the past at all, except for the strange sayings of servant girls or the remarks they considered amusing that came from the men, like Noah, who took them into the country to hunt. The economic history of Newfoundland was a subject as taboo in their house as a discussion about religion in Belfast.

"It's an academic subject anyway," I said, "all this talk about the influence of television. You can't pick up a glimmer of it. We're hundreds of miles from the nearest transmitter."

"Mr. Carter has promised us a relay station at Pass Island, and that will reach Baleena," Jane said confidently. "When I was talking to him on the wharf last Sunday, I told him we simply had to have it."

"Yes, I guess he did promise television. He's got an election right now," Victor Moss added cynically. "He promised it last election too."

Chesley Carter, our Member of Parliament, was already on the campaign trail, even though he would certainly be re-elected. For most people a vote for any party but the Liberals was to risk losing the benefits of Confederation— the Family Allowance cheques, the pensions and the Unemployment Insurance. The 1963 election was scheduled for April the 8th. For the candidates the ordeal of campaigning during February and March was formidable. Yet Mr. Carter dutifully spent weeks travelling on the coast boats, going ashore on icy wharves at awkward hours to shake hands, make promises and listen to complaints. He had been a school inspector on this coast before he entered politics and so had the supreme advantage—for a politician—of knowing every family by name.

One prime reason the election had been called was to resolve the matter of whether or not Canada should instal nuclear warheads in the missiles on our NORAD bases. The Conservatives, a minority government led by John Diefenbaker, were resisting pressure from the United States that Canada should accept nuclear weapons. The Liberals had stated that they would comply, if they were elected. But as critical as this issue was for mainland Canada at the time, it didn't raise a ripple of interest among the constituents of our coast. *They* wanted to know when they would get that long-promised highway which would magically connect them to the rest of the world, and that elusive television transmitter which would let them take a better look at it. The bolder fishermen dared to ask why the price they received for landed fish hadn't risen for twenty years when all their expenses had. Almost no one—except perhaps Victor Moss—bothered their thoughts with faraway and abstract issues such as Canada's commitment, or the lack of it, to the North American Air Defence organization.

Victor Moss was the manager of the plant—a quiet, well-liked man of about fifty, short and heavy, with thinning grey hair. He liked to read and to discuss issues and ideas. He might have become a closer friend of ours if it hadn't been for his family situation. His wife, Glynnis, whom he'd met and married during his years in Britain in the R.A.F., didn't go out anywhere and didn't invite anyone in. She may have been reclusive by nature. Or perhaps she had never been able to adjust to her life in a series of outports where life was not at all like the small Welsh city where she'd grown up. Whatever it was, she busied herself with solitary pursuits like growing tropical plants, and needlepoint. Victor, when he went visiting, went alone. Apart from his occasional appearances at the Drakes' house, we seldom saw him.

When dinner was announced, we shelved our ongoing debate and moved into the elegant dining room. There was a mahogany table that could seat sixteen people. When the drapes were drawn, the room shimmered from the light of eight tall candles in silver candelabra. The food was served on Spode china dishes and eaten with sterling silver cutlery. Some of the most noteworthy meals I've ever tasted were eaten there. Friends in other places may have imagined I was roughing it in the bush in Baleena, yet paradoxically I was learning the knack of presiding over dinner parties while I lived there. I learned a lot from Barbara Drake.

Most of the food came from the sea or the land around us. Our first course was usually smoked salmon—smoked by Barbara herself, who had learned how to do it from Noah Joseph. It had only been a generation since most outport people had put up a supply of smoked salmon and smoked herring to tide them over the winter months. But smoking fish was a time-consuming job and almost everyone abandoned it when the arrival of a money economy made it easier to buy food from the shops. What had once been poor-man's food was now a delicacy for the rich. Noah didn't smoke any salmon for his own family. They didn't like it. They had lost the taste for it, something I found hard to fathom. I could have eaten it every day.

Barbara tinkled the little silver bell she kept beside her dinner plate and Edna and Ruby, the servant girls, came in and discreetly cleared away the plates. They wore black dresses and white aprons and caps. They had been trained entirely by Barbara, a task she had to repeat often, for most of the girls did not remain long in this prestigious job. They were soon snapped up as brides. Many evenings a chair in the kitchen was occupied by some patient young man waiting for the interminable dinner to end so he could take his girl-friend out to the movie at the Orange Lodge.

Edna was the exception. A shy girl with a long face, a large nose and small eyes, she did not have a boyfriend and she was already twenty-five years old—an old maid by outport standards. For the previous six years she had been doing things like clearing away silver serving dishes, pouring wine, cleaning up messes, and helping to raise the Drakes' growing family. "Indispensable" and "devoted" were the words that Barbara used to describe homely, patient Edna. Ruby, on the other hand, got no such commendation. A pretty girl who always looked as if she was suppressing a laugh, she was married within the year.

The girls passed around the vegetables while Freeman carved the roast of caribou—his favourite dinner. There was a tossed salad—and *that*, in Baleena in any season, was something to exclaim about. Commodities like lettuce, spinach, radishes or cucumbers were only available at random intervals, as they didn't often survive the long, erratic journey from California. After we had devoured a delicious rum trifle for dessert, we wandered back into the living room for coffee and liqueurs.

Barbara once told me that her parents used to separate the men and women after dinner so that the men could smoke, drink port and discuss matters that weren't discussed in front of ladies. I've often wondered what those subjects were. I knew that this after-dinner segregation had taken place at one time in Upper Canada too, but it had been long before my parents or even grandparents could recall it.

Edna came in with a note for Dr. Billings, too shy to look such an important man in the eye. He opened and read it and stroked his chin. Then he handed the note to Freeman.

One of the company's draggers had just docked after a week at sea. On board was a crewman who had injured his knee when he fell on an ice-covered deck two days earlier. The captain wanted the doctor to take a look at it before the man attempted to walk home.

"Can't someone drive the chap home in a truck?" Roger asked.

Freeman told Edna to usher in the man who had delivered the note. It was Gus Barnes, the night watchman. He told them that the injured man lived on the far side of Hann's Island, which could only be reached by a trip in a dory. Even if the truck did take him to the wharf, there was still a ladder to climb and a long uphill walk after that.

"I'll go and see the laddie," Iris volunteered. "There's a first-aid box in the plant office. I could tape his knee, if need be, until tomorrow. He'll be wanting away home to his family."

"Would you? That's first class," Roger responded.

"Iris, you'll need a key to get into the office," said Victor. "I've got one with me. But I think I'd better come along too and see what this is all about. Besides, there's ice all over the road. We don't want you getting injured too."

Iris and Victor bundled themselves into their respective coats and boots and mitts. Iris was looking very attractive that night. She had done something to her hair so that it fluffed around her face. It was usually held at the back of her neck with an elastic band. She was wearing a pretty dark-green dress of some clinging material, and her legs in sheer stockings and high-heeled shoes had taken on a new shape.

We watched briefly from the picture window as the two of them set off up the road, struggling against the wind and clinging to one another as they tried to stay upright on the frozen road. Then we went back to the fire.

Barbara put a record on the stereo—*The Sound of Music*. They had seen the Broadway production on their last trip to New York. They loved the theatre. The music, the fire and the brandy were hard to resist. We curled up on the carpet, postponing the moment when Farley and I would have to face the icy road ourselves. I kicked off my shoes and wiggled my toes in the tingly warmth.

My shoes were black suede pumps, with high heels, and the dress I was wearing was a black velvet sheath. The tight skirt made it difficult to sit on the floor. It had been even more difficult to surmount the snowdrifts and the boulders on our way to the party. Furthermore, the dress was sleeveless and the wind could blow right up the sleeves of my coat and chill me to the armpits. Even though I had worn my snow boots (carrying my shoes in a handbag), the whole outfit was totally unsuitable to the climate and the place. I was like some nineteenth-century missionary wearing hoop skirts into the jungle. I marvel that it took me so long to discard that kind of costume, but logic is rarely the reason we dress the way we do. We take our banners with us when we migrate. And that kind of dress was the last word in city fashion in the early sixties.

Farley, on the other hand, always wore what he pleased. He preferred his comfy old tweed jacket and his corduroy trousers. He brought his carpet slippers in the pockets of his parka.

I was content to listen to Mary Martin singing a song about being a rebellious nun, but Jane Billings got into a discussion about hunting. Jane loved to hunt.

"Carcasses everywhere," she said sharply. "These people have no notion at all of conservation. Game has always been

93

plentiful and, as they see it, it always will be. You can't convince them otherwise. Heaven knows, I've tried to tell them."

She was always trying to convince someone of something.

"Back in November when I was hunting with Jacob," she went on, "we walked for two days before we saw even one animal."

Jacob Swift, her hired man, was the equivalent of the Drakes' Noah Joseph.

"Then on the way back we came across three moose carcasses—just left there to rot. People are too lazy to bring out the meat. They hunt, I'm convinced, out of blood lust. They don't even begin to understand the spirit of sportsmanship."

"It's a way of life," Freeman tried to explain. "Men have always gone hunting. They like to get back in the country. Away from the sea. The sea means work. I don't think they're lusting for blood so much as they just want a chance to get away for a while. Same everywhere."

"I'm the only woman in Baleena who goes hunting at all," Jane bragged and pulled herself up in her chair.

"Well, they're lucky," I said, trying to ignore Jane, "to have so many places to go. And it's all free. I mean, a man in a city would have to own a car and probably drive for hours to find anything like it."

"Yes. Very true," Freeman was quick to agree with me. He liked to emphasize any possible advantages that *his* workers might have over their less fortunate brothers in the cities.

"But they don't use what they do have properly," Barbara interjected tersely.

"And they don't appreciate what's done for them either," Jane added.

Barbara and Jane were at it again. Jane was convinced that the local people needed supervision at every turn. Barbara saw them as children in need of an inspired example. It struck me that neither of them appreciated the good qualities in these people whose existence—either as workers or as patients—supported both their families. Roger Billings didn't denounce the people—his patients—but then he rarely ventured an opinion on anything. As far as Freeman was concerned, they seldom worked hard enough nor did they spend enough money.

I suppose if anything held us together, it was probably our divergent views about the people among whom we lived. We pontificated about them, about what needed to be done for them, like a congress of theologians. Sometimes the air fairly crackled with the tension. It was usually Barbara who manoeuvred the conversation back to some less abrasive subject like the weather or food or travel. She could well have had a career as a diplomat. She knew it was easier to manipulate friends than enemies. We were treated as friends; although Farley unnerved them. He was an anomaly—an independent man living in a place where direct or indirect dependence on the merchant was the lot of everyone. Farley's income came from books and magazine articles that were sold in other places. He was, in the medieval sense of the word, a free man. It was anyone's guess what he might do or say.

Neither Iris nor Victor returned to the party, and we left around midnight. By then the ice was turning to slush, so it was easier to walk.

You could never count on the same weather for more than a few hours, but even during those storms I loved the long walks back to our house at night. We trudged up the main road—past Middle Class Row, the name Farley had given to the three identical split-level bungalows that housed the plant's managerial staff. Then we walked on past the plant buildings, on beyond the barn that contained the Drakes' horses and ponies, until we came to the end of the road. Then we climbed up a hill and reached a stretch of frozen barrens which led us to Long Pond and Short Pond—the winter shortcut to Dog Cove. Since it was marshy ground for most of the year, no houses or other buildings could be built anywhere nearby. If we stood in the centre of Long Pond on a winter night, out of sight of people and far enough from the fish plant not to hear the constant roar from the engine room, we could fantasize momentarily that we were standing in a virgin world that had barely emerged from the last ice age. On a clear night the stars seemed as close to us as those sleeping households just over the hill.

Beyond Short Pond we left our fantasy and came back into the real world as the dark, familiar shapes of the houses of Dog Cove loomed ahead. We had only to cross the foot bridge and then we were in our own snug house.

Eight

"SEEN YA'S COMIN' OVER T'HILL t'other night," said Ezra Rose, squinting against the glare of the sun on the snow. He was in his yard, holding a can of paint in one hand and a brush in the other. It was one of those rare March days when you could, for the first time, feel some warmth from the sun. Every clothesline in Dog Cove, including mine, was laden with undulating sheets, towels and clothes. And every able-bodied man appeared to be busy doing something outdoors.

"Near one o'clock in t'morning 'twere. So I said to meself I knowed where you was to," Ezra rambled on unabashed. "I figured you and the old man was down havin' a visit with Mr. Drake."

Ezra stared at me for confirmation, or denial. Our comings and goings, he reckoned, were as much his business as ours. Ezra and Matilda Rose, both seventy-two years old, were our nearest neighbours. They lived in a tiny, single-storey house painted emerald green, located alongside the Dog Cove bridge. From their kitchen window they could handily see us, or anyone else, leaving and returning home. I had always assumed that late at night, with their house in total darkness, they were asleep. But I was wrong.

How did I feel about this blatant inspection of my life? Well, I resented it at first. Where I grew up, it was a point of pride not to notice what your neighbours were doing, or at least not to mention it to them. Here our life, even to its most inconsequential detail, was a matter of public interest.

As time went on, I realized it was more than simple snoopiness. A bedroom light that wasn't turned off at night might mean that someone was ill and help was needed. And failure to return home from an evening out might mean that we had fallen into the sea or met with some other disaster.

The Roses and ourselves were the only other residents of Dog Cove who were not related to the prolific Quayle clan. The Roses' children had long since left home and their house, which once had had two storeys, had been decapitated. Removing the second floor of a house was a common alteration made by elder couples since it reduced both the amount of fuel needed to heat it and the housework needed to keep it clean. So now Ezra and Matilda lived in the three rooms of what had originally been the ground floor. Apart from the kitchen, which was the sitting room as well, there was a tiny bedroom for themselves and an even smaller one reserved for the day one of their married children might come back for a visit. They never did.

"Niver had no family to speak of," Ezra told me early in our friendship. "Only a girl and a boy. Then another boy we took and reared."

The statistics of the Rose family—two children of their own, and one adopted—would have delighted the advocates of zero population growth, but in Newfoundland no one offered them congratulations. Having such a small family was a pitiable thing. But not as pitiable as a couple who had no children at all. Like us. No one was ever unkind enough to mention our childless state to us directly. Like confronting a cripple with the fact of his lameness, they would never be so uncharitable.

"Nice pile o' freight come fer you on the last steamer," Ezra continued. This was good news; a floor lamp, a desk lamp and a carpet I had ordered three months earlier from Eaton's mail order in Moncton, New Brunswick, had finally arrived. The wharfinger, a man employed by the federal government to look after all incoming and outgoing freight, always stacked our incoming shipments with the freight for Dan Junior's shop, which in winter was delivered to the far side of the Dog Cove foot bridge by a horse-drawn "slide"—as sleds were called. The children who then transported it across the bridge in their weekly unpaid stevedoring would note what we had bought and pass the news along.

Ezra, like all the older men, was in league with the children. Like them, he had time to look at the smallest details of his world.

"Now me woman's after me to git the 'lictric lights," he said, knowing that we had two new lamps. "I can't see the need for 'em myself. Done fine without 'em this far."

Only two houses in Baleena were still without electricity. The Roses, who had lived for seventy-two years without it, and the Pointings, who didn't have the money to pay for it. The progressive Quayles all had their houses wired as soon as the municipal diesel-powered electric generator had arrived five years earlier. Electricity was not cheap in rural Newfoundland. In our own house, with half a dozen light fixtures, a refrigerator, a water pump and the once-weekly use of the washing machine and iron, we were paying about twenty dollars a month. In Ontario and Quebec at the time, the same amount of electricity would have cost less than five dollars.

"So what's the old man up to today?" Ezra asked of Farley, who was thirty years his junior.

"Oh, he's hard at work. Writing his book."

"Tellin' lies again, is he?"

I protested that Farley only wrote the gospel truth.

"Those writer fellas only tells lies," he persisted but with a grin that was part mischief and part challenge.

"He'll be tellin' lies about we people one day," Ezra ventured. "Sure as I'm standin' here."

Ezra Rose had never been to school in his life but, after he was married, with the help of Matilda, he worked on learning the alphabet until he was able to make some sense of the written word. He read English about as well as I have since learned to read Russian, by sounding out the letters and syllables one at a time. There had been a teacher from time to time at Outer Island, where Ezra was born. A community of a mere five families two miles south of Baleena, it had been abandoned fifty years earlier. The teacher always arrived in the winter—the season Ezra spent back in the country helping his father with the trapline and the firewood. Matilda, however, the youngest of a large family, had grown up in Grand Anse and attended school for seven years.

With only a limited reliance on the printed word, Ezra's view of the world was not clouded by the opinions of people he did not know. He had drawn his conclusions in life from watching, listening and asking. He listened to the buzz of news the children disseminated and he collated the gossip from among the other men. He even listened to me, though usually it was I who listened to him, for I didn't have much to tell him that he needed to know. He also listened to his battery radio, and with a shrewd ear. He was one of the few people in Baleena who did listen to the CBC, spurning the quiz games and the Nashville music that spewed forth from the rampantly commercial station at Marystown.

Ezra liked to add his own commentary after he had heard the news, explaining things like why it was that the Tories were going to lose the next election. He never missed the fishermen's broadcast at five o'clock and could tell anyone the daily fluctuations in the price of landed fish at Boston. He had once tried to follow the National Hockey League broadcasts but had given it up. He had never seen hockey played, and the impassioned commentary made no sense to him. Grown men carrying on like youngsters! All that squabbling over who pushed a puck into a corner. And the radio using up everybody's Saturday night to tell about it. Such carryings-on just proved what an idle place the mainland was, something he had always suspected anyway.

Ezra and Matilda had been married in 1919. The same year the families of Outer Island decided to abandon their rocky perch and move to the more sheltered harbours of what was now known as Baleena. The other families had dismantled their houses, board by board, and then rebuilt them at a site at Round Harbour. But Ezra, newly married, preferred to build a new house in the then uncluttered space out at Dog Cove. There he and Matilda survived two lean decades in which the price of salt fish dropped lower and lower, and the economic depression of all the western world made their lives even more stringent. In 1939, when war broke out, Ezra was one of the first men in Baleena to volunteer for service in the British Merchant Marine. He was then close to being fifty years old. He made many stormy crossings of the North Atlantic in submarine-hunted convoys, oiling machinery in the throbbing engine room of an ancient freighter.

In the port cities of England he first encountered a way of life that was not the way of Baleena. He had never seen so many buildings so close to one another and he marvelled that human beings could bear to live like that. No one ever invited him into a house there, and the pubs and teashops he visited were damp, chilling places that numbed your feet and soul. He was never warm in England. Even the poorest house in Newfoundland, he reckoned, had a kitchen that was warmer than an English castle.

"Them poor people over t'other side," he told me pityingly, "lives worse'n dogs. That's truth. I had a team o' dogs one time and they was better off."

When Ezra was retired from active duty in the merchant navy after three years' hard service, he returned home with his back pay and a small grant for having served his King and country on the perilous North Atlantic. He spent the final war years dory fishing, thankful that his son did not reach the age of eighteen until the war was almost over. Though he was still trapped in an inequitable barter system where the merchant held all the winning cards, the mariners' pay, while it lasted, made those good years for Ezra. The family was all at home. Florie helped her mother make salt fish on shore, while the boys—first his own son and then the orphan boy—went fishing with him in his dory.

It was when the war ended that things started to change. One by one his children drifted off. First it was Florie, who went over to Sydney to work as a servant girl. Soon she was married to a man from Sydney Mines. Then the boys decided they would emigrate to Canada too, where jobs were reported to be plentiful. Had they waited two more years, they wouldn't have had to bother with the formality of emigration because in 1949 Newfoundland held a referendum and 52 per cent of the population voted to become the tenth province of Canada. And that was the beginning of the biggest change of all, for almost overnight everyone had cash money to spend. It arrived, without a word of explanation, as Family Allowances for everyone who had children and Old Age pensions for those who were over seventy years of age. Furthermore, a man could apply for a service pension if he had served in the Armed Forces. Ezra got one when he was sixty-one.

Then Mr. Drake arrived and built his new fish plant, where they froze the fish instead of salting it. He didn't operate the way the Jersey merchants had, writing each man's catch in a ledger and then settling the account against goods from the store. Mr. Drake paid both the fishermen and the plant workers cash. You could spend cash money anywhere. And if that wasn't riches enough, the Canadian government even began to pay out money to fishermen during periods when fish were scarce. This was a benefit called Unemployment Insurance. A welfare officer gave out forms with questions that had to be answered and sent away. And a few weeks later a cheque arrived and, for the first time ever, healthy men found themselves being paid a wage for doing nothing.

Ezra and Matilda each received a monthly cheque for seventy-five dollars, and that, plus Ezra's service pension, put them in the previously unimaginable position of having more money than they needed. Ezra had recently made a loan to Dan Quayle Junior so that he could buy a freezer for his shop. Ezra had never expected to see the day when he would have surplus money to lend anyone.

Matilda Rose was a frail woman with white hair, arthritic hands and a bent spine—a contrast to her still-robust husband. Forty-four years earlier, she had arrived as a bride from the small community of Grand Anse, twenty miles westward. Grand Anse was one of the prettiest places I've ever seen, in sunshine or in fog. The rocky harbour was lined with tidy houses and on a hill behind them stood a picture-postcard clapboard church. Right beside the church was a cascading waterfall; and beyond that, the terrain ascended to form a hazy purple backdrop for the scene below. Yet Matilda had never looked at her former home the way I did. She once said to me that "scenery" was scarce in Grand Anse. For her, scenery was the picture on the calendar from Dan Junior's shop, which hung on her kitchen wall (and on everyone else's kitchen wall in Dog Cove). There were four fat cows standing under a large tree in a green pasture on a sunny day. In the distance two immaculate children played in the lee of a large red barn.

Though it took less than two hours on the coast boat to reach Grand Anse from Baleena—and the fare was less than four dollars—Matilda Rose had not once been back there for a visit in forty-four years. She didn't like to travel, she said. "Besides, my people come up here times enough."

They did too. Her Grand Anse brothers and sisters, and nieces and nephews, came often to Baleena, mainly to visit the doctor. They stayed in the spare bedroom in the Roses' house until the westbound boat arrived to take them back home.

Matilda was known as "Aunt Til" in Dog Cove, even though she wasn't really anyone's aunt hereabouts. She seldom left the house, but a surprising number of people came to see her. I often dropped in myself.

Ezra Rose, his morning's work done, washed his hands in the basin on the pantry counter. Then he came in and sat down on a chrome and red vinyl chair by the kitchen window. There he commanded a fine eye-level view of the Dog Cove bridge and all who passed over it on foot or under it by dory. No view of any other bridge in the whole world could have been so intriguing to him.

"Be fine all day, 'twill," he said with conviction, scanning the sky. "West wind will hold. Like as not, be fine tomorrow besides. T'inks I'll walk to Round Harbour this evening and buy 'nother can dory buff. Dan got nary can left in shop seein' all hands has it to paint boats today."

Dories were always painted dory buff, a yellowish-beige shade of marine enamel. Though a wife was granted an opinion or possibly the entire choice about the colour a house might be painted, a man's dory remained the traditional colour.

A kettle of boiled vegetables and salt beef was simmering on the range, and fresh bread was cooling on the pantry shelf. It was almost noon, time for the main meal of the day in Baleena—and indeed almost everywhere in Newfoundland. In Dog Cove, Dan Quayle Junior closed his shop for an hour. The noon whistle at the plant brought Dan Quayle Senior, his son Clarence and his several working daughters puffing up the hill and down over the foot bridge, heading for home and a hot meal. The school children came just behind them. Then Dog Cove sat down to eat.

We were the exceptions. The only meal we ate which coincided with the local pattern was breakfast at about eight in the morning. It wasn't until one o'clock in the afternoon that we ate again, and it was a small meal—soup or a sandwich or something left over from the night before. Our main meal of the day was eaten at seven in the evening. This was the pattern I had grown up with and never questioned until I found my timetable was at variance with that of my new neighbours.

The amount of time Farley and I spent eating was another habit that set us apart. Lingering over a leisurely meal or chatting over a second cup of coffee seemed peculiar to our household. Dan Senior, his son Clarence, and his daughters were usually on their way back to the plant a scant twenty minutes after they had arrived home for dinner.

Though we never adjusted to it ourselves, their meal schedule made better sense than ours. It meant, for one thing, that much of the cooking, baking, peeling and chopping—plus the cleaning up afterwards—was over and done with each day by early afternoon. Their subsequent meals, "tea" at five o'clock and "lunch" at ten o'clock—cold meat, pickles, bread, biscuits, cheese and cakes—were much easier to assemble. For all I know, they may have been easier on the digestion at the end of the day.

As I got up to leave the Roses' kitchen, I heard the latch lift on the storm door and the sound of boots shuffling on the doormat. It was Dorothy Quayle. Each day she visited the homes of the sick or the old on her father's behalf. She collected grocery orders on the way home from school at noon, and delivered them on the way back.

"Want anything from shop?" she asked in a business-like manner, her face glowing from the sun.

"Two pound cabbage, Dorothy, my dear," said Aunt Til in her frail voice. "That be all now."

I left with Dorothy and we dawdled along the path together, soaking in this intoxicating warmth. Days like this were a gift. Dorothy's brother Leroy, too young for school, had been waiting for her. Half sliding and half running, he came down the hill and marched jubilantly along beside us, not saying a word.

"You divil. You're goin' to catch it," Dorothy admonished him. "Where's your jacket to?"

He grinned at her, and then at me, and still didn't say anything. On this lovely day, Leroy, who was four, had abandoned his coat somewhere and was giddily running around in just his sweater and the lower half of his snowsuit. Defiantly happy, he unbuttoned his snowsuit helmet and began swinging it back and forth in great arcs, as if it had the momentum of a pail of water.

"You're some idle, Leroy, my son," Dorothy added like a little mother, and then gave him a hug. "All youngsters is idle," she said to me sagely.

As we walked along, Dorothy reported the news. Since she was in and out of many homes every day, she was a fountain of information, and sharing the news was as much a part of her daily routine as delivering the groceries.

"Grandfather John's took real bad," she said. "He finds his stomach, he does, and doctor cain't do a thing for 'im neither. Right old, 'e is."

At eighty-nine, John Quayle was the patriarch of Dog Cove, the great-grandfather of Dorothy and Leroy and innumerable other children whom I had yet to know by name. His failing health was a matter of interest to an infinite number of people.

"Is he in hospital?" I asked.

"Etta won't 'low 'em to carry him off to hospital. Seems he got to die home, like he was born home."

Etta distrusted hospitals. In her youth they had been regarded as places where people went to die, often from tuberculosis. She did not share the optimism of the younger women that the hospital was a place in which to get well.

"Blanche is goin' to hospital. Right soon," Dorothy reported.

"Blanche? Now tell me, who is Blanche?" I asked.

"Charlie's Blanche," she said impatiently, wondering how I could be so dim that I didn't know who she was talking about.

"Blanche's havin' a baby. And nary truck can git up road neither 'cause of ice. She got to go in dory. They're choppin' now so's to clear the way"

She pointed towards the far end, the "bottom" of the cove. Two men in a dory were leaning over its side, hacking at the ice with axes. They were about fifty feet from a fishing stage where they hoped to load the pregnant Blanche into a dory. Fortunately, the ice was not very thick. If Blanche could hold on for a few more days, and the weather stayed mild, the problem would be solved. But neither pregnancies nor weather are entirely predictable, and so the two men chopped all day.

When we reached Dorothy's house, we could see Jackie and Susie inside wiping peek holes in the steamy window panes. Leroy and Dorothy ran up the path and pressed their noses against the glass of the kitchen window.

Just before she turned into the porch, Dorothy called to me, "I got me poem wrote off. I'm comin' over with it this evening!"

"Good. I want to read it," I called back.

She darted into the security of their kitchen, both pleased and embarrassed.

I meandered up the path towards our house, then checked my laundry to see if it was dry, savouring the good smell of clothes that have been dried by a sea breeze. Because of the high cost of electricity, very few families, including ourselves, could afford to operate a clothes dryer.

I heard my name being called. "Claire! Wait for us!"

Heading across the foot bridge were Iris Finley and little Nancy Drake. They caught up with me, a bit breathlessly.

"Is this no a grand day? Come away with us. We're off to the beach for a picnic. Get Farley and pack a sandwich and we'll have a grand time."

"Iris, you're daft. A picnic in the winter?"

"What matter. A fine day is a fine day any time," she insisted with Scottish sensibility.

She was absolutely right. The temperature on our kitchen window thermometer was 54 degrees (F), which wasn't all that far off the temperature of most summer days. The sun was bright, the breeze was gentle, and the visibility so keen we felt we could have seen all the way to Bermuda.

Farley was happy to go on a picnic, eager to get out of the house and away from the typewriter where he had been slogging for four months. His book was nearly finished. So we hastily packed sandwiches and a thermos of tea and the four of us headed off into the country.

From Dog Cove we had to cross a second foot bridge to reach the countryside. The "swinging bridge" was a narrow suspension bridge about a hundred feet long and just wide enough for a person or a sheep to walk across. It swayed with the impact of footsteps, and it was always a major undertaking for the Drakes or the Billings to persuade their high-strung horses to cross it. It bridged a narrow arm of the sea that formed a natural boundary between the settlement and the country. No one had built a house beyond it, for reasons that may have been psychological rather than physical. Beyond the bridge was a well-worn path that led up an incline to the top of a vast rock. From there you could look back and see the confetti-coloured houses of Dog Cove and Muddy Hole and Round Harbour and Hann's Island and The Gut—all of Baleena laid out below you like an aerial photograph. Far beyond them were the long-deserted settlements of Outer Island and Offer Island, with only the collapsing stick fences of their cemeteries as barely visible reminders of the human lives they once harboured. And beyond that was the lonely Seal Island with its brave white lighthouse standing guard over the mosaic of reefs that lurked under the sea. On days like this, the sea was a deep indigo blue, a deceptive colour that made it look like the colour of the Caribbean on a travel poster. It lapped timidly at the shore as if it was a summer day and gave no hint that you would freeze to death in a few minutes if you fell in. Even on the hottest day in August, it was perishing. One summer I bravely attempted to swim, but I was out again within the minute. It took my breath away.

In late winter the snow lingered in gritty grey pockets in the crevices of the rocks. We trudged on through a wet marsh and then crossed over to a level place that was covered by springy juniper plants. From there we followed a path through a thicket of spruce trees. Finally we reached the edge of a precipice down which the trail plunged dangerously. Then it was smooth sailing because this was where the beach began, a stretch of pure-white sand that continued for seven miles. And there wasn't a soul living any closer to it than we did.

Nancy had already started running down the cliff towards the sand. Why do beaches have such a magnetic appeal for children? Or for any of us? We followed her down, picking our way with adult caution. Finally on the firm sand, we plodded along in our winter boots, listening to that pleasing gurgling sound of pebbles being washed together along the shore with each wave.

The end of winter is the best season for beachcombing. As the ice and snow melt, the bounty that has been hurled ashore by months of storms begins to appear. Driftwood and sea shells were everywhere, along with the occasional fragment of whale bone, the skeletons of birds and a lot of other mysterious jetsam that we could never quite identify. Less intriguing were the hundreds of fragmented plastic bottles and bags that were altogether too easy to identify. Plastic doesn't erode beautifully like wood or bone. Nor does it sink to the bottom of the sea like glass, or disintegrate like cardboard containers. Nor is it eaten by the scavengers—conners and flatfish—who devour the edible garbage that gets flung into the coves. The sea has no way to rid itself of these intractable containers. Like bad pennies, the detergent and the bleach bottles come back again and again.

It was too cold to sit on the exposed beach, so we walked inland to a field of pale beach grass. We found a smooth rock the size of a chesterfield and, using it both as a backrest and a windbreak, we sat down in a row, like birds on a power line.

"We've a new nurse come last week," said Iris as we delved into our lunch. "Miss O'Brien from St. John's. If it wasna for her, I'd no be away here the day."

"That's good news," I said.

"She'll no stay long, that one," Iris added.

"Why?"

"Tsk. She told me the first day that she hadna been in an outport before, and she didna think she would like it. She's scarce been out the door since she got here. Only place she goes is the post office. Spends all her time writing letters to her boyfriend."

"Bloody St. John's," Farley muttered. "The damned townies have been bleeding these outports for three centuries and they can't put themselves out to take care of the poor souls who've been maintaining them in their bastion of civilization."

"Och, Farley, that's no fair," Iris challenged. "There's some do."

"Name one."

"You surely canna say that Miss O'Brien's folk have been bleedin' the poor folk on the coast. She told me her father is a city policeman in St. John's."

"It's the St. John's attitude. They're all the same. They think they're inside a fortress. They won't budge if they can help it. Just look around you, Iris. You came from Scotland. Roger Billings came from England. Dr. Lee is from Hong Kong. The doctor before that came from Italy, and the one before that from . . . where did you say he was from?"

"Ireland."

"See what I mean? There are nurses and doctors in St. John's. Surely to God some of them could come and work for part of their careers in the outports. But they don't. And there's never been a dentist here, ever. People lose their teeth before they lose their hair."

"There's Reverend Way. He's a Newfoundlander. From Heart's Delight. He's looking after his own."

"Well, yes, he is in one area," Farley admitted. "There's no shortage of clergymen. Must be the only profession with a surplus to export."

Nancy had been listening to this conversation with solemn interest.

"When I grow up I'm going to be a doctor and a nurse and look after all the sick people," she announced.

"Are you, my dear-ee-o? A doctor *and* a nurse. That's grand. We'll all be waiting for that," said Iris, winking at me.

Unlike her older sister, Megan, who already had the air of a crown princess, Nancy at five and a half was shy. She preferred solitary pursuits like drawing or reading or playing with her dolls. Most of all, she loved to go anywhere with Iris, who, a younger sister herself, was understanding of her.

We finished the picnic by sharing the box of shortbread that Iris had brought along. Then we walked back over the beach, where I had a wild urge to take off my snow boots and socks and feel the cold sand squishing between my toes. I didn't do it, of course, but a beach in winter can be almost as inviting as a beach in summer.

Returning along the same trail through the spruce trees and the marsh, we saw a man and a boy coming in from another trail that led into the country north of us. They moved at the fast clip of men who are used to the country and, as they got nearer, we recognized the inscrutable Garland Pointing and his son, Harold. They were less than happy to see anyone else because they had been hunting, and hunting was illegal at this time of year.

"'Tis a civil day," Garland grunted. Harold, a glum boy, managed a glimmer of neighbourly recognition. Both were dressed in ragged wool jackets, worn trousers and tattered rubber boots that looked as though they leaked. None of the Pointings ever looked warm enough. But Garland obviously had something in his bulging pack that ought to be the basis for several substantial meals.

The two of them soon outdistanced us and, when they were out of earshot, Iris, in a disapproving voice, leaned close to us and said, "That lot! Their bairn's in the hospital just now, poor wee soul. Pneumonia. Just one year old. He's well now but I havena the heart to send him home yet. And her about to have another one. Tsk," she clucked.

"It's amazing that they survive," I said.

"It is that. And it's no use talking to that madam. She doesna heed a word. There's no many like that around here, thank the Lord. Most folk take their medicine and stick to their diet, you can be sure. Mind," she chuckled, "they've their own remedies too. I've one old dear comes in with her granddaughter, and she's a string around her neck with a packet full of hair tied on it."

"Hair? What kind of hair?" Farley asked.

"Seemingly it's the hair of someone who's never seen their father," Iris harrumphed.

"What on earth is that supposed to cure?" Farley wanted to know.

"Asthma."

"And does it work?" I asked.

"No fear," Iris snorted. "Mind, neither does the treatment we're giving her, poor lassie. I canna scold them altogether for trying to treat it their own way."

The Pointing family didn't have any remedies, either useful or silly, of a bygone era. They had discarded them, yet they hadn't replaced them with any new ones either.

They had abandoned the old nutritional virtues, such as picking berries and preserving them for the winter. Though Garland still went out hunting, it was easier to sell the meat and take the money to the shop and buy something. Something sugary in a bright package. Garland and Rosie had been exposed to a money economy for a decade, but they were still bewildered by the decisions they were forced to make as to what to discard and what to keep from the time of their childhood.

When we got back to our house, I found a folded piece of paper on the kitchen table. It was Dorothy's poem. I had forgotten that when she said she was coming over in the "evening," she meant that part of the day which I had always understood to be the afternoon. Written in her neatest handwriting, the poem read:

A FRIEND OF MINE

by Dorothy Quayle

Sometime when I have nothing to do
And like to spend an hour or two
I go up to a friend of mine
And there I spend a lot of time
Sometimes I wash the dishes
Sometimes I sweep the floor
And when it's time to go
Then I can do no more
I like to write my poems
And sing songs any old time
But I'll still wash the dishes
For a friend of mine.

Nine

IN APRIL FARLEY FINISHED HIS BOOK about wolves—
three hundred and fifty typewritten pages, which I had
typed twice through myself! With this monumental task
behind us, nothing, not even the long spell of dismal weather,
could dampen our spirits. It was the slop bucket end of
winter, a day as depressing as the resurgence of an old
ailment. But finishing a manuscript, with all the final revi-
sions in place, is a euphoric experience, almost like childbirth. We wanted to celebrate. So on that dank evening
with wet snow underfoot and a gunmetal sky overhead, we
went looking for some friends and fun.

In slickers and boots we plodded down the muddy road
to see who might be available to share our buoyant mood.
First we tried the RCMP detachment and the McEacherns.
I rang the doorbell but no one answered. Farley rang the
bell at the door of the police office. No answer there either.

"Out," Farley said with some disappointment. We stood
and wondered where we should try next. We couldn't visit
Iris as she had gone to St. John's to take a one-week course
in pulling teeth.

We considered calling on the Billings, but Jane's long-
awaited thoroughbred horse had recently arrived and she
could talk of nothing else. Once again there was no second
doctor. Dr. Lee, who had proved to be a pleasant though
subdued companion, had resigned as the travelling doctor
and was by then on his way to join a group practice in Nova
Scotia. We thought about dropping in on the Reverend

Matthew and Thelma Way but were hesitant to barge in there on a Saturday night when he might be writing his sermon.

There was only one other place we could think of going where anyone might comprehend the nature of our jubilation, and that was the Drakes. We headed for the Gut Road, reasonably sure they would be at home. Their choices for an evening out were even more limited than our own.

"Farley and Claire! How nice to see you. Come in," said Barbara through a forced smile. She was by then in the middle of a pregnancy. She looked tired, but her terse greeting hinted that something besides the pregnancy was unsettling her. If there had been a graceful way to do it, we should have left then; but because of the general unwritten protocol of outports, we felt obliged to remain for a polite few minutes anyway. Just as she was obliged to extend a welcome to us, however inconvenient it may have been for her.

"Miserable weather, isn't it? Take off your coats and come in and have a drink with us," she insisted.

Freeman was standing by the fireplace with a drink in his hand. He looked angry. To our surprise, Doug McEachern was also there, and so was Victor Moss and Noah Joseph, all of them looking solemn. Freeman was making a dark pronouncement about someone being "up to something."

"Farley, my son, come in. Claire, you're looking lovely. How are you?" said Freeman, snapping into a state of cordiality and giving me a kiss on the cheek. "Let me get you a drink . . . let's see, that's rum for you, Farley. And Claire, you'll have a . . . scotch and soda, right?" he asked, recovering some equilibrium as he went through the ritual.

"It's Jersey Island," Barbara explained hastily, since it was obvious we had walked into the midst of some turbulence. "They've walked off the job. This afternoon. They say they're on strike. Can you imagine such a thing?"

We could easily imagine it. It was a storm that had been brewing for a long time. Freeman must have known it was coming.

"Victor says he knows who's behind it," Barbara said triumphantly.

"Hold on there, Barbara. I only said that I had a few suspicions. I don't know for certain who it is," he explained calmly.

Ever since he'd come to work for Freeman Drake, Victor Moss had been pouring oil on troubled waters. Somehow he had maintained the delicate balance between Freeman's obstinacy and the growing discontent among his workers, which was no small accomplishment. Without it the labour and management clashes would have been a lot worse.

"Victor, you'll come with us tomorrow, of course," Barbara commanded.

"If I can be of any help," he said with a trace of resignation in his voice.

"And Corporal McEachern, too . . . Doug," Barbara added, deciding to call him by his first name and thereby include him in the circle of management.

"Not unless I'm needed," he replied matter-of-factly. "I'd have to know first what charges you intend to lay."

Freeman exploded. "Good God, there has to be something on the books! Vandalism. Trespassing. Rioting. Drunk and disorderly . . ."

"You know if any of that happened? Any damage to the plant itself? Got any witnesses?" our corporal asked, switching to his policeman's voice.

The answer to all of Doug's questions had to be "no" and Freeman knew it, but Doug's reluctance to accompany them to Jersey Island the next morning was nearly as unacceptable to him as the strike itself. Doug's mere presence— six feet four inches, dressed in his sombre winter uniform —would lend an air of stern authority to Freeman's arrival. The only problem was that there isn't any law to prevent fish plant workers from leaving their jobs.

Doug, who had grown up in a pulp mill town in British Columbia, had no great love for the people who ran "company towns." The mill would have been his life too, if he hadn't escaped it by joining the Mounties. Now he lived in another kind of company town—four thousand miles from the one he had left behind.

Freeman suddenly turned his attention to Noah Joseph, who had been sitting like a good school boy, listening but saying nothing.

"Noah, my son, your sister's married down to Jersey Island, isn't that right?"

"Yessir. That's true, Mr. Drake."

"Well, my son, I wondered if you happened to have heard anything about this so-called strike at our plant there. I've got a hunch it's some of those fellows who go away to work on the Great Lakes ships. They could be the trouble-makers. Your sister's boy goes away to the Lakes, didn't you tell me that?"

"Yessir, I b'lieve he did go away last year. Levi must be seventeen, maybe eighteen years old now. Like as not, he'll go back again this spring," Noah offered.

"Here, let me get you another drink, Noah," said Freeman as he headed for the bar.

"Thank you, sir."

"You know, it would be a terrible thing for the folks at Jersey Island if there was a strike. We wouldn't have any choice but to close down the plant. All those lost jobs. Be too bad."

"Yessir. Wonderful bad."

"I just thought, oh, seeing as how you've got some of your own people down there, Noah . . . well, you'd hate to see the hard times come back. And if you happened to hear who the troublemakers were . . . well, we would certainly like to know their names. Get to the root of the trouble."

"Yessir. Be some big trouble."

Noah had to sit through another drink and another round of questions. But he revealed nothing that might have reflected badly on his relatives or friends. After his third drink, he got to his feet and insisted that he must be off, explaining that three of his children, as well as his wife, Minnie, were all in bed with the flu.

"So what do you hear about all this, Farley? You seem to have an ear to the ground around here," Freeman asked my husband.

"Not a thing that you don't know," Farley told him truthfully.

During the final solitary weeks of unrelieved writing, neither of us had talked to anyone beyond our immediate neighbours. Rumours had wafted through our kitchen but then they always did, whatever the season.

"I'm curious to know what it is they want," Farley asked. "Why have they stopped working, anyway?"

"It's a totally illegal strike," Barbara corrected him. "Because of stupidity and just plain stubbornness."

"Troublemakers. A crowd of rowdies stirring up trouble," Freeman added.

"But you didn't answer my question," Farley persisted. "What is it they want? More money? Shorter hours? Paid holidays? Pensions? What?"

At this point Victor interjected. "I believe they want one dollar an hour for the men and ninety cents for the women. Oh yes, and the chance to form a union besides."

Farley considered this and then put it to Freeman. "Well, why don't you give it to them? That would settle the whole matter and then they'd go back to work."

Freeman gave Farley the exasperated look a man gives a fifteen-year-old offspring who announces he wants his own car.

"My son," he said, barely containing his temper but using the only chummy salutation he ever used, "you don't know what you're talking about. We can't pay them that much. The fish business, my God, you wouldn't believe it. Plentiful one year and scarce the next. There's no money in it, no money at all."

"I really think it's sentiment that keeps us in this business, Farley," Barbara added. "There's so little profit to be made."

Doug McEachern and I exchanged glances. Victor was tactfully inspecting his fingernails. It was difficult to believe that there was no money to be made in the fish business.

"Ninety cents then," Farley went on, assuming the role of negotiator. "Ninety for the men, and eighty for the women. That would be meeting their demands halfway. I bet they'd settle for that."

"Can't be done," Freeman said angrily. "If you give in, they just go on wanting more and more. There won't be any unions in my plants. Not now. Not ever!" he boomed.

"If it becomes uneconomical to run the plant, then we'll have to close it," Barbara added. "Lock the door. Bring all the draggers over here. There can't be many of them behind this. We've always treated the Jersey Islanders like our own family. As soon as we find out who those troublemakers are . . ." She gave Doug a demanding stare. "Now, do let's change the subject. We'll have enough trouble tomorrow morning when we have to deal with them. Farley, tell us how that book of yours is coming along, the one you've been writing all winter."

"Well, as a matter of fact, it's . . ."

"Is it finished yet?" she interrupted as she left the room to replenish Doug's drink.

"It's finished, thank God," said Farley, his answer falling on Victor and Doug. They were suddenly quite interested in the book and full of questions, relieved not to have to listen to any more emotionally charged discussions about the strike. What was the book all about, they wanted to know. When could they get a copy? What was its name?

Victor was an omnivorous reader, but Doug had only started to read something besides police reports and magazines since he had been posted to Baleena.

"Haven't got a name yet. I hate naming books. Don't know why. Maybe because you spend so much time writing the damn thing that when it's finally done you just want to hand it over to the publisher and forget about it," Farley explained.

"I thought he could call it 'Farley and the Wolf,'" I said.

"Not that kind of wolf story," Farley said.

"How about 'Who's Afraid of the Big Bad Wolf'?" Doug suggested.

"Or maybe 'The Boy Who Cried Wolf,'" added Victor.

"Won't do, won't do. The wolf is the good guy in my story," Farley explained. "For centuries he's been blamed for everything from baby snatching to the decline of the arctic caribou. I know better. That's what I'm telling people in the book. If anyone reads it."

"Tellya something, Farl, I bet a lot of people will read that book," Doug said sincerely. "Out where I come from —Vancouver Island—that's what a lot of people are interested in, wild animals."

"Well, you never know about books. The ones you think will sell, often don't, and the ones you figure are write-offs, often catch on. Who can say?" Farley shrugged. "Anyway, my working title for this one has been 'Cry Wolf,' although my publisher favours 'Never Cry Wolf.' We'll probably use one or the other."

"Having trouble naming your book, Farley?" asked Barbara, breezing back in with drinks and picking up the tail end of our conversation. "We're having the same problem—trying to think of a name for the new refrigerator ship. We just don't have any talent for that kind of thing, do we, Freeman?"

Freeman's new ship—the one they were trying to find a name for—was ready to leave Pictou, Nova Scotia, where it had been built. But the Gulf of St. Lawrence was still choked with ice. If it didn't arrive within two weeks, the next shipment of fish wouldn't reach the Boston market on schedule. That meant the loss of a good deal of money. Their present refrigerator ship, the old *Bosco*, had passed her last marine survey by the federal government inspector, but she was too slow and too small for the job.

I tried to think of some ships' names. The three draggers were called the *Sheldrake*, the *Wood Drake* and the

Eider Drake. Their yacht was called *Sir Francis Drake*. Although as far as they knew, they weren't directly related to the famous Devon sea dog and buccaneer, they liked to believe there was an ancient, distant connection.

"So, what else starts or ends with drake?" I asked the gathering.

"We seem to be running out of drake names," Barbara said.

"Say, what about Mandrake?" Doug offered. "You know, like Mandrake the Magician?"

"Drake's Drum?" suggested Victor.

"Drake's Progress?" suggested Farley.

They weren't taken seriously.

"This is a refrigerated vessel," I said. "I think it should have a name that makes you think of ice or frost, something like that. It should be named after a glacier. Or a snow-capped mountain maybe. How about Mount Drake? Is there such a place?"

None of us had ever heard of one.

"How about Montcalm?" said Farley.

"Monte Carlo?" said Victor.

"Montreal?" said Doug.

"I've got a good idea," I said, "how about Mount Snowdon? That's a mountain in Wales. It sounds kind of, oh . . . grand and cool."

I had only the vaguest idea where Mount Snowdon was, the idea having come to me from the fact that Princess Margaret's husband had recently been named Lord Snowdon, presumably after the same mountain.

"That's rather nice," said Victor, who had a Welsh wife.

"Mount Snowdon," Barbara repeated, mulling the name over, saying it several times. Names that sounded as though they belonged to the British aristocracy had a special place in her affection. "Mount Snowdon isn't bad at all. Do you like that, Freeman—Mount Snowdon?"

Freeman was beyond caring about ships' names. His thoughts were somewhere else. He grunted and then abruptly changed the subject.

"Tell me, Farley, my son, what is it you do now that you've finished this book? Send it off to Toronto, or to the States or somewhere? Or do you take it there yourself? What happens next?"

Freeman seemed oddly curious about the process of publishing a book, a subject which hadn't captured his interest before.

"I have a publisher in Toronto and another one in Boston. I should go down to Boston and see my editor one of these days," Farley explained. "I generally see him once a year. He looks over my manuscript, we talk about my future writing, that sort of thing," he went on, trying to explain the subtle relationship which exists between a writer and his editor.

"Well," Freeman's voice took on a hearty tone, "why don't you and Claire take a trip to Boston on the new ship. The, um . . . what did you say you wanted to call her, Barbara?"

"Could be Mount Snowdon. I like the sound of it."

"Well then, the Mount Snowdon. With any luck, she'll be going from here to Boston in a couple of weeks. There's a comfortable cabin on board—the owner's cabin. You might enjoy it."

"Not a bad idea," said Farley, a bit surprised by the offer and looking to me for a reaction. "What do you think, Claire?"

"I'd love it," I said.

"Good. Call it settled then," said Freeman generously. "We'll keep a weather eye open. Let you know when she gets here."

We left the Drakes' house with Doug McEachern and walked along the road with him. In this slushy season, the ice was no longer safe and so we had to take the longer route home, which wended its way through the entire community. The snow had turned to cold, piercing rain, which met us head-on.

"Light's on in the kitchen. Marj must be back. C'mon in. Have some tea," Doug said as we approached the detachment.

"Hi, there. Come in out of the rain," said Marjorie, who was preparing a lunch. She had spent the evening at a neighbour's house, teaching a woman to crochet. She was one of the few younger women who had any skills with a needle. Perhaps it was because she had been raised by her grandmother. Most of the young wives of Baleena had never learned to knit or quilt or crochet. They had brushed all that aside, along with the less charming aspects of the old life, such as scrubbing boards and chamber pots.

"So how did it go?" she asked Doug, curious to know why he had been summoned to the castle.

"That Free Drake . . ." Doug grumbled through the crumbs of his first chocolate chip cookie.

"Are you going to Jersey Island with him?" Farley asked.

"Farl, there's not one good reason why I should go. Not one bloody reason—unless someone down there is stupid enough to start fighting or destroying property. Jeezus, I hope they don't. Then all hell will break loose. I'll have the sergeant from Cornerbrook sending in a plane load of rein- forcements. We'll have a bloody war on our hands. Lookit,

I was one of the ones the feds sent in to Badger back in '59 when the Woods Workers went out on strike. I already know what happens when they send in the Force to break up a strike. Bloody hell, and I don't want any part of it. No, sir."

"How are they ever going to organize a union in a place like Jersey Island?" I wondered out loud.

"Not a snowball's chance in hell," said Doug. "But I envy you guys, takin' off in that new ship to Boston. Sure beats walkin'," he added.

"I know. I'm excited about it. I love the sea."

"And am I looking forward to a nice rest," said Farley. "Days and days with nothing to do but watch the seagulls."

"Didja stop to think why he might have offered you that trip?" Doug asked.

"Probably figures I'll write something about it. You know, 'Iron Men in Wooden Ships,' that sort of thing. Maybe he wants to immortalize the business he's in."

"Could be kiddin' yourself, Farl. How's about he wants you off and gone somewhere. Maybe figures you got something to do with this fracas, on the side of the strikers."

"Me, for Christ's sake? I've been glued to my typewriter for months."

"Yeh, but he can't be sure. He doesn't know who you've been talkin' to. He's got more suspicions right now than farmers have hay. See, it was real bad luck for Free they let that fish get unloaded over at Jersey. If he'd known there was a strike comin' up, he would of got those draggers over here instead in one hell of a hurry."

Doug was the antithesis of those hard-nosed, trouble-seeking cops who are the heroes of television sit-coms. He tried to prevent trouble before it happened. But when we got to know him better, we teased him that he had the cushiest police job in Canada. Most of his complaints involved disputes concerning dogs—whose dog had bitten whose child, or which child had tormented which dog. He had to deal with the occasional domestic squabble and once in a while he had to cope with drunks.

When he first learned about his posting to Baleena, he hadn't looked forward to it, largely because it meant three years without a car. However, it hadn't taken him long to discover that this deprivation had a good many advantages. For one thing, he didn't have to spend his weekend patrolling the roads for traffic violators or impaired drivers. He didn't have to investigate grisly accidents in which people were injured or killed. And not having a police car to drive around in, Doug had effortlessly lost fifteen pounds in eight months.

"I sure don't want to still be here whenever the road gets through and people start gettin' cars," he once told us. "Nothin' worse than guys that never had cars, once they get 'em. I seen that back home—a fishing village on the coast—the province punched a road over the mountain where there'd only been a wagon track before. Suddenly everybody and his brother got a car. Awful old wrecks. Spent every cent they had to keep 'em goin' and drove 'em like a bunch of wild men. The first year three men and a girl got killed and another guy lost an arm, all in separate accidents. They just couldn't handle the speed. And I'll betcha dollars to doughnuts the same thing will happen here. Just hope I'm off and gone somewhere else before it does."

"You will be," Farley said. "With a hundred miles of muskeg to cross, and the Annieopsquotch Mountains to get through besides, it would cost millions to put a road in here."

"Aha, but Mr. Carter says the highway survey is underway," Marjorie reminded us.

"Yes, but surveys are cheap, and so are promises," said Farley. "Honestly, I don't know why everybody believes that a road is going to improve their lives or make them happier. It would take hours and hours to drive out of here, even on the best of roads, which isn't what they'd get. For all the money it would cost, the government would be way further ahead to build an additional coast boat or two."

"Lookit, Farl, it's cars themselves," said Doug, after giving the matter some thought. "People just gotta have a car even if there's no place to go."

"Yes, I guess," Farley nodded. "The new religion—machines. They should have stuck with Christianity."

"Now, Farley," Marjorie scoffed, "such foolishness. You surely don't mean to say you can't be a Christian and own a car or a washing machine or whatever?"

"It's not that simple," Farley explained. "It's a matter of what you believe is the ultimate good. Either you have a spiritual god with a tangle of obligations and rewards, or you choose technology with all its attendant gadgetry and the obligation of getting enough money to pay for it all. I just don't think human beings can reconcile the two."

"They can, sure," Marjorie insisted.

"Maybe they can right now, while they still have a foot in both camps. But the passion for one is going to out-distance the passion for the other. Just look around. It already has in most of North America. Why the hell do you think I want to live *here*? Nobody here has yet to hear the word that if they get hold of enough bulldozers they can build paradise on earth."

"Jeez, I drove a bulldozer one summer," Doug suddenly reminisced at the mention of the machine. "Year before I joined the Force. I kinda liked it too. Sittin' up there, shovelling up the earth. Funny thing, most of the guys I knew who worked at it—they were really happy."

"Never mind the bulldozers," said Farley, nonplussed by Doug's nostalgia. "Around here most people still believe there's a good life to be lived without changing the shape of everything. Can't you see that someone who builds his own house, catches a few fish, grows a few potatoes and keeps a cow and a sheep and a few hens is in a safer position than, say, someone who works in a city for thirty thousand bucks a year?"

Doug and Marjorie both shook their heads. They didn't see it at all. They could both remember stories about their grandparents, who had lived the old-fashioned way.

"Now you look here, Farley," Marjorie replied. "If you weren't making money from your writing, why, you wouldn't have the time to *do* any writing. Would you now? You'd be out there milking the cows and catching the fish and chasing the hens around the yard. not to mention all the spinning you'd have to do before you could get enough wool to knit yourself some winter underwear."

She winked at me, and we both started to laugh, trying to imagine Farley sitting in earnest concentration, knitting on a suit of long johns.

"Ah, the irrefutable logic of women," Farley said with a mock sigh. "You've got me there. Alas, I'm a lousy knitter."

When we left at midnight, it was still raining. Farley called back to Doug, who was standing in the doorway, "Don't let them bully you into anything tomorrow. It'll be a case of a man getting his Mountie if you do!"

Ten

I AWOKE TO THE SOUND of grinding and scraping. I wake up sluggishly and it was a minute or two before it dawned on me that I wasn't dreaming. I listened—wide awake suddenly—to a searing crunch, the sound that gives you a sinking feeling when you're parking a car. But I was on a ship, not a car, a ship that shuddered like a whale with a chill. Pale, cold light streamed over me from a porthole opposite my bunk. It was 6:10 A.M., a time of day that poets with a different metabolism from mine have been moved to write about.

As far as I could see, we were surrounded by ice—great and small chunks of it, floating and submerged. Ragged ice pans the size of backyards cracked like plates as the ship ground its resolute way. It was an eerie sunrise. The eastern sky was streaked with gold and pink and turquoise, nursery colours that cast an incongruous delicate glow over the chunky miles of blue ice. Seagulls, brighter than I am in the morning, perched saucily on the ice floes, taking flight and circling the ship as they scolded us for disturbing their hitherto quiet morning. A band of harp seals sitting on an ice pan stared curiously at our approach, then slid into the inky depths.

"Some sight, eh?" said Farley, wide awake in the upper bunk. He was as absorbed as I was with this other-worldly vista. I crawled in beside him and we continued to watch, as fascinated as children.

We had left Baleena just ten hours earlier and there hadn't been a trace of ice. Farley calculated that we were somewhere to the east of Cape Breton Island and in the middle of the great ice pack which descends from the Labrador Sea to assault Canada's east coast every spring.

I could smell bacon frying.

"Come on, sleepyhead, hurry up and get dressed. They eat early around here. She's not the *Queen Elizabeth*, you know," Farley said.

Indeed, she wasn't. The *Bosco* was the well-worn wooden vessel belonging to Freeman Drake that had been converted from a World War Two mine sweeper into a refrigerated freighter. Due for replacement and officially listed for sale, she was nevertheless proceeding through a frozen sea laden with a hundred tons of frozen fish. The *Mount Snowdon*, hindered by a similar ice jam, had failed to reach Baleena in time to make this trip.

Though we were warm and comfortable in the "owner's" cabin, it was scarcely luxury. It was a bare little room with an upper and lower berth, a couple of chairs and a table. There was a small wash basin with hot and cold running water, but the toilet was next door in a large washroom which we shared with the crew. This posed no problem for Farley, but it did for me. One woman travelling aboard a ship with fourteen men faces some unique obstacles. Farley reported that there were two toilets in separate cubicles, one urinal and one shower.

"I guess I'd better go when you do," I suggested, thinking that would be the best arrangement. But what would I do if one of the crew came in? I would have to just sit there like a mouse until he had gone on his merry way.

Farley nobly offered to stand on guard outside when I was inside.

By 6:45 most of the crew were in the dining saloon enthusiastically eating breakfast. It was a cramped, hot little room scarcely deserving the name of "saloon" which was stamped on a small brass plate above the doorway. There was a long wooden table with a bench on either side. We wriggled past the backs of the men in order to squeeze into two vacant places on the inside bench.

The captain—Vince LeBlanc—sat in the one free-standing chair at the end of the table.

"Morning," he said to us cheerfully. "Fine day. Eat up. No chance of getting seasick. Cook! Two more here!" he called to a thin man back in the galley.

Although the captain had spent the night on the bridge piloting the vessel through the ice, he was still alert and amiable. He was an unimpressive-looking fellow in his mid-forties, perhaps, with thin, drab hair. His face might have belonged to a bank manager, and he didn't look like someone who had ploughed his way across the mighty oceans all his life, although that was what he had been doing for twenty-three years. He wore no uniform to indicate his captaincy, nor did any of the crew.

The cook, whose name was Cyril Oxford and whose weathered face bespoke a lifetime spent somewhere other than in a ship's galley, strode in and plonked down two big plates covered with bacon and eggs. His good humour compensated for any lack of finesse in either cooking or serving. In the middle of the table was a platter piled high with cold toast. Alongside that was a large assortment of marmalade and jam, pickles and sandwich spread, peanut butter and mustard. This same array of bottles and jars appeared at every meal.

The other crew members stole glances at us over their mugs of tea. They were a mixture of young and old, and none of them fitted my image of sea-going men. Where did I get my preconceived notions? From the movies? From high school productions of *Pinafore*? They were dressed in the same Terylene shirts and Orlon sweaters that could be seen anywhere ashore. And only one of them had a visible tattoo.

"Fine day," remarked a young man with a carefully combed ducktail haircut.

"Smooth as oil, she is," said another.

"Don't say as you'll be seasick," one of the older men said, grinning at me warily.

Newfoundland men teased women about seasickness as routinely as they teased each other about women. On those rare occasions when any outport woman went to sea, they usually faded away to their bunks at the first hint of rough weather. I love ships and I'm rarely sick on board. I'd crossed the Atlantic seven times on ocean liners, as well as all the harrowing voyages with Farley in our schooner. But I wasn't going to let these facts spoil the fun. They could tease me if they wanted to.

Somewhere in my mental packsack of ill-found folklore, I had read or heard that seamen consider it unlucky to have a woman on board. A woman, or a clergyman. I was probably a century out of date because no one aboard the *Bosco* acted as if I, like Jonah, should be thrown overboard to ensure a safe passage. Quite to the contrary, I got the impression that they rather liked having a woman in their midst. I was a rarity because women were never hired as crew members and maritime regulations make it nearly impossible for anyone but the crew or the owner to travel aboard a working freighter. Insurance doesn't cover the hazards that might befall a passenger. So in order to legally be aboard the *Bosco*, Farley and I had had to sign ourselves on as crew members.

When we finished breakfast, it was only 7:15. Everyone else on the ship was occupied with his duties or, having finished them, was asleep. For us the whole day stretched ahead in idleness. Captain LeBlanc had invited us to come up to the bridge any time we felt like it, and so after an hour or more of reading in our bunks, we did.

There is a sanctity about a ship's bridge, even aboard a small freighter. The men quietly perform the rituals of their appointed tasks. Despite all the technical equipment—the wheel, the radar, the binnacle and all the other nautical and navigational machinery—there is a curious hush. It's almost like being in a library where you're not expected to talk, but you're free to browse.

People came and went. The chief engineer came in and sat on a stool, drinking a mug of coffee and thoughtfully regarding the ice. He was followed by Cyril the cook, who, during the mid-morning lull in his work, joined the silent vigil for a few minutes.

I think I understand why sailors have long been regarded as great tellers of stories. They are alone with their thoughts for many hours every day. For much of their time they are waiting for something: a departure, a change in course, a floating object to avoid, a docking. They have more time to think than most men do. We joined them in their silence, dazzled by the glare from the ice which stretched all the way to the horizon. The *Bosco* continued to lurch and shudder as she nuzzled her way cautiously through the narrow leads of water amid the ice.

The only intrusion into this peaceful communion was the cackling and static from the ship's radio—unintelligible outbursts that were ignored by the crew. It takes a practised ear to make any sense out of the sputtered conversations which are tossed from ship to ship. I tried to identify the languages—Norwegian? Portuguese? Russian?—though most of the time it was English of one sort or another.

The captain spent a lot of time in the chart room at the back of the bridge, trying to choose a course to avoid the worst of the ice. He relied on the radio talk to help him judge the extent of it. Its size and location varies from day to day—sometimes from hour to hour—depending on the temperature and the winds. The skipper's skill, plus a little luck, still determined whether a vessel would get through or be trapped in a frozen ocean.

Captain LeBlanc was like some bird who had just heard the call of his mate as he picked up the handset and replied to some distant static that had been aimed at him.

"Bosco calling the Meelpaeg Lake. Bosco calling the Meelpaeg Lake. Can you read me, Captain? Over."

The reply sounded as if it was coming from the moon.

"Bosco. Bosco. Read you good there, Captain. Over."

"Meelpaeg Lake. Meelpaeg Lake. Right you are, Captain. I heard you talking to Cape Smokey there. We're into the ice here. Twenty miles off Halifax. Been in it five hours and not getting any lighter by the looks of it. Over."

"Bosco. Bosco. Yes, bye, it's a whore, ain't it now? I'm off Shelburne here meself and it's thicker than a pan o' duff. Over."

"Meelpaeg Lake. Meelpaeg Lake. That's the way everywhere, Skipper. A rough go of it. Would you say I can haul over to the land and get inside of it? Over."

"Bosco. Bosco. No, Skipper, I don't say you could. She's tight to the land as far as Cape Sable. A son of a bitch to get clear of it. Over."

"Meelpaeg Lake. Meelpaeg Lake. Well, thanks then, Skipper. Over and out."

When the shouting and sputtering ended, the tranquility of the bridge was restored. We were scarcely moving. The captain slid open the door to the wing of the bridge and we went outside with him. He scanned the horizon with binoculars, looking for a patch of darkness that would indicate a bigger lead of open water. There was only a hypnotic whiteness as far as anyone could see. Cold wind whipped around us, but the heat from the reflected April sun bathed our faces in delicious warmth. It was a tingly combination of hot and cold, like a baked Alaska. Had we stayed there long enough, we would have been both sunburned and snow-blind.

In retrospect, I marvel that I wasn't afraid, that no one seemed afraid. Ships have been crushed in the ice and people have died as a result, but no thought of it entered my head then. Perhaps it was the commonsense manner of the captain and the crew as they went about their work that lulled me into that fearless state. Was this the way regiments went marching into war, blindly loyal to some general who may have calculated his enemy with less accuracy than Captain LeBlanc did the ice pack?

Though he was uncommunicative and unsmiling most of the time, Vince LeBlanc—a Cape Bretoner—proved to be more convivial as we got to know him. Momentarily off duty at noon, he invited us back to his cabin for a predinner drink. It was a room behind the chart room, similar to the cabin we occupied, and there he kept a bottle of rum in a desk drawer. He relaxed a bit and seemed eager to talk to us. He was curious about us and found it hard to understand why we, a couple of bizarre Upper Canadians, had chosen to go and live in a Newfoundland outport, something that no Cape Bretoner in his right mind would have wanted to do.

"When the war ended, I shipped out of Halifax for a few years. All kinds of jobs then. I tell you, we had a real merchant marine in those days. Fifth biggest in the world, Canada. But one by one the Canadian shipping companies folded up. Sold out. So where did that leave someone like me, with a foreign-going ticket? I suppose I could have gone working for the Yanks or the Brits or the Greeks, but that would have meant uprooting Louise and the kids and, oh, I don't know, we just wouldn't feel at home anyplace but Cape Breton. Funny thing, when I was young everybody wanted to get away from home as fast as they could. Seems as if I had to look all over the world just to figure out where I belong."

Vince had his name on a waiting list for work with the marine division of the Canadian National Railways. He was hoping for a permanent job on one of the ferries between Nova Scotia and Newfoundland. His employment with Baleena Fish Products was temporary, one assignment at a time.

Vince didn't go down for dinner with us. Since the ice was getting thicker, he didn't leave the bridge. His meal was brought up to him on a tray.

In the galley, Cyril banged down two weighty plates in front of us with the same cheerfulness he had shown at breakfast. It was a meal of codfish—apt, I figured, on board a ship that was carrying a hundred tons of the same thing. We were also served a small mountain of mashed potatoes, boiled turnips, carrots and cabbage—the traditional "cooked" dinner. Every day we ate the same basic meal, the only variation being that the fish was replaced by boiled salt beef on alternate days. Cyril, who whistled while he worked, was not bothered by the chore of planning meals.

Obi Kendal was the newly hired second engineer on the *Bosco*, and he greeted us like long-lost friends. Although he had finished his dinner, he took a second mug of tea to keep us company. This was his first trip and he was glad of the job after a long, unemployed winter. At last his experience on the Great Lakes ships had got him a job at home.

When we had finished eating a bowl of doughy, steamed pudding with raisins in it, Cyril cleared away the dishes.

"Thanks, Cyril. It was delicious," I said.

"They really know how to feed a man on this ship," Farley added.

"And so they should," Obi added in a whisper, so that Cyril couldn't hear him. "Considering what they pay for it."

"Paying? Surely the crew don't pay for their meals?"

Obi glanced around and leaned in closer. "Well, not paying like it was a hotel or anyplace, but there's a hard racket going on here, I can tell you. See, there's this new law come down from Ottawa, a minimum wage for seamen who go outside Canada. By rights this crew has to be paid according to that. Three hundred dollars a month minimum."

"Is that what you get?"

"We gets two hundred and ten."

"Where's the other ninety?"

"That's took out for our room and board."

139

"Why the hell doesn't someone tell these poor bastards how they're being used? Why don't you explain it to them, Obi?"

He went on, his voice low. "Jumpin' Jesus, I can't do that. I'd be out of a job sure as there's shit in a crackie dog. What good would come of it? Nobody could do a thing about it 'cept quit. And you know how scarce jobs is on the coast."

"Obi, what do you hear about the strike at Jersey Island?" I asked. "They haven't got a union behind them. How can they make it stick?"

"Not a hope, missus. When the company finds out who started it, they'll git fired, and then the rest of 'em will say they never wanted a part of no strike and they'll go back workin' like before. That's the jigs and reels of it."

Obi headed for his bunk as he had to be back on duty in three hours. We had nothing but time to spare, so we decided to take a tour of the steaming little galley. Cyril was proud to guide us. There was a huge oil-fired range with a metal fence all around the top to prevent the cauldrons of food from sliding off in a heavy sea. Behind the stove was a kind of pantry that contained a barrel of salt beef, a fifty-pound sack of potatoes and a crate of other vegetables. There was a hundred-pound bin of flour which Cyril was scooping out in preparation for baking bread. He baked twelve loaves at a time, he told me, which was three times the amount of dough I was able to heft at home.

Apart from canned milk and canned peaches and pears, everything else on board was cooked from scratch. No one would ever write about it in *Gourmet* magazine, but it did have the virtue of not coming from a package or tin.

"I b'lieves you knows my brother, sir," Cyril said to Farley. "He was up to your house in the fall of the year to get 'er fitted out."

"You're Frank's brother?"

"That's right, sir," he smiled, glad that we had established the connection.

"And you live in Wilfred's Harbour too?"

"All be leavin' the harbour, sir. Closing out altogither. Everyone got to be gone by end of summer. Those of us what can is gettin' work away. I come up to Baleena on first steamer when I hear'd they was cook's job this trip. I figure I could cook as good as anyone when I had to."

"Where are you going to go then when they close Wilfred's Harbour?"

"I'm shiftin' me family to Baleena come summer. Gover'ment give we seven hundred dollars fer to shift. Job Hann sold me a place fer me house down behind his. All we got to do now is git our house up on drums fer to float her off and tow her down the coast. Hopes we git a spell of fine weather."

I knew where Job Hann's house was. You couldn't miss it. It was perched on a high rocky ridge and painted bright red. But it was surrounded by nothing but muskeg and little ponds. The possibility of being able to erect anything nearby, except something resembling the Leaning Tower of Pisa, seemed very slim. But Cyril was undaunted by the difficulties. If he could learn to be a ship's cook almost overnight, presumably he could master the art of replanting his house firmly in a bog, a house that first had to survive a journey along thirty miles of open coastline.

"That's a very big undertaking," Farley said.

"I hope you'll be happy in Baleena," I added.

"Well, missus, we got to do what's best these times. Youngsters got to git the h'education now, don't they? I got a crowd of boys meself. Way we used to live is not fittin' fer the youngsters comin' up. Thing is, we can't git no teachers 'ome. They come one year and they's gone the next and 'tis a divil's job to git another. Then there's the 'lectric and the water and sewery. Man from gover'ment came down and explained how we won't niver have those t'ings in Wilfred's Harbour 'cause of there bein' too much rock.

"Me woman don't want to shift," he went on. "Figures to be lonesome in Baleena. And me father what bides with us—I don't say he's too content to shift neither. Seventy-one-year-old and right smart he is too. Fished all hees life, he did, and don't know nothing else."

"Your father can still fish when you move to Baleena," I suggested, sounding like a well-intentioned guidance counsellor.

"Don't seem likely," Cyril said. "Down back of Job Hann's there's no place fer to put a stage. Besides, you got to know where the fish is to."

Fishing, like farming, is territorial. Fishermen don't encroach on each other's territory, unless they're prepared for minor warfare. Cyril knew better than I did that his father would be redundant in Baleena, his wife would be lonely, and he himself would spend the rest of his life working for Baleena Fish Products. Yet he believed that his children, by some arcane process called education, would be transported into a brave new world of perpetual school teachers and electric lights.

During the night the wind changed and the captain altered course. By heading east and then south, we circumvented several hundred miles of pack ice. By morning we could feel the motion of the sea again, and the sound of the wind replaced the abrasive grinding of the ice against the hull.

We fell easily into the ship's routine and I was in no hurry to reach our destination. I was almost sorry when I awoke on the fifth morning to the sound of screeching gulls and the realization that we were in the process of being moored at a large wharf. Through the porthole I saw a long wooden building which housed a company of fish distributors.

Behind the building was a vista which took me by surprise. There were a dozen large deciduous trees budding in the pale yellow-green leaves of early spring. I hadn't seen a large tree for half a year. My eye had adjusted to the look of a land where they didn't grow. Seeing those trees had the impact of seeing a long-lost friend.

This fish warehouse in Gloucester, Massachusetts, was as stark a building as all its counterparts in Newfoundland, but those trees ameliorated the ugliness. They softened the landscape. Though I loved the stormy coast from which I'd sailed, the green leaves of Gloucester were hard to resist.

The day was warm and still and the crew were all out on deck in their shirt sleeves. Below, Cyril served us our last breakfast while a United States customs officer sat drinking coffee, checking the list with the names of the crew and scanning a lot of other documents related to our cargo. He was a big, relaxed-looking man. He seemed to be enjoying his work. Not for him the hard-eyed pursuit of drug traffickers or smugglers in some crowded tourist town. It was a gorgeous spring morning in Gloucester and drinking coffee with the cordial captain of a Canadian fish freighter was a pleasant way for him to start the day.

Another man joined us in the galley. He was the manager of the fish distribution company, a former Newfoundlander who, after twenty years in Massachusetts, still met every ship from his native land. He took the trouble of explaining to me where our cargo was going. It was to be unloaded into refrigerated trucks that same day, and by night it would be on its way to Chicago. From there it would be redistributed to several midwestern states—Wisconsin, Minnesota and Iowa.

"The Midwest. That's our big market. Big R.C. population. Big Friday sales."

I wondered if anyone in those inland states ever stopped to think, as they laid the fillets in the pan, about the men who had caught them, or the people who had cut them and packed them, or of the risky voyage we had just made to bring all this fish to them. Only rarely do we think about the complexities of the production and distribution of food. It is so mindlessly easy to ignore the human involvement when we simply reach into a freezer.

Farley's editor, Peter Davison, was on the wharf waiting for us. We loaded our suitcases into the back of his Volvo, waved our farewells to the crew, and then headed for Boston. There was a second surprise that morning—the sensation of speed. I hadn't been inside a car for seven months and travelling at fifty and then sixty miles an hour felt like driving in the Grand Prix. It didn't feel safe. Later, Farley admitted that he had had the same reaction. I kept my fears to myself but it took about a week until I felt at ease again with traffic lights, pedestrian crosswalks, subway trains and speeding cars.

The masses of people in downtown Boston startled me too—a sea of well-dressed strangers who would never know my name or nod at me or remark on the weather. How quickly I had become accustomed to the social patterns of the people of Baleena. When I went shopping in the Boston department stores, I was overcome by the massive amount of merchandise and the confusing choices I was presented with. In Baleena we could only buy the bare necessities and considered ourselves lucky when we found the most ordinary things—socks in the right size, curtain material that wasn't too tawdry, a can of percolator coffee instead of instant. The monumental display of everything in Boston made me feel like someone from the Third World. When I had lived in a city, I had been immune to it all. I had to go away to a poorer place before I even noticed what we had.

However, it was comfortable to again be among people who were involved in things that particularly interested us but were never discussed in Baleena. We stayed with the Davisons in a charming old house a stone's throw from Harvard University. There was a magnolia tree in blossom in the front yard. They and their friends talked about books and the world of publishers and authors—which books were selling well, who had won a literary prize, who had changed publishers, who was getting a divorce. It was our other community, one that we also cared about, and it existed a universe away from Baleena.

Nevertheless, within a few weeks we were glad to make our way back to Baleena—though not aboard the *Bosco* this time, since she had only stayed in Gloucester for two days. From Boston we flew on an Air Canada Viscount to Halifax, Nova Scotia, and then waited several hours to catch another flight which took us to Sydney, Nova Scotia.

From there we took a taxi for the fifteen-mile journey to North Sydney, where we again waited for several hours to board the ferry for the overnight crossing to Port-aux-Basques, Newfoundland. And there, on a cold Saturday in May, with not a green leaf in sight and the ponds still covered with ice, we waited for one more day to board the weekly coast boat for the journey back to the treeless place we called home.

Eleven

BY THE TIME WE RETURNED, the abortive strike in our sister community of Jersey Island had been squashed. Just as Obi Kendal had predicted, the threat of plant closure had sent most everyone scurrying back to work.

More young men than ever from both Jersey Island and Baleena went away to the Great Lakes to work, and when they came back, there was time to talk and time to ask questions. Why were wages so low in Newfoundland and so much higher in Ontario? Why didn't fish plant workers and dragger crews get together and try to do something about this unfair situation? There were no answers, but the questions remained.

There was a new government in Ottawa by then. In the election of 1963 the Liberal party defeated the Conservatives, and Lester Pearson became the Prime Minister. Although the long-promised television still hadn't arrived, another technological wonder was about to appear.

"Telephones is comin'," Ezra Rose announced grandly as he placed a large codfish on our kitchen counter, a gift to us from his morning's catch. "Just like they got up on the mainland and all them places. Just pick 'er up and talk to anyone anywhere in Baleena. Won't be no time till you can't tell the difference 'tween here and Port-aux-Basques. They got a paper put up down the post office. If you wants the telephone hinto your house, you puts your name onto it."

"Are you going to get a telephone?" I asked.

"Now what good I be havin' telephone? Them as wants to talk with me can come up and bide in me own kitchen. 'Sides, me woman don't want one. Feared she might get bad news."

"I know how she feels. Maybe we won't get one either."

"When you gets a message," Ezra said with certainty, "you'll get two more to follow. And one of 'em has got to be bad news. Last week the missus got a message that her brother was comin' home from the Boston states. Then she got another one come that said her sister's girl got a baby boy. Then the third one come to say her brother had passed on. What I say is, if you git the telephone there's no sayin' how much stormy news you'll git. I'm steerin' clear of it altogether."

Until then the telegraph had been our only means of quick communication with the rest of the world, a world that was comfortably inaccessible after six o'clock each night and all day Sunday. Later in the week I stopped in at the post office and read the notice from Canadian National Telecommunications announcing their plans to change all this. Initially there would be a telephone system within Baleena and ultimately a microwave link with the rest of Canada and, presumably, the rest of the world.

Although the monthly rate was to be only $3.50, there had not been any great rush of clients. There was a blank paper underneath the notice so that potential subscribers could sign their names. There were only five signatures—Freeman Drake, Dr. Billings, the RCMP detachment, Mr. Dollimount, the wharfinger, and Hann Brothers, the largest merchant.

It had been the absence of intrusions such as the telephone that made this place so appealing to Farley and me. Yet I knew that in many ways our life would be easier with

148

a telephone. Finding message-carrying children was rarely possible during school hours or after dark. And if we could make long-distance calls, it would eliminate those lengthy telegrams Farley had to compose whenever there were last-minute changes to one of his manuscripts. Editing books and correcting proofs was not a simple matter by telegraphy.

Old habits die hard. After a few weeks of debating the issue, we succumbed and put our name on the list. Eventually the number of potential subscribers reached the minimum required and a crew of installation men arrived on the coast boat. We got used to seeing them asking directions to this house or that, and then climbing to the top of those skinny poles to instal equipment. They had been sent from Gander, a journey of two days by train and ship, and they regarded their safari to this coast with the enthusiasm of exiles who had been ordered to Siberia.

"Will one of you be staying on here for maintenance and repairs?" I asked the unsmiling young man who came to instal our phone.

"None of us'r stayin' here. That's for darn sure. I'm gettin' outa here on the next boat. Don't care what the boss says," he replied in a militant voice.

"Won't there be anyone stationed here then?"

"Nope."

"Well, what's going to happen when something goes wrong, say, when a storm blows the wires down, that sort of thing? Doesn't the phone company know about the gales on this coast?"

"Guess not," he said indifferently. Then he added, "They got a repairman at Hermitage. He can come down if something goes out."

"But there's only one steamer a week between here and Hermitage. The phone could be out for a week or more."

He stared at me in some exasperation. Who was this uppity housewife who was daring to complain before the phone service had even begun? Why couldn't I be properly grateful and keep my mouth shut? Hadn't he endured enough—three weeks in this fogbound place, sharing a room with two other men in Mrs. Parsons' boarding house, not to mention Mrs. Parsons' cooking? And here he was already getting flak from a woman who seemed to think the phone service would break down before it got started.

"Well, that's it then," he said after affixing the round piece of paper with the number in the centre of the dial. "Your number is 3111 and your ring is three longs and two shorts."

"But that sounds like a party line. We applied for a private line," I objected.

"They got no private line out this end of Baleena," he snorted.

"And why not?"

"Not enough subscribers. There's just the one line for everyone out the west side."

"How many families are on it?"

He sighed and consulted a small notebook. "There's eight," he said flatly, "and you're the ninth."

Before he left he gave me our telephone "directory"— four mimeographed pages of names and numbers.

I didn't know how to break this news about the party line to Farley. A party line would be ringing all day, not to mention the obvious lack of privacy. The lineman hadn't been gone more than twenty minutes before our first call came in.

"That you, Clara?"

"Yes."

"'Tis you talkin', Clara?"

"Yes, it is. Who's this?"

"My dear, 'tis really you?"

"Yes. Yes, this is Claire Mowat. Who is this?"

"My Gawd. Never thought the day'd come when I'd be talking to you up in Dog Cove. Some nice, inn't it?"

I finally recognized the voice of Minnie Joseph. I should have known who it was since she was one of the few women I had been able to persuade to call me by what was approximately my first name. But Minnie hadn't yet realized she would need to identify herself when she used this exotic device. All previous conversations in her life had been face to face.

"I didn't know you were getting the telephone, Minnie. That's very nice," I said, trying to think of something appropriate to say.

"Yes, m'dear! Noah got 'en. Mr. Drake wanted it so's he could talk to 'im handy. And don't the youngsters love it! Been listenin' all day, carryin' on with that Pointing crowd. What a racket 'twere. I drove 'em all outdoors at the last of it. Well, dear, I got to go now. Time to bile the kettle."

I put the phone down with a sense of doom. It hadn't occurred to me that the Pointings would also have ordered a telephone. Their contacts with anyone but their immediate family were so few and their cash income so small that I would have imagined they would be the last family to want or need a telephone.

Garland Pointing had found work that spring as a helper on a lobster boat. The price paid for lobster had risen dramatically that year, and a number of fishermen had made lobster traps during the winter. Most lobster fishermen work in pairs, and as the helper in a boat owned by his brother-in-law, Garland could be reasonably sure of eight or nine weeks of work. That was long enough for him to qualify for several months of Unemployment Insurance. The only uncertain factor was the brother-in-law, Manuel Tibbo. He drank. Not socially at weddings, like everyone else, but in erratic bouts—benders—whenever he could find a quantity of alcohol. Everyone knew about this. And no one ever offered Manuel a drink unless they were prepared to endure him until the bottle was empty.

The first time we were jarred awake by the party line at 3:00 A.M. we bore with it, believing that some emergency had occurred in one of the other eight households on the party line. Farley muttered something savage about Mr. Bell's bloody invention, and we went back to sleep.

It wasn't until the third consecutive night of being awakened in the pre-dawn hours that Farley stumbled out of bed and lifted the receiver to find out what was going on.

"Naaaaah, me son. Be nary lobster today."

"Sure, bye. She's smooth as 'ile."

"Nary lobster. Naaaah."

"Yis, bye. T'ousands."

"G'wan."

Farley banged down the receiver and came storming back to bed, cursing, "It's goddamn Garland phoning goddamn Manuel and they're arguing about whether or not they're going fishing this morning! Honestly! Fishermen have been quietly getting up at daybreak and going about their business for hundreds of years on this island, and now all of a sudden they have to wake up the whole bloody community while they discuss it over the phone."

"What is there to discuss this morning?" I asked sleepily.

"It sounds like Manuel has been drinking again and won't go out in the boat. Garland was ready to go—it's nice and calm this morning—but he can't go out single-handed. Boy, what luck. I'm on a party line with the worst drunk in town. Don't they *know* they're waking up dozens of people?"

"Guess not," I mumbled as I drifted back to sleep.

Garland and Manuel were not the only two fishermen who made a habit of phoning each other before dawn. It was a curious thing that men who would not ordinarily have dreamed of disturbing other people in the middle of the night now phoned each other at all hours with total indifference towards the sleeping habits of other families.

The new technology cancelled the old rules. During the daytime the same children who had so often sat in my kitchen in solemn silence now took to phoning each other all day long, dialling wrong numbers, laughing, whispering, shouting, and often just breathing into the receiver to sustain the link.

Their mothers didn't admonish them for this. Discipline tended to be a group endeavour. Children were only scolded in the interest of their own safety—from real dangers like falling into the sea, or else if they became too "idle," a word that bespoke mischief. Obviously the telephone posed no apparent threat to anyone, and mothers and fathers were as intrigued with it as the children.

When they dialled a wrong number, they treated it as an unforeseen social encounter.

"Who's that?" they demanded when my "hello" failed to identify me.

"It's Mrs. Mowat."

"Miz Mote? Miz Mote up in Dog Cove?"

"Yes."

"My dear! And I be callin' Emmy Barnes," came a reply of genuine surprise, as if she had walked into the wrong house. "Wonderful bad weather we got today, Miz Mote."

"Yes, it is, all that rain."

"Can't get a day to put out the wash."

"True."

"We deserve a civil day now."

"Yes, we do."

Eventually the infatuation with the telephone subsided and the incessant ringing lessened. However, the guidelines of telephone usage and phraseology that I had learned at my mother's knee did not appear to be taking hold in Baleena.

The first time I asked, "Is Minnie there, please?" at the Joseph household, the child who answered replied simply, "Yes." And there our conversation ended. He had answered my question. I had to ask a second question— "Could I speak to her then?"—before he summoned her to the phone.

Noah and Minnie kept hens and I bought eggs from them. Once we both had the telephone, it was a lot easier to find out if Minnie could spare me a dozen. Fresh eggs were a luxury. Though we ate lobsters and salmon till we were sick of them, what to me had always been commonplace food—hens' eggs—were an expensive delicacy here. Eggs were sold in all the Baleena shops, but they were imported from Nova Scotia and tasted of some chemical that was used to preserve them for months, exactly as supermarket eggs taste everywhere. Minnie catered to a carriage-trade clientele of people like ourselves who could afford these few fresh eggs. Since all the hen food had to be shipped in on the coast boat, it put the cost of these precious eggs at just about double the price of store eggs. They were delivered to customers by the children. With water to haul and eggs to deliver, the Joseph children had not yet become redundant as part of the family function.

Those families who had been reluctant to sign up for a telephone were soon clamouring to have one. Unsure at first about the benefits which would come from this new machine, they soon began to feel that they had been left out. Dan Quayle Junior, who spent his money prudently, had originally decided that he didn't need a telephone. After all, he had four healthy children, and what were children for if not to help with chores like carrying messages. However, he eventually realized that there was one tiresome chore he might be spared if he did have a telephone, and that was the Saturday-night vigil awaiting the steamer bringing in supplies for his shop.

Trying to gauge the arrival time of the weekly CN ship was like betting on a horse race. The odds were against you. So many imponderables—storms, fog, blizzards, the amount of freight and the destinations of the passengers—all played havoc with the schedule. And every once in a while the boat would arrive early and throw everyone off base. That was because occasionally they had to skip some of the smaller outports when the tide or the wind made it too dangerous to enter their harbours. So they would be bypassed and the boat would come on to Baleena. Sometimes the wharfinger got word of these alterations, though often he didn't, with or without the telephone. But Dan realized that if he could call Billy and ask about the boat, and if Billy knew, then he would be spared those long hours of hanging around, waiting, waiting, waiting.

Until then he had stoically accepted this weekly guessing game as one of the trials of being in business for himself. He worked six full days a week, and often six evenings as well, including every Saturday night, when he had to retrieve his freight—by dory in good weather, or else by a hired truck or horse and sleigh in the winter.

As soon as we got a telephone, Dan became our regular Saturday-evening visitor, calling around to see who had heard anything concerning the vagaries of the steamer schedule.

He often talked to us of the problems of making a living from his small but bulging shop. He had no trouble selling the things he stocked—it was getting them that was so difficult. The damaged freight, the dented cans, the torn packages, the bruised apples, the rotten potatoes—these made his shopkeeper's life a torment. Returning such things to the wholesaler at Port-aux-Basques involved hauling them back to the wharf by dory to put them aboard the westbound steamer, which might arrive any time from two to four days after the eastbound one. It was hardly worth the effort since the refund often took six months to arrive. Dan usually tried to salvage what he could and sell it quickly at a reduced price in the hope of breaking even.

He had been running his shop for a dozen years. As a young man he had gone away to work—to Nickersons, a large fish-processing plant in North Sydney in Canada.

"A crowd of us worked over there regular one time. Those times you had to have papers to git work. We'd send to git the papers and when they come back, spring of the year, then we'd all pile aboard the steamer. Spring of '48 seemed like most everyone was going away to work. The

Cabot Straits was only supposed to carry eighty passengers but there was over three hundred of us altogether from this coast. Wonderful crowded she was, so's I had to sleep on top of me two suitcases. When we got to Port-aux-Basques we had to wait four, five days to git across to Cape Breton. Wouldn't allow us into Canada packed in like sardines. And those as come without papers was turned back and had to go home.

"'Tweren't no life at all. So the year after that I put me head to it and figured there was enough of us here in Dog Cove so's I could start a shop, specially since LeDrew the merchant had cleared off. First two years never made a penny, just got me food out of it. But by the third year I started to make a living."

He made a reasonable living from his shop. Farley had helped Dan with his income tax return and so we knew that in the previous year he had cleared almost four thousand dollars, which in 1963 was about double the amount of money that a fisherman or a plant worker could have earned.

It was almost eleven o'clock when Billy Dollimount, the wharfinger, called to say that the steamer was leaving Grand Anse and could be expected here within two hours. That was good news for all of us. Dan could judge the correct time to set off for the wharf, and it meant that we were free to go to bed once Dan left.

As we snuggled up close under the blankets to keep warm, we heard the distant, repetitious wail of the Seal Island foghorn. It was June, the month of everlasting fog. Fog is no one's friend. It doesn't water the garden, it doesn't fill up the well and you can't skate or ski on it. It is the bane of all seafaring men.

I've only found one effective use for fog. It provides an ethereal background for coloured photographs. Perhaps fog is treasured by filmmakers and poets alone. Certainly it would make Dan's cold and lonely journey more risky that night as his dory chugged towards the dripping wharf. His was not the easiest way to make four thousand dollars a year.

Twelve

LATER THAT YEAR OUR HOUSE was finished. Frank Oxford, our migrant carpenter, came back to us nearly a year after he left and put the finishing touches on Farley's office. After that he built an addition which doubled the size of our dinky little parlour, and in it he installed a large window overlooking the sea. The difference was dramatic. We had a living room with a view. A window facing the sea was an architectural aberration that was popular only among those of us who had moved in from somewhere else. The Baleena people, if they had a choice of where their windows could be, always built them facing the road. They preferred to see who was passing by, rather than to stare at that stormy abstraction that so fascinated us—the Atlantic Ocean.

We didn't see Frank again after that, not as a carpenter anyway. When Wilfred's Harbour was officially closed, he moved his family to Port-aux-Basques. There they would be much closer to the ferry, the link with the province of Nova Scotia, where their son would soon have to attend the regional school for the blind in Halifax. He found steady work there as the janitor in the bank.

Farley's book, *Never Cry Wolf*, had been a modest success in Canada and also in the United States. He was soon immersed in another major project—a chronicle of the early exploration of the Canadian Arctic. He was reading volumes of the journals and diaries of the eighteenth- and nineteenth-century explorers—books that were obtained for him through the inter-library services of the Gosling Library in St. John's. They were mailed to him in Baleena free of charge. None of these books was ever lost or damaged or even delayed. In 1964 the Canadian post office worked like a charm.

I used to pick them up on Mondays when I made my weekly journey to collect our other mail, stopping, as usual, to chat with Percy Hoddinott, who was keenly interested in our rather unusual mail.

"My oh my, look at this," he said as I handed him a letter that Farley had written to the Arctic Institute in Leningrad. "Thirty-five years in the post office and this is my first letter to Russia!"

He insisted on getting out his postmaster's manual and describing to me the route that the letter would take—first to London, England, then to Helsinki, Finland, and from there on to the Soviet Union. I was as absorbed by the prospective journey as he was.

From the day we arrived in Baleena we had both let it be known that we would like to do something for our local library. It was disorganized and seldom used by anyone except a handful of children. Farley is the son of a librarian and he grew up in a series of libraries in Ontario and Saskatchewan. However, there had been no rush to enlist his services or mine. We were, we had to remind ourselves, outsiders. Also, it was still not clear to many of those around us just what Farley really did for a living. Writing all those stories—who were they for? Who paid him for this seemingly trivial occupation? Though the economics of his work remained a mystery, after a couple of years in the community the man himself was gradually accepted as sufficiently trustworthy to serve on the library board. My status, being directly linked to my husband's, meant that we could begin to contribute something to the life of the community.

The people who tend the machinery of any municipality—those who serve on school boards and library boards, or as church wardens or town councillors—are usually from the middle class. In Baleena this differed only insofar as the bourgeoisie was a smaller segment of the population than would have been the case in a mainland community. It included the more prosperous small shopkeepers, the few people who held permanent government jobs like postmaster or wharfinger, and the managerial staff of the fish plant. Skippers of the draggers or freighters also belonged to this social level, but since they were away at sea most of the time, they were rarely asked or expected to help run things ashore. The doctor, the clergyman, the teachers and the school principal were usually outsiders, and they hovered on the edge of this group, their status linked to the number of years of service in the community. The nurses, being unmarried women as well as outsiders, and the Mountie, whose stay was transient, did not qualify.

It was this middle group we knew the least. They lived in a well-established circle of their own and they were not particularly accommodating of people "from away." They clung tightly to their belief that they were a cut above the fishermen and the plant workers—those people who comprised the other eighty or ninety per cent of the population.

Service on the library board was the only civic role open to women in those days. Reading, it was thought, was primarily a women's and children's pastime. Very few men served on the board. Of the eight people asked to serve that year, Farley was the only male.

The library was a small white clapboard building which stood at the edge of a pond directly across the road from the United Church. Our first meeting there took place on a cold November evening. A tiny glimmer of light glowed from the small, high windows of the square, clapboard building. Inside it was cosy and welcoming. It is a curious thing the way shelves of books can transform even the plainest room. The library was about twenty-five-feet square and the fact that most of the bookshelves held dog-eared volumes by third-rate authors of fifty years ago did not detract from the warmth they seemed to radiate. In the middle of the room was a long, linoleum-covered table surrounded by chairs, a place where readers could browse through books and magazines.

The newly formed library board sat at that table facing each other like two opposing teams. We were in fact equally divided into two groups—four who were born there and "belonged," and four who didn't. On one side sat Barbara Drake, Jane Billings, Farley and me. Facing us sat Mrs. Stuckless, Mrs. Dollimount, Mrs. Northcotte and Mrs. Pink, the librarian. The clergyman and the school principal, both of whom were honorary members, had failed to appear.

No one seemed quite sure how to begin the meeting. Barbara Drake was impatiently trying to extract information from Mrs. Northcotte and Mrs. Pink, who had been members of the previous board. It took some discussion to discover that there hadn't been a single meeting during the preceding year and Mrs. Northcotte had missed the one meeting held two years earlier because she had been ill. She had, however, been the treasurer through all that time.

"Good," said Barbara with authority. "You'll carry on then as treasurer, won't you, Mrs. Northcotte?"

I'll never know if shy Mrs. Northcotte wanted to carry on or not. She didn't have much choice. Her husband worked in the engine room at the plant and she wouldn't have refused this request from Mrs. Drake. She nodded acceptance. Then she produced a scribbler from her handbag and showed us how the library's finances stood. Her handwriting was precise and even, with great flourishing tails on the letters, a relic of the days when Mrs. Northcotte had been a school teacher and penmanship was a subject to take seriously.

The provincial library service, we learned, provided us with an annual grant of two hundred and fifty dollars, of which two hundred dollars went to pay Mrs. Pink's salary and fifty dollars to pay for oil for the space heater. Nine dollars and fifty cents had also been spent to replace three broken window panes. That would have left us with a deficit but for the two federal elections of 1962 and 1963, when the library was used as a polling station. This windfall had added another fifty dollars to the treasury, so we had a credit balance of $41.50. Mrs. Northcotte now proudly produced the actual cash in a change purse which she laid on the table so we could all see it.

There was a murmur of approval. We were all glad not to have any debts.

Once our finances had been dealt with, there was another long, awkward silence during which Mrs. Pink got up and checked the space heater.

Farley broke the silence. "How about buying some new books with the balance?"

Mrs. Pink cleared her throat. "Money's very scarce to buy books. Time to time St. John's sends us some." And there she stopped, leaving us waiting to hear more about the subject.

"Mm. Hmm. How often, I wonder? And, ah, how many books do we get, say, in a year?" Farley asked as carefully as he could, trying to avoid any implication that this library may have been last on the list of priorities among the province's fifty-four libraries.

"Parcel came on last steamer," said Mrs. Pink, pointing to an unopened brown paper parcel on her check-out desk. She had evidently been in no hurry to see what it contained.

Barbara insisted that we open it there and then. Inside were six story books for young children. We duly admired each one. However, six new juveniles could do little to rescue this library's collection of deadwood. The novels all appeared to be ancient imports from England, set in country houses and rose gardens and filled with titled ladies and gentlemen. The non-fiction portion was clogged with antiquities such as a six-volume history of British diplomacy prior to 1930. Apart from a collection of sermons by a St. John's clergyman, written during the 1920s, there didn't appear to be one book about Newfoundland, or by a Newfoundland author on any subject, or indeed by any author from any other part of Canada.

"I think," said Farley diplomatically, "that we could do with a little housecleaning here."

Mrs. Pink looked wounded.

"What I suggest is that we have to discard books to make room for some new ones."

"Smashing idea," said Jane Billings. "If we'd only thought of it sooner, we might have had a jolly big fire on Guy Fawkes Night. Got rid of the lot."

"Burn our books! Oh my dear!" said a horror-stricken Mrs. Pink.

"Shocking," muttered Mrs. Northcotte.

"Sinful," added Mrs. Stuckless.

"But we have to operate on the premise that books are to be *read*," said Farley reasonably. "And when we find that some books haven't been taken out by any readers for a while, for a few years. say, well, then we should remove them and make room for some new ones."

"We shouldn't burn them, sure," pleaded Mrs. Dollimount.

"Perhaps we could sell them. A nickel each. That way we'd make a little money besides," suggested Mrs. Stuckless.

Everyone seemed pleased with that idea except our librarian, Mrs. Pink, who sighed. "These old books been here a wonderful long time. I'll miss them when they're gone."

We talked on about how to raise money to buy new books and how to attract more readers. Jane suggested that those of us who had personal libraries might sift through them and donate what we could spare. Farley said he would write to his publishers and ask for donations of recent books. Barbara said there were people in the fish business who owed Freeman a favour and she would ask them for donations of money. We were soon carried away with enthusiastic ideas about acquiring more and more books until the shelves would threaten to collapse under their weight. But it was we four outsiders who were doing all the talking and dominating the meeting.

"Now then, ladies," Farley addressed himself to the four cautious faces across the table, "how does this sound? If we can round up three or four hundred books . . . wouldn't that bring the people in?"

"Mr. Mowat, m'dear," said Mrs. Stuckless, who when confronted head-on could easily rise to the occasion, "don't you be too sure now." Hilda Stuckless was a recently widowed woman who had returned home with three teenagers after living in Gander for fifteen years. "What we got to consider is what the people want. Let's hear what you think, Nellie," she said, turning to Mrs. Dollimount beside her.

"Well, dear, if we could get some of them books by Grace Livingston Hill . . . there's plenty reads those. And nurse and doctor stories. Haven't seen any new nurse stories in here for a long time now."

"I hear'd tell those stories not fit for the library," said Mrs. Pink apprehensively, but, lest anyone think she was betraying the opinion of Mrs. Dollimount, she quickly added, "Still and all, there's plenty of them does get read. A nice lot."

Barbara had been listening with mounting impatience. "Surely a few new books would be a welcome change. There must be people here who want to read them."

"The majority of the adults don't want to read anything at all," said Jane Billings. "We're beating our heads against the wall. I suggest that we should only be considering the children, enticing them to learn to enjoy reading before they drift into . . . well, whatever it is they're going to do with their lives."

We all agreed that special emphasis should be put on books for children and teenagers.

"Too bad Mr. Pardy isn't here tonight," I said. Mr. Pardy was the school principal. "We could arrange with him to have the students come over here from school. One class at a time. They could start to feel comfortable here even if they didn't read very much right away."

There was a chorus of agreement from Barbara, Jane and Farley. But only a blank stare from the other four.

"You mean . . . interrupt their lessons . . . and have the whole crowd come over to the library?" asked Mrs. Pink incredulously.

"Yes," I said. "That was how we did it when I went to school."

"I don't say Mr. Pardy would go along with that," she said flatly.

"'Twould be time away from their school work," added Mrs. Northcotte.

"That Mr. Pardy is a hard ticket," said Mrs. Stuckless. "Not once he ever lets the youngsters get away home before four o'clock. He says nothing should interfere with their lessons."

"But they'd be learning something from reading!" the four of us said, like a Greek chorus bursting with our faith in the printed word.

"Who the hell is this guy Pardy?" Farley demanded loudly, wondering what sort of Dickensian schoolmaster we had in our midst. The four women winced at his rough language. The few men who came into the library were not in the habit of swearing. "Let's make damn sure he's at our next meeting."

"Exactly," agreed Barbara. "And I move we meet again in one month. I want to talk to Mr. Pardy too about a lot of things!"

Barbara believed in education with the fervour of a zealot, and the quality of education at the Baleena school displeased her. By then she was the mother of four daughters, and though they eventually would be educated in private schools far away, their primary education had to begin here. Barbara would have liked to reform the Baleena school totally, but as a non-Anglican, she was ineligible to sit on the board of what was ostensibly an Anglican school. The best she could do was to hassle the principal and the teachers whenever she could.

We adjourned our meeting feeling pleased that the problem had at least been spelled out, even if the solutions were still hazy. We resolved to get the legendary Mr. Pardy out to our next meeting in December. As it turned out, I didn't have to wait that long to meet him.

A few weeks later I was asked if I would volunteer to be the art teacher at the high school. Matthew Way, the progressive clergyman who was also chairman of the school board, did his best to seek out local talent, Anglican or not, and incorporate it into the school. Newfoundland's clumsy multi-denominational school system had traditionally excluded qualified local people who were not members of the particular denomination which administered the school—often the only school in the community.

My qualifications to teach art were considerably greater than those of the current art teacher, whose total training in art had been a few hours during a summer course. I was a graduate of a four-year course at the Ontario College of Art and had had a brief career as a commercial artist afterwards.

Yet once it had been arranged that I should become the teacher, I felt a little uneasy. Was it such a good thing that I foist my opinions about art on people who had been managing nicely without me? Would I be interrupting a system that worked, and insulting a teacher who felt that he was doing an adequate job? Maybe I should have kept quiet about my art training. However, Mr. Pardy, like it or not, had an art teacher on his hands and he sent me a note to say he would be expecting me on Friday afternoon.

I arrived at our spanking new school for my first class on a cold December day. The building was a focus of much local pride despite the fact that it was singularly ugly. There was a bareness to the long, two-storied structure. Sheathed in wood siding, painted a stark white, it was perched on a rocky ridge and was as unembellished as a boiled egg. There wasn't so much as an alder bush nearby. Lumber was stacked against one wall, and wood shavings blew around the stony yard. Empty paint cans were piled under the stairs waiting for someone to haul them away.

I entered through a massive set of double doors that closed behind me with a thunderous bang. After that, there was a resounding silence. All the students were in their classes behind the half-dozen closed doors that faced the hall. Not a soul was in sight. I moved slowly along the wide, vinyl-tiled hallway, tiptoeing as if I were passing the room of a sleeping baby. I felt more like a burglar than a teacher. How on earth was I going to find combined grades ten and eleven? I had to resist an urge to run or, more likely, to tiptoe quietly out of the building and extricate myself from the whole ordeal.

"Mrs. Mowat."

The voice came from behind me, shattering the silence like a rifle shot. It was Mr. Pardy, the principal, standing at the door of his office. Feeling caught like some unlucky student who had been trying to skip school, I turned quickly and faced him.

"You can leave your coat in here if you like." Those were his opening words. Practical matters first. I peeled off my coat and hat and mitts, my extra sweater and my boots. I put on my shoes and then, uninvited, sat down in the one extra chair in his office, an office as devoid of frills as everything else about the school.

Mr. Pardy was, I guessed, about twenty-five years old, with a face as solemn as the traditional undertaker. He looked across his desk at me with forlorn eyes.

"I don't know very much about art myself," he stated firmly. I didn't know how to respond to that. Should I have said I was sorry to hear it?

"It seems, however, that we have got it on the school curriculum. Everyone has got to have it, right up to grade eleven," he explained in the manner of an accountant explaining some unreasonable tax law. "Mr. Crewe has been teaching it up to now but he has not got much training to speak of. Not much at all." Mr. Pardy spoke very precisely, enunciating his words with care, like someone reading aloud.

"Some of these young people here are not interested in getting an education. No. They just stay in school until the school-leaving age and then they go and work in the fish plant. That is what looks good to them."

I wanted to tell him about Dorothy Quayle, who wrote poems and songs and who was learning to use my type-writer. I could have told him about a dozen other children who, now that they were getting to know me, displayed a lively curiosity about everything from archeology to zoology. They pored through the magazines they found in our kitchen and asked thoughtful questions. I wondered if there ever would be an appropriate time to tell him. His opinions seemed as unyielding as the pilings under the new government wharf.

Instead, I said I hoped he would join us at the next meeting of the library board.

"I don't get out many evenings," he replied. "I have got lessons to prepare and papers to mark."

"We really would like to have you there, Mr. Pardy," I urged. He was about the same age as I was but he never suggested that I call him by his first name. "We do need the presence of the school principal. We would like your opinion on the important decisions we have to make."

He brightened a little. I had flattered him.

"Yes. Well, perhaps I will come out one of these times."

It was time for my class to begin. Armed with a small booklet which outlined the art curriculum for Newfoundland schools for grades nine, ten and eleven, I followed Mr. Pardy as he led me wordlessly down the hall to one of the unmarked doors. He opened it and preceded me into the classroom. Twenty-three pairs of eyes stared at me, and to my amazement all the students got to their feet and stood mutely by the side of their desks.

In that same expressionless voice, Mr. Pardy announced, "This is Mrs. Mowat," and unceremoniously departed.

There are times when we are faced with situations in which all our former experience fails to help us. I had never been a teacher and had never tried to impart anything I knew to a large group of other people. Suddenly I was facing two dozen teenaged youngsters who expected me to teach them something. It didn't help that most of them had familiar faces, faces I had seen in my own kitchen.

"Do sit down," I said.

The first item on the curriculum was perspective drawing, but I decided that could wait. Like scales and chords in music, it is a necessary drill but it's the dullest visual subject to learn or to teach and the one least likely to interest an indifferent student.

I decided to start the course with "Still Life" so my students could draw something they could see. I looked hopefully around the room for any group of objects that could be assembled into a still-life arrangement. There was absolutely nothing. Not a globe or a potted plant or any of the flotsam and jetsam that usually gathers on classroom window sills. The room was as bleak as the rest of the school. There was only one place to look, and that was out of the window towards the ice-covered pond down behind the school, to the great rocks and the distant spire of the church. There were colourful houses with the ultramarine ocean beyond them and a menacing winter sky above—a dramatic scene that would have gladdened the heart of any painter.

With a mixture of desperation and inspiration, I faced the class and said, "I want you to draw a house today, any house. It could be the house you live in, or possibly a house you might someday like to live in." I thought the latter suggestion left room for creativity. "Don't worry about accuracy too much. And if anyone wants to come up and stand at the window and draw any house that can be seen from here, please feel free to do so."

Everyone started looking in their desks for paper and pencils. I had no idea what kind of art supplies they had, and I was disappointed to see that even in the final two grades of high school they had not been introduced to any drawing materials other than the standard HB pencil and

172

the shiny paper of the scribblers that were used for all school subjects.

With these inflexible tools the possibility for any kind of artistic subtlety was extremely limited. It was like playing a piano with only two octaves. Everyone got down to work right away, though I noticed that no one was taking up my suggestion to stand at the window and draw what could be seen. Apart from visits to the pencil sharpener, everyone was glued to their desks.

"If you have any questions or any problems, don't hesitate to ask me for help," I added, scanning the heads that were all turned towards their work. A few students looked up at me from time to time, but no one raised a hand or a voice. Not wanting to interfere with the creative process, I decided to wait a while before I walked around and looked at their work. That left me with the unforeseen problem of what to do with myself.

On the corner of the teacher's desk there was a pile of leaflets distributed by the Canadian National Railways describing career opportunities for young people. I browsed through these persuasive brochures and read about the bright future of a waiter, a cook, a teletype operator and a brakeman. After that there was nothing left to do but glance at the class and try to identify as many of my students as I could. There was Muriel Quayle, the next-oldest sister of Ruth Quayle (and aunt of Dorothy Quayle), and endowed with that same head of thick mahogany-brown hair that all the Quayle sisters had. Then I noticed a boy at the back of the room who was also a Quayle—a son of either Clarence or Charlie, I wasn't sure which. Mary Joseph was in my class—the eldest daughter of Noah and Minnie—a petite girl with her father's olive skin and green eyes. One of

Cyril Oxford's sons was there—was it Heber or Eddie? I couldn't tell. There was a tall blond boy who looked so much like Effie that I figured he had to be her youngest brother, the last of the eight Green children who was still living at home. Others looked familiar but I couldn't attach a name to them.

The slapping sound of wooden rulers on wooden desks brought me to my feet. Why were they using rulers? That wasn't the way I wanted them to be drawing a house. Flustered, I made another announcement.

"I want you to draw this house as freely as possible today. Don't worry if the lines aren't precisely straight. Just draw this house in any way that interests you, and I hope some of you will go to the window and draw the houses you can see from there."

They looked at me perplexed. They glanced sideways at each other. But no one said a word. Had they understood me?

When I looked at what my class was doing, I realized that we had a communication problem. Every student was making a perspective drawing, complete with vanishing points and lines of vision, as rigid as their rulers and as sterile as their school. Neither whimsical creations nor attempts to recreate reality, not one of these houses looked anything like an outport house. They all had peaked roofs sloping conveniently away to a fixed point on an arbitrary horizon. Their own houses had flat roofs.

I wondered where I had gone wrong. It was too late to change the assignment that day. The following week I would have to explain the lesson differently. While I had been learning to understand the words and phrases of Newfoundland's dialect, they of course had not been learning mine. Analyzing my own words, I tried to remember exactly what

I had said: "Feel free to . . . Don't worry about . . . Don't hesitate . . ." I couldn't remember if I had heard anyone use those phrases here. Perhaps they would have phrased it another way. It might have been easier for all of us if I had spoken a different language. Then our problem would have been obvious. The misunderstandings of our common language were as tricky as sunkers.

Speaking in what I hoped was plain, unadorned English, I suggested that they add some people, some dogs, some flowers or bushes near the houses of this featureless subdivision, but almost no one did. Unsure of what I wanted them to do, they had reverted to the prescribed, mechanical method of drawing a house that their previous art teacher, Mr. Crewe, had taught them. Mary Joseph was brave enough to draw curtains on the window of her house. She was a rugged individualist.

My students were remarkably well behaved. I had been worried about what I would do in the face of a student who was rude or disobedient or who persisted in talking instead of doing his work, but it never happened. On the other hand, they didn't speak to me either. The "good" student was apparently one who never spoke, and that included not asking questions.

I finally decided to approach them one at a time. I wandered up and down the aisles, stopping at the desk of anyone who was having obvious difficulties. Even then they said nothing beyond a polite "yes" when I asked directly if they had understood me. I badly needed some input, some hint from them that they were interested or, conversely, that they hated what they were doing and wanted to try something else.

Teaching the visual arts to anyone is a happenstance business. You can't appreciably alter the ability of the brain that connects with the hand that wields the brush or the pencil. What you can do is encourage people to see—to look closely at what is there, and then to translate their vision into pencil marks on paper, or paint on canvas, or masses of clay or wood or plastic, or whatever media of expression to which you may introduce them. I could see that no teacher here had ever done that.

I glanced through several of my students' scribblers, marked "ART" on the first page. Their season of geometric pictures—rigid drawings with as little spontaneity in them as Mr. Pardy—weren't the appropriate drawings for these children, who laughed and sang songs in my kitchen and made up stories. Wherever their gaze had been directed, it was not to the surroundings in which they had grown up. Where were the pictures of dories and fish stages? Of fishermen in their rubber clothes? Or the fish they caught? Their homes or their kitchen tables?

My watch said five minutes before four o'clock. How, I wondered, was I supposed to dismiss this class? Did they just pack up and go? Or did they stand at attention once again, and wait for me, like visiting royalty, to leave first?

"Next week," I announced, and suddenly all eyes were on me, "I'm going to bring some objects for you to draw. I'll put them up at the front of the room and then we'll draw what we can see."

They continued to stare at me without comment.

"Does anyone have a drawing pencil?" I asked. "A charcoal pencil perhaps, or a pencil with a soft lead like a 2B or a 4B?"

I was surprised that I got a response. Three students opened their desks and held up sets of Eagle Verithin coloured pencils. It wasn't exactly what I hoped to see. The inflexibility of coloured pencils doesn't teach much about the use of colour. Still, it was a beginning to find that a few students had been interested enough to buy some art materials on their own initiative. However, none of them had ever heard of drawing pencils with soft leads.

At one minute before four o'clock, Mr. Crewe came back to the classroom, thereby solving my dilemma. Oblivious to my presence, he opened a small black book and stood before the class, all of whom were hastily stowing their books and pencils. They faced their bare desks with that suppressed joy that everyone who ever went to school remembers about the hour of four o'clock. It was time for closing prayers. Lest I be caught in another ritual that was unfamiliar, I decided I would leave immediately. In one fell swoop, I collected my handbag and pencils and was gone.

Thirteen

I can be of considerable help to the people of Baleena because of the fact that I have to visit St. John's quite often on personal business at no cost to the community, and during these visits I can talk to the right people in government who can assist in getting more money to:

1. Give Baleena better roads.
2. Give Baleena a water and sewage system.
3. Build a new post office in the centre of town which will contain a new telegraph office besides. Such a building would be a credit to the community and everyone would be proud of it.
4. Give Baleena television so that the people of this community can see and hear what is going on in the rest of the world.
5. Give Baleena a garbage collection system to keep it clean.

Because I can help get these things, I want you to vote for me as a Councillor of the Town of Baleena. Remember I cannot help you unless you elect me. Please get out and vote for me on Election Day, July 15.

Thank you
Freeman G. Drake

A copy of Freeman Drake's election platform was sent to every home, delivered by a band of children who were intrigued to be participating in the event. There had never been a municipal election before. By some process I never quite fathomed, the first town council had come into being, by acclamation, when seven men volunteered to be members. They decided among themselves that Billy Dollimount was to be the mayor. Apart from one new member who replaced another who had died, the same group had remained the acclaimed mayor and council for twelve years. By provincial law, municipal elections were supposed to be held every four years, but I suppose that if no one contested them, the result was a repeat performance with the same cast.

Billy Dollimount was a solid, grey-haired man with a heavy jaw and a trustworthy air about him. He had been the wharfinger—a federal government job—ever since Confederation. At one time he had been the chairman of the school board, and for as long as anyone could remember he had been a lay reader in the Anglican church. As a wharfinger he went to great pains to track down freight or luggage if it went astray. He was, by anyone's yardstick, one of Baleena's most diligent and reliable citizens.

Billy and the council met on Monday evenings and tried to make wise decisions about allocating money for road repairs, garbage disposal and the everlasting problem of the shortage of fresh water.

The "road," all three and three-quarter meandering miles of it, would hardly have qualified as a road in any other part of Canada. Having evolved from a series of footpaths, it was blockaded with steep inclines, deep potholes, blind curves, and in several places ran perilously close to the sea. There were no guard rails nor any form of highway punctuation like STOP signs. They were scarcely needed since not one of the trucks, nor even the newly arrived taxi, could navigate the road faster than ten or fifteen miles an hour.

What to do about garbage was a more serious concern for the council. Until recently it hadn't even been a minor concern. People had always used the time-honoured method of heaving their refuse into the ocean, but lately that didn't seem to be working very well. At Round Harbour there was a problem with rats. In a cove where there had once been a dozen families, there were now thirty-five families crowding into the same space. Consequently, at low tide the shoreline revealed an appalling collection of bottles, cans, fish guts and human sewage. Even at high tide the murky water was strewn with floating debris. Although a weekly garbage collection had been discussed many times, the council still couldn't figure out where they were going to locate a dumpsite or how they could find the money to pay a trucker to collect it.

The drinking water. or rather the lack of it, was even more urgent. There simply weren't enough wells for the mounting number of people. Most of them ran dry in summer, and those that didn't were reduced to "droughty" water that was unsafe for drinking. In warm weather gastroenteritis was a common complaint among infants and small children. Some enterprising families travelled several miles in their dories to fresh-water streams back in the country to fill barrels and buckets. But that wasn't a solution for families where the husband was away working, nor for the elderly or the sick.

In truth, the cost of supplying those basic public services that are so much taken for granted elsewhere—safe drinking water, garbage disposal and graded roads—was very much higher when they had to be undertaken in such an impenetrable landscape.

Town taxes were five dollars a year per household. The tax was the same for every family regardless of the size or opulence of the house or the number of people living in it. Thus, the Drake family paid exactly the same tax as, say, the Pointing family. There was another tax levied on retail business based on volume, and a few additional dollars were collected from dog licences. The tax money collected by the town was matched dollar for dollar by the province, but the grand total was still minuscule.

The fish plant was not taxed at all. Freeman Drake maintained, rightly, that it was neither a retail business nor a household. There had never been a taxation category for industry and there wasn't going to be if Freeman had any say in the matter.

He wasn't shy about extolling the advantages of his connections in St. John's. He would be like a saint with a direct line to God. A word with the right people, and all those insoluble problems would be solved. Though the streets wouldn't exactly be paved with gold, they would at least be paved, and that was unquestionably a good thing, he proclaimed. It would surely follow that those marvellous modern streets would soon be connected with that long-awaited highway that the Canadian government was going to build. If Freeman was elected, he promised, the place would soon be a modern town, just like everywhere else.

Freeman was backed by a slate of new candidates. It included both Dr. Roger Billings and Jane Billings, Victor

Moss, the plant manager, and George Cossar, the plant accountant.

Roger had a definite political advantage. Most people were afraid not to vote for him. Although it would not have happened, they feared that he might refuse, at some later time, to come to their aid when they were sick. Most outport doctors didn't stay long, and so people were nervous about antagonizing their one and only medical practitioner.

Jane Billings, the first woman candidate ever, was in a category by herself and her campaign to be elected eclipsed all her previous endeavours. She organized a meeting in the basement of the new high school and invited everyone to come, especially the women. No one had ever paid any political attention to the women before, and they turned up in droves, bringing sandwiches and husbands with them.

Billy Dollimount had let his name stand for election, but since he had never waged a campaign before, he was reluctant to wage one now. It was brazen, he believed, to stand up in front of a crowd of people and tell them he intended to do things he knew couldn't be done. People knew how carefully he spent the taxpayer's money. They would surely vote for him because of that.

There were other new candidates. One was Fred Fudge, the man who had realized the business possibilities of the telephone and started a taxi service. One Wednesday he had taken the coast boat to Port-aux-Basques, and on Sunday he had returned with a worn-looking metallic blue Ford station wagon perched proudly on the deck. It was the first automobile in Baleena and it was regarded with awe by children and adults alike. He charged fifty cents a ride to any place, and from the start he was busy day and night. He then had a vested interest in the state of the road, and he also had ample opportunity to tell his passengers that he intended to see that a modern road be built right away, as soon as he was elected He had reason to be insistent. He had at least one flat tire every day.

The dark horse in the race was Obi Kendal. In his twenties, he was by far the youngest candidate. He was also in favour of improved roads, but he was more interested in seeing a water supply and a sewage system installed. But, he explained to anyone who would listen, there was only one way to get these things, and that was by taxing the plant. How else could the money be raised to pay for everything?

There was scant interest in Obi's commonsense attitude to town finances. It made a lot of people nervous to talk about crossing Mr. Drake. It was more entrancing to listen to his lofty visions of the future and believe that his high-placed friends would pay the bills.

I had been subtly trying to persuade Farley to run for a seat on the council.

"I'm not a politician. I'm a writer. I just can't get involved in this," Farley said. "I know how frustrating the whole thing can be and how it eats up your time. Meetings, meetings, meetings. I can't be distracted by people calling me up to find out what I'm going to do about the potholes in the road or why the garbage truck didn't show up. Besides, people wouldn't vote for me. Voters don't trust authors. We're too bloody independent. Nobody can figure out what our vested interests are."

"Well, they certainly know what Freeman Drake's are," I said.

"Sure they do. He'll get elected. You can bet on that. Wouldn't surprise me if he tops the polls."

"He's already got too much power. All the jobs, the money . . ." I complained.

"Just the man they want."

July 15 is a date rarely designated for municipal elections elsewhere in Canada when summer lassitude and thoughts of holidays lower the public interest in the electoral process. But in Baleena the lobster season had just ended, the salmon season had just begun, and the mackerel were starting to appear in the hundreds of thousands. Prosperity and optimism clothed us in those few warm weeks when we didn't need a coat. Even before the polling station closed, Jane Billings had organized a victory celebration at their house. "Someone's going to be victorious, aren't they?" she chirped over the telephone when she called to invite us. "We can all be here together when the results come in! We'll be expecting you!"

Curiosity drew us to their house. When we got there, Roger was in the kitchen opening the first of a dozen bottles of champagne. The dining room had been turned into a bar that was awash with bottles of hard liquor and beer. Jane, for a change, was wearing an attractive dress, complete with a string of pearls.

Their guests that night were not the people they usually entertained, and most of them had never been inside that house before. Billy and Nellie Dollimount sat uneasily on a pair of dining-room chairs, politely refusing anything except tea. They felt that drinking alcohol in the doctor's house wasn't fitting. Fred Fudge, however, was not similarly inhibited. Having only been in the Billings' house before to await a passenger for his taxi, that night he swaggered between the living room and the bar, spilling part of each drink on the pastel broadloom. It was a strange gathering, and by the time the election results arrived, the house was filled with people in varying states of timidity, awe and inebriation.

Mr. Harvey Spencer, the town clerk, arrived with the results shortly after nine. He was a hunched man in his fifties with a pale complexion. He had learned his trade in that school of hardest knocks, the tuberculosis sanitarium. He had lost one lung and four years of his life, but it had inadvertently put him in a unique position when he finally came home. In the sanitarium he was taught to type and to write official letters, the kind advising people of civic matters such as the date their taxes were due. He did his work in a small office which had been built on the front of his house; and there, with tender precision, he composed his officious letters and carefully filed all the municipal red tape.

In his hand was a piece of paper on which he had typed the names of the eleven candidates, listed in descending order of their numbers of votes. But he was too shy, and had too feeble a voice, to bring himself to read the results out loud in front of this august assembly. So he handed the paper to Freeman Drake, who stood up and cleared his throat. He was wearing a natty navy-blue blazer and grey flannel trousers, and he straightened his tie and looked appropriately dignified.

"Mr. Spencer has asked me to read the results of the election," he said in a loud voice which stopped all other conversations. "I'll read the names of those elected in order of their number of votes."

He began. "Freeman Drake." His own name, right at the top of the list. He would be the mayor. There was a round of applause and Barbara came over and kissed him.

Roger shook his hand. Victor Moss slapped him on the shoulder, and someone else patted his back.

"Thank you. Thank you all very much," he said rather grandly, already sounding like a mayor. "I'll do my very best to live up to this great honour. And we can look forward to growth and prosperity in the coming years. And now I'll continue reading the list with those others who have been elected."

Those elected were Jane Billings, Victor Moss, Roger Billings, Fred Fudge, Dan Quayle Senior and Billy Dollimount. Billy, the mayor for twelve years, had come in last. And Jane Billings had come in second. That made her the deputy mayor, who would be in charge when Freeman was away.

"So, ladies and gentlemen, those are the results," Freeman said with finality. "Now I suggest we all enjoy this fine party that Dr. and Mrs. Billings, our new town councillors, have provided for us all tonight."

When the town clerk put his list on the coffee table, I went over to read the results in more detail. George Cossar, the accountant, had just missed being elected by four votes; and only two votes behind George was Obi Kendal. Obi had done surprisingly well despite his reputation as a radical.

The only two people on the council who were without connections or obligations to the fish plant were Fred Fudge and Billy Dollimount. They couldn't outvote Freeman Drake, even if they dared to.

Billy Dollimount and his wife were in the hallway putting on their raincoats when Doug and Marjorie McEachern arrived.

"Good thing we've still got you on the council, Billy, old man," Doug said. "They need somebody with experience, that's for sure."

Billy chuckled quietly. "Well, bye, that's progress. I been mayor for a nice while. Now we got a new one. Nothing stays the same, do it now?"

They left, and Doug and Marjorie drifted over to where I was talking to Iris Finley, who was loyally supporting her friends, the Drakes. "Get you girls a drink?" offered Doug as he glanced at the bar. "Will ya take a look at that champagne? Jeez, we never had that much even at our wedding," he hissed.

"Champagne makes me belch," said Marjorie.

It wasn't my favourite drink either. We concluded we both wanted a cup of tea. Since we didn't feel we had anything to celebrate, we would have that over in the McEacherns' kitchen. Marjorie had just baked a chocolate cake, a sure incentive to lure Farley over.

I went looking for Farley. I heard him before I saw him. He was in the pantry at the back of the kitchen, his voice rising in a noisy debate. He was with Freeman.

"And if you don't care . . . don't feel . . . The days of telling people what to do are over. They're going to have a voice in their own destiny . . . in their own . . ."

He was delivering an eloquent but disjointed plea on behalf of fair play, democracy, brotherly love—a whole range of civic virtues. This had become a regular occurrence lately, whenever he and Freeman got together.

"Why should I give a damn what you think, Mowat . . . I do care about these people. And they care about me too. They've just elected me mayor, for Christ's sake. Look, my son, they *know* who provides their livelihood around here. The facts of life. The butter on the bread . . ."

The two of them might have gone on all night but luckily someone came in and delivered a note to Freeman.

That gave me a chance to inveigle Farley away to the McEacherns'.

As we were putting on our coats, we could see Fred Fudge sprawled in an armchair, his eyelids at half mast, waving his umpteenth drink around as he conducted an argument with someone in an earnest but slurred voice.

"I hope he don't think he's going to drive his taxi home in that condition," Doug said, giving Fred a policeman's glower. The first charge of impaired driving had yet to be laid. Until then, both motor vehicles and alcohol had been scarce. Fred caught the admonishing look of the Mountie and looked away.

We were almost out of the door when we heard Freeman's voice. He was making some official announcement.

"Ladies and gentlemen, I have just received the news that Mr. Billy Dollimount, our former mayor, has decided to resign his seat on the new council. Now I'm personally very sorry to learn of this decision and I know you will be too. His experience would have been valuable. So I think that in this case the only thing we can do is have the candidate with the next-highest number of votes fill that vacancy. And that candidate is, ah, Mr. Cossar. Am I correct there, Mr. Spencer? Yes, that's right. Mr. George Cossar in seventh place."

So Freeman's plant accountant moved up to fill the vacancy. He stood up and looked around the room as though he expected some applause, which he didn't get. He was a thin-lipped sombre man who made much of the fact that he neither drank nor smoked.

"Let's get out of here," I said to Marjorie. "This is too depressing."

We tried to persuade Iris Finley to come with us, but she was engrossed in a conversation with Victor Moss and didn't seem to want to leave just then.

Once we were out of the house and heading up the road, Doug said, "Poor Billy."

"He wouldn't have got a word in edgewise with that crowd and he knew it," Marjorie added.

"That can't be bloody well right, can it?" Farley demanded loudly of the drizzling night.

"What can't?"

"Just appointing the next guy who came closest. Surely to God they have to have a by-election or something."

"Don't know, Farl," Doug said after giving the matter some thought. Policemen were expected to stay out of politics. They enforced the rules, and any thoughts Doug may have had about the people who made them had to be kept to himself. "Municipal Election Act is not my strong point. Tellya what, I'm gonna find out, though."

"Come on, let's get in out of the rain," Marjorie urged us along. "Let's have some cake and forget about it for tonight anyway. There must be something happier in the world we can think about."

Fourteen

IT WASN'T UNTIL THE LAST SUNDAY of July that Farley and I started loading gear and provisions aboard our small schooner. The *Happy Adventure* had been moored out in the cove for months—waiting for a spell of favourable weather so that we could make a voyage. We were the least intrepid sailors, and the longer we spent living alongside that ferocious body of water, the less inclined we were to sail anywhere. Particularly not in that cramped old jackboat that had brought us here in the first place. If we hadn't lingered until it was too late to move on, we might never have become infatuated with the place. Our destiny seemed connected with that boat.

We didn't have a wharf or stage of our own, but Ezra Rose invited us to make use of his. We carried things from our house down to the stage—saucepans and ropes, sleeping bags and navigational charts, canned food and books—and loaded them into our dinghy and rowed it all out to the schooner. We were going to have a holiday—a cruise to some unknown destination, perhaps to a cove or bay where no one had ever been before. It was the kind of day that quelled our fears and lured us out to sea. The air was so still that when the Sunday-morning church bell started pealing, it sounded as if it was beside us instead of a mile away. It was hot that day—a situation so rare that I can still clearly remember it.

Ezra Rose and Dan Quayle Senior were sitting on a bench on the stage, carefully noting all our preparations, mentally tabulating every item. They were having a discussion about town politics, but I'm not sure whether the recent town election or the preparation for our voyage was more engrossing to them.

"Clement LeDrew left here a rich man, and I'll live to see the day when Mr. Drake will do the same," I heard Ezra say as I climbed up the ladder on the side of the stage. He spat out the words and then spat into the sea. "Didn't I work for Mr. LeDrew all them years back, twelve hours a day makin' salt fish, and all we got was five cents an hour? That's the rights of it. 'Twas all he gave us. That 'n art'ritis in me spine from bidin' on that cold stage all them years."

"'Twere fifty years ago, Ezra," Dan Quayle argued. "Altogether different them days. Five cents would buy more than these times."

"Don't matter one pick. A millionaire is what he was when he left. Now how did he get so rich and we poor people stayed so poor? Tell me that."

Dan didn't have an answer. He had heard Ezra's harangue about the economics of the fish business before. We all had. Like a Punch and Judy show, we all recognized the villain and the victim. Yet, like an actor, Ezra brought the same old lines to life. A clutch of Dan's grandsons, who were fishing for conners under the stage, had heard this diatribe many times.

"You heed that Obi Kendal," he said with a note of warning in his voice. "When them young rascals takes over, then we'll see Jack's as good as his master!"

"Likes of Obi Kendal gets everyone into trouble," Dan Senior said sententiously, though he believed in his heart that the fish plant should have been paying taxes right along. Once, years before, Dan had almost convinced his fellow councillors that they should pass the motion—just go ahead and tell Mr. Drake that he was going to be taxed like everyone else who was in some kind of business. But that had been back around the time of the earlier labour troubles, and with Mr. Drake talking about closing the plant and moving away, the other councillors had been afraid of a confrontation. So the motion had been dropped. And Dan knew it wasn't going to be passed by this new council either.

By noon our boat was loaded. There was a slight breeze from the west and we were eager to be off. We rowed out to the schooner, climbed aboard and tied the dinghy to the stern.

"Fine breeze, Skipper. Carry you straight to Oporto!" called Dan Senior, who many years before had survived a shipwreck off the coast of Portugal.

"Not going that far," Farley called back.

"You'll make the Azores then sure," Ezra added.

Farley laid out the chart on the table in our small cabin. The west wind gave us a choice of anywhere to the east. We decided to head first for the abandoned settlement of Cul-de-Sac West, about ten miles away.

"Looks like the perfect place to spend tonight," Farley said as he charted our course. "Good anchorage in the lee of the headland. Okay, mate," he said, sounding like a comic-opera captain, "prepare to haul the hook!"

As a sailor I never achieved a rank above that of deck-hand and galley slave. I was decidedly more at home in front of the stove than I was at the tiller. The ancient skill of harnessing the wind so that the ship moved in the direction we wanted did not come easily to me. We did have an engine in the ship, a thudding old diesel that could extricate us from the tricky harbours and adverse currents, but it was a point of pride with Farley to use it as seldom as possible.

Sailing eastward, the rocky shoreline gradually rose to an infinity of high majestic cliffs. On that clear day it seemed as if we could see forever. There were no other ships to be seen. We were alone on a vast, quiet ocean, and on days like that I felt sorry for everyone else in the world who couldn't be there to share it.

For lunch we ate bread and cheese and sardines out on the deck, and drank part of a bottle of wine. That was our standard meal when we were underway, one that always tasted better at sea than it did ashore. Our ship had no electricity and, consequently, no refrigerator. However, we scarcely needed one, not even in mid-summer. We stowed butter and cheese and bacon and potatoes in a locker under the floorboards, where they stayed cold. Of course the trouble was that in such a climate I was always cold too. At sea I wore a heavy sweater, a waterproof jacket, denim jeans, thick socks inside rubber boots, and gloves. Farley, who has a body thermometer set several degrees higher than mine, could be comfortable in less bulky clothing.

"We could keep on going," Farley suggested, scanning the shore. "It's only four o'clock. Still lots of daylight and a good following breeze. What do you think?"

"How far?"

"Maybe Enragée River."

"Why not?"

"Adieu Cul-de-Sac West." Farley saluted the distant harbour as we sailed on by. "We'll visit you another day. Today faraway outports look greener."

We sailed on past the impenetrable cliffs for another couple of hours. Farley studied the chart very carefully and finally pointed the bow of our schooner towards a barely visible cleft in a thousand-foot wall of rock. It was the mouth of the Enragée River. We lowered the mainsail and under power cautiously steered into the forbidding chasm. Suddenly, and violently, a wall of turbulent green water rose dead ahead and washed over our bow. Plastic cups and plates rolled into the scuppers as the boat pitched and tossed. Bursting spray drenched my face and hair. Farley clung to the tiller, desperately trying to keep our little ship heading straight into the river and away from the fearsome walls of the canyon. I frantically grabbed the charts, binoculars and jackets as they scattered across the deck. Then, as suddenly as it had come upon us, the turbulence was over. We were inside the sheltered haven of a wide and placid river. About a mile ahead of us we could see the clustered houses of a little village, hemmed in by brooding hills, catching the glow of the late-afternoon sun.

"Dear God," I said, "I can see why the French called this place *enragée*."

"We hit the outgoing tide," Farley explained as he changed into a dry shirt, "but that's nothing to what it must be like in a real sou'wester."

The prospect of facing the furious waters of that river mouth again gave me pause. Would I have to stay in Enragée River and start life over? Had that been the fate of the people who lived in the village we were approaching?

I did my nautical best to furl the foresail and we proceeded slowly up the river.

The distant houses were as vivid as a colouring book. They were all bunched together at the base of a huge promontory of rock, and they looked as if they had been built on top of one another's shoulders in the manner of some hill village in Italy or Spain. High above the settlement, a trickle of sparkling water plunged down into a stream that disappeared among the maze of houses. As we drew closer, we could see people—dozens of people—heading towards the wharf. By the time we reached it ourselves, I'm sure the entire population was awaiting us. The small government wharf was as crowded as the Toronto subway at rush hour. As Farley swung *Happy Adventure* alongside with a flourish, every eye was on us. There was not a word of greeting—only an uncanny silence.

This settlement, like many in Newfoundland, had one name which appeared on the map and the post office, and another by which everyone knew it. Enragée River had become Rosey River to those who lived there, and only greenhorns called it by its formal name, which was a relic from long ago when the French had occupied this coast. The French names they left behind after the English conquest had long since been corrupted beyond recognition.

On the coast, Rosey River was a legendary place. Like fabled Cathay, I had never expected to see it myself. It was not on the route from anywhere to anywhere else, and the coastal steamer, when conditions of tide, fog and storm permitted it to enter the river at all, only stayed for five or ten minutes. Very few people from Baleena had ever been there, yet the people of Rosey River were the butt of their jokes, the kind of jokes that would ultimately be told by mainland Canadians about all Newfoundlanders. The "River" people were the country cousins, the people who allegedly talked with a funny accent, wore shabby clothes and couldn't fathom the more worldly ways of their sophisticated cousins in Baleena, Jersey Island or beyond.

The Dog Cove children who visited my kitchen claimed they knew about Rosey River and its sloth and poverty. They told me that the people there had nothing to wear but rags. Rosey River was where you sent your used clothing. There was even a song about Rosey River. Dorothy and Ruth had sung it to me gleefully one time:

Up Rosey River
The sun's shining down
You see all the young folks
Lyin' around

Waitin' for the steamer
To come down the shore
To bring them their cheques
From the government, sure.

Numerous attempts had been made to relocate them to some larger centre like Baleena. Several government relocation officers had tried to inveigle them into it, but not one family seriously considered the idea. Though months might pass without so much as one visit from the doctor, a year without a school teacher, or several weeks without postal or freight service, the Rosey River folks were unshakable in their conviction that this was their home and they intended to stay in it.

So, finally, there I was face to face with this legendary band. They stared at us, absorbed by every move we made. When we were moored, I busied myself with deck chores, glancing into the crowd from time to time and trying to veil my own curiosity. True to the folklore, they seemed a shabby crowd—little girls in faded cotton dresses which hung to a matronly ankle length, little boys in pants with missing knees and shirts with tattered elbows. Three young girls sat on the edge of the wharf with their feet dangling over the side. They wore identical pairs of red plastic sandals. Then I noticed that almost every child on the wharf wore this same style of shoe. It must have been the major shipment of new footwear to arrive there that year. The less lucky children wore the threadbare sneakers of other years.

The women who stared at me were indeed wearing the cast-off clothing of other outports, an incongruous array of dresses of moiré taffeta, rayon crepe and faded pastel cotton. This was where Barbara Drake's old clothes were dispatched in their final phase, and I couldn't help looking for things that might have been hers. All the women and girls over the age of about ten were crowned with the same style of home permanent—corkscrew curls as tight as a Persian lamb coat. My own hair, straight as a ruler, must have intrigued them for its lack of style.

In the midst of the crowd a group of older men stood together. Dressed in baggy pants, heavy flannel shirts and cloth caps, they smoked pipes, chewed tobacco and watched us fixedly. Perhaps we seemed like ghosts from another time. We had arrived in a wooden sailing ship of a kind that hadn't been seen around there since the 1920s. What's more, the captain sported a long beard of the kind their fathers had worn but which had been out of style for forty years. Maybe our little ship was some sort of Flying Dutchman that had been adrift on the cold ocean these many years while life moved on apace on shore.

After what seemed like a very long time, one of the men ventured a few words to Farley.

"You and yer woman be all you got, Skipper?"

"That's right. Just the two of us. We just sailed in from Baleena."

"He's the captain and I'm the crew," I added. It was my favourite pat explanation of how we manned our ship.

No one said anything. They continued to stare in silent wonder. These women didn't go to sea, except reluctantly as passengers. I looked up at the little girls whose feet dangled over the wharf and smiled at them. They were blondes and pretty, despite the fuzzy permanent waves. But they didn't smile back at me, nor did they utter a word. The camaraderie of mariners apparently did not extend from woman to woman.

"Would there be any way a man could buy a fresh fish around here?" Farley asked of no one in particular.

"No, sir. We don't fish Sundays. 'Tis a sin."

Of course. Sunday. The mandatory day of rest. I wondered what people did do here on Sunday. There was a church but there wasn't a clergyman.

I went below deck and resigned myself to making a supper out of that old standby, canned bully beef and potatoes. With any luck, tomorrow someone would be going fishing.

The crowd didn't disperse during the hour we spent preparing and eating our meal. A few of the onlookers wandered away, but they were replaced by new ones. Clearly, we were not going to be left alone. Despite this continuing vigil, we took our coffee up on deck, something we always liked to do to savour the sunset and the satisfaction of having made a voyage. When the last glow faded from the western sky, the final watchers drifted away from the wharf. Then I saw something I had never seen before, nor have I seen since—the sight of an entire village lighted by lamplight, a gentle golden glow behind a hundred lace-curtained windows. Farley and I sat looking at this rare scene for a long time until, one by one, the lamps were blown out and families went to bed. Then we too went below, blew out our lamp and crawled into our sleeping bags. I fell into an impatient sleep, eager as a tourist for the morning to come and the chance to explore Rosey River.

Fifteen

THE THIRTY-FOUR HOUSES of Rosey River stood on a patch of land that covered no more than a city block. It was stony, sloping land and directly behind it was a monolithic wall of rock. It looked about as accessible as the south slope of Mount Everest. No one, I was told, had ever attempted anything so foolish as trying to climb it. Life in Rosey River looked sufficiently demanding without this challenge.

After breakfast we left our ship and ambled through the village. A freshly gravelled path led uphill into the knot of houses and sheds, intersecting here and there with other narrower pathways. The houses were as close to one another as if they had been in a city. They were square, two-storey structures—no room here for the luxury of a bungalow. The colour of the houses particularly intrigued me. Every possible combination of the spectrum of commercial paint had been used. There were turquoise houses with yellow window sills, pink houses with blue doors, orange houses with green porches. As house painters the people of Rosey River were as uninhibited as New York abstract expressionists.

There was not one motorized vehicle in the whole place. The pathways abounded with sheep; they were everywhere, foraging where they could—on meagre patches of grass that crept out from under fences, and on the small tufts of greenery that managed to grow in the crevices in the rocks. They even foraged in the cemetery, the one patch of level land that hadn't been pressed into service either for a building site or a garden. Every tiny patch of usable soil was surrounded by a stick fence to protect a small potato patch. In a curious inversion of agrarian law, in Newfoundland a family was obliged to erect a fence to keep animals out, not in. These unpainted fences, made from the vertical trunks of skinny spruce trees, were everywhere and gave the whole place a palisaded appearance. And on this washday Monday, I noticed that the laundry was hung on horizontal poles made from the same thin trees.

It seemed a model of ingenuity that any agriculture could be undertaken in so small a space. An urban planner, faced with the limitations of this cramped corner of the earth's surface, would have thrown up his hands in despair and opted to move the whole population somewhere else. But there *was* nowhere else for dozens of rocky miles in any direction. It was Farley's guess that Beothuk Indians had surely used this place for a camp long before the coming of Europeans. They too would have appreciated its natural advantages—shelter from gales, an abundance of fresh water and access to both the sea and the interior country.

As we wandered through the community, people drew back their curtains to look out at us. We were still a top news item. And we attracted a coterie of children who made no attempt to disguise their blatant interest in us. They followed us everywhere we went, their numbers steadily growing until the procession began to look like the Pied Piper's exodus from Hamelin.

We led our entourage along various footpaths and eventually came to a halt at the door of the two-room school. It was a frame building in need of paint, which stood unobtrusively at the back of the community. Beside it was a small, steepleless Anglican church in similarly shabby condition. These buildings were obviously not the source of pride that the crayon-coloured houses were.

On we ambled, and though the children chattered amiably, few of the adults we met along our way gave us more than a polite nod as they went about their business. But a hefty woman with an inquisitive face and a worn apron over her dress waited bravely by her garden gate as our procession came by.

"I hear'd 'twas strangers comin' round and I said I got to see 'em fer meself," she proclaimed as she stared straight at us. We might have been performers on a stage.

"Well, it's a fine day," Farley offered.

"Foine day," she agreed.

"Good day for hanging out the wash," I added in a spirit of accord, though actually it wasn't all that good. The weather was muggy and still, and swarms of blackflies were all around us.

"Yis, dear, foine day fer d'wash," she said. She wasn't going to disagree with me.

We stood there chatting for a while, swatting blackflies, agreeing about the weather, the potato gardens, and about our "pretty" little boat.

"Oi loikes to go in boat up river. When me man gits home, we be goin' in boat. Gits lonesome when he's gone," she said.

"Is your husband away at sea?" Farley asked.

"No, me dear man, he's gone bukams," she told us. "Be gone a nice while he will. Plane come fer 'im. Pitches right 'ere on river." Then after a pause, she added, "He gone bukams last year besoides."

We didn't understand what she was talking about and, after we were out of earshot, Farley asked one of the children what the lady had been trying to tell us about her husband. What had happened to him?

"Gone bukams," one of the boys repeated as succinctly and mysteriously. He didn't seem inclined to elaborate, so we dropped the subject. Perhaps the poor man was in a sanitarium or an asylum.

I wondered about the kind of life that woman lived. I tried to imagine a life in which strangers were as memorable as hurricanes or droughts or fires. How many strangers would she see in a lifetime? How many had I seen in a day in a city? I was full of questions about this place. Were the sheep owned communally or individually? Did anyone grow anything besides potatoes? Where did people go to pick berries? I asked the children who persisted in following us, but they were either so shy or so uncomprehending of my own speech that they seldom answered. One brave little boy ventured to tell me that there were "t'ousands blueberries up t'river." We eventually discovered that "up the river" was the source of a lot of things that made for a pretty nice life—salmon, trout, moose, caribou, ptarmigan, wild berries and firewood.

On the porch of a large yellow house, a grey-haired man sat whittling with a knife. He was surrounded by a pile of wood shavings. A large elderly dog and a dozen or so hens kept him company.

"G'day, Skipper," he called out cheerfully.

"Fine morning," Farley called back and, encouraged by this friendly greeting, he asked, "And what is it you're so busy making?"

"Me brooms is all. Come in. Come in now," he beckoned. "You and your woman have a look."

We unlatched the wooden gate, leaving our gaggle of followers behind, and climbed the flight of steps to discover that the old chap was carving an implement which looked as ancient as the concept of living in houses—a broom consisting of a rough stick handle about four feet long, at the bottom of which he had made, with a thousand deft strokes, paper-thin shavings. These shavings were bent back in an "S" shape and tied to form a thickly tufted head. A bundle of finished brooms stood in a corner of the porch, and he got up and handed one of them to me for closer inspection.

"I makes 'em from the birch trees I get upriver," he explained.

"They're very good," I said, examining his craftsmanship.

"Take it along wid ya, me dear maid," he insisted.

"Oh now, I can't . . ."

"Yis, yis. You take that home now. I makes t'ousounds of 'em. Sells 'em to d' fish plant."

"The fish plant in Baleena?"

"Yis, and Jersey Island besoides. Pays I forty-five cents each broom. That bundle there goes up on steamer tomorrow."

It was fascinating to find this independent artisan making a living from such an ancient craft.

"How did you learn to make them?" Farley asked.

The fellow looked puzzled, as though no one had ever asked him that before.

"Most everyone knowed how to make a broom around here one time," he said. He couldn't recall exactly when he had learned to do it. Like hauling water or felling trees, it was just something every boy of his generation had learned.

"Chesley Green's me name, Skipper," he said to Farley, "and what be yours?"

"Farley Mowat. And this is my wife, Claire."

I sat down on the top step of the porch to watch the long shavings grow magically at the end of the new broom. Chesley's wife came bursting out of the front door.

"Come in now, come in. Can't bide out here. Come in kitchen," she said solicitously, insisting I shouldn't sit on the porch steps with the men.

I followed her into the kitchen. Or rather, I thought we had walked into a kitchen. When I took a closer look, I realized that it was actually the parlour—that sacrosanct part of a house reserved for celebrations. It was a room of many shiny surfaces. The walls had been painted in a startling shade of high-gloss orange. The congoleum floor was buffed to a mirror finish so that the chrome legs of the chairs were reflected in it. Everywhere there were gleaming surfaces of Arborite and vinyl. Even the fibreglass curtains reflected light. The whole room shone like some fancy teapot that was never used. We went on through into the kitchen. There I was invited to sit down on an old pressback wooden chair to which a coat of paint must have been lovingly added every year since about 1910.

The kitchen was at least twice as large as the parlour, and equally shiny. There was a large black wood-and-coal range with gleaming nickel trim. The wooden table and chairs had been painted a glossy yellow. The walls were red as poppies and the linoleum on the floor, a bit worn in places, was another shade of red. On a corner table there was a cheerful clutter of dishes and teapots, a mail-order catalogue or two, and a big Bible.

"Name is Pearl," Chesley's wife said with a wide smile. She didn't have any teeth at all. "I'll bile the kittle and git some tea. You loikes tea, me dear?"

I told her I did. She shoved a big cast-iron kettle over to the hot side of the range. I was surprised to see that she was still making use of this ancient, cumbersome kettle. When I first saw it I thought it was some kind of decoration—a treasured link with the past amid a profusion of more contemporary artifacts like the plastic piggy bank and the ashtray with a picture of Confederation Building in St. John's.

"Foinest kind, this old kettle," she said with downright affection. "Belonged to my poor grandmother, it did. I leaves the water into it all night and it never colours."

On the mainland that kettle would have been part of a folk museum. In Baleena it would by then have been chucked over the end of the wharf.

Pearl, who was about sixty, was dressed in a flowered dirndl skirt, a pink sweater and a rhinestone necklace. She wore men's dress socks inside black suede pumps. Her light-brown hair had only traces of grey in it, and if it hadn't been for the absence of teeth, she would still have been a good-looking woman.

Once the ice was broken, she was as friendly as a puppy, and kept up a steady patter of conversation, only part of which I understood. It was not the same dialect that was spoken in Baleena. Similar, but with a different cadence. Pearl had never been to Baleena, not even to the hospital. Chesley had been there three times, and she recalled the date and the purpose of each of these visits.

Our tea was served in elegant English cups and saucers covered with primroses, violets and other faraway flowers that had never been seen in Rosey River. Where had they come from? I wondered. They were too elite an item for the mail-order catalogues. Had a sea-going ancestor brought them back from a voyage to Halifax or St. John's, Bristol or Liverpool? I was too polite to ask.

When I left to return to our boat, Pearl gave me a loaf of her homemade bread—the best gift anyone can give to people who live aboard a small ship with only a two-burner gas range on which to cook.

I went below into our little galley to warm a can of soup to accompany our welcome loaf of bread. Farley stayed up on deck to repair our radio antenna, which had been torn from our mast during our tumultuous entry into the river. As I was setting out the plates, I heard another boat's engine chugging close by. A few minutes later someone shouted a greeting. There was the sound of a length of rope landing on our deck, followed by the creaking of wood against wood. The new arrival had moored alongside us and I went up on deck to see who was there.

It was a shabby, grey workboat from Baleena, a vessel known to the plant workers as "The Lumpfish." She was used for such messy chores as taking out loads of fish gurry to be dumped at sea, though that summer she had been dispatched along the coast to collect herring from the inshore fishermen. Herring is one of the bait fish for cod fishing and some years it is in short supply. Though we recognized the vessel, it was a surprise to see our clergyman, Matthew Way, alongside the skipper. We seldom saw him in Baleena since he was constantly in transit to one or another of his three parishes.

"We didn't expect to see you here!" Farley called.

"Have a good voyage?" I asked.

"Oh yes, thank the Lord, it's a mausey day," he said as he took a handkerchief and wiped his brow. "I'm no sailor, you know I don't make any secret of that. But this morning it was smooth as oil, as the saying goes. We had a good passage," he laughed, looking a little hot under his clerical collar.

"Well, come below," Farley invited him after the Lump-fish's skipper had headed off into the community. "We'll see if we can't find a little something to settle your nerves." Farley spirited a bottle of wine from under the floorboards.

"So you're no sailor and the bishop sent you *here*—to this coast?" Farley asked incredulously.

"Somebody has got to come," Matthew said with cheerful stoicism. "And I am enjoying being here, apart from all this going to sea. So many good people. And there is so much work to be done in the parish. So much."

"How often do you get here to Rosey River?" I wondered.

"As often as I can. I take the coast boat or I catch a lift when one of the plant boats or the medical boat is coming this way. I rarely get here on Sunday, but the people don't seem to mind. Rosey River people have never had their own clergy. They don't expect miracles." He laughed. "Perhaps they should. After all, I got here this morning without being seasick. Now there's a minor miracle!"

"They're staunch churchgoers then, are they?" I asked.

"I wouldn't exactly say that," Matthew laughed, but with less gusto than before.

"The church doesn't look to be in the best shape," said Farley.

"We're going to build a new church! It's long overdue. We have to remember that this place, this community, has special needs. These people have been on their own here for a long time, with little help from anyone outside." He went on, groping for the right words, reluctant to describe his smallest and poorest parish in any way that might be unkind. "They're very independent, these River people. They have had to be, or they never would have survived."

"Matthew, have you any idea how long they've been living here as a community?" Farley asked.

"Not exactly. The old headstones in the cemetery were made of wood and they only lasted a few generations. My oldest parishioner here is a woman of ninety-eight, and she told me that her grandmother was born here. So that takes us back to, oh, about 1800, 1810, by my figuring. Of course, her grandmother's antecedents might have been here even before that. We just don't know. The history of settlement in small places like this is obscure. No known records of them at all. We only know from their surnames that somehow they got here from England—probably Dorset or Devon, like most of the people on this coast."

"Easy to see how Rosey River could be overlooked. You can sail along the coast, and even on a clear day you wouldn't see the entrance," Farley said.

"True. And isn't it surprising, once you get in here? This wide river, all the trees, a land of plenty. Have you been further up the river, into the arms?" Matthew asked us.

"We're planning to go right after lunch," I said.

"Come with us for the afternoon," Farley suggested.

"No, no," he said a little wistfully. "Thank you anyway, but I have a great deal to do here before the westbound steamer comes tomorrow, if it's on time. I've got to organize a shipment of lumber so work can start on the new church, not to mention the church services, a baptism and some sick people to visit. And I've got to do something about a second teacher. School opens in three weeks and I'm still without one."

"You've got the first one, have you?" I asked.

"Yes, luckily a few years ago a young man came down here from Pass Island to teach and he married a local girl and stayed on. But trying to find that second teacher is always a problem. Not many want to spend a year in such an isolated place. I've got a couple of bright young people in Jersey Island who finished grade eleven this year—they could teach on my recommendation, but they just don't want to come."

"Matthew, why does everyone look down their nose at this place?" Farley asked.

He shook his head. "Most people tend to feel superior to someone else. The darker side of us, sure."

"You should advertise for a teacher in the *Toronto Star*," I urged. "Or maybe the *New York Times*. You'd get dozens of replies. Why not try that?"

"Saints preserve us," he said in genuine amazement. "I can't imagine anyone from those big places wanting to come here. Not to Rosey River. The salary is very modest, very modest indeed."

"The money wouldn't matter. There are all kinds of people—and I mean young people with some education, maybe a B.A.—who would want to come here just for the adventure."

"Oh, but they surely wouldn't stay."

"They'd stay the school year, I'll bet. That's as good as you're getting with the local teachers," Farley reasoned.

He mulled the idea over, doubting us, doubting that anyone from a modern city would want to trade life there for ten months in Rosey River. "Well, I must be getting along," he said, putting down his plastic cup. "Flora May always has dinner for me when I arrive."

"Flora May?"

"Flora May Green. A fine woman, very kind, very strong. She usually boards the teacher, and she runs the telegraph. You could say she's something of an unofficial leader here. No one acknowledges that she has any special position, you understand, but not much gets done around here without her instigation or approval."

"Any relation to Chesley Green, the broommaker?" I asked.

"No, I don't think so." He pondered the matter. "No. You have to remember that about two-thirds of everyone here has the surname of Green. It might appear that they're all related, but it's not the case. I still haven't sorted out who is whose cousin or aunt. But they know who's related, sure, even if I don't."

"Matthew, before you go, there's one thing you might be able to tell us. What does it mean when someone here says 'gone bukams'? Do you know?"

"Gone bukams? Bukams?" he repeated. "Oh, you mean Buchans! Gone to Buchans. That's a big mine right in the middle of the province. A lot of the men from Rosey River go there to work every summer. For about the past five years. They work with the prospecting crews, way into the interior. Isolated work, but these fellows don't seem bothered by it. On the face of it, it's not unlike the way they've always lived, except that they don't have their wives and families along. The mine sends them home every fourth weekend, and then collects them again. They have a float plane for the job. The children rave about it. You'll see it if you're around here for a while. Those jobs have made a big difference to the prosperity of this place. When the men come home to stay, in the fall of the year, they have quite a sum of money."

"More affluence than meets the eye?" Farley concluded.

"Right. So we'd better get our new church built while the going's good!" he exclaimed and headed off towards the settlement.

The same eager crowd of children who had followed us took off after Matthew Way, and they all disappeared into the labyrinth of houses and sheds.

North from the settlement, the Rosey (or Enragée) River gradually widened into a large fiord. We were surrounded by towering rocks and, above that, a thick forest of spruce trees. The basin branched into three arms; one led to the north, one to the northwest, and a smaller one due west. We stopped our engine and drifted in the powerful silence while we studied the chart and tried to decide which way to go.

The first usable charts of this sombre coast were made by the celebrated Captain Cook long before he sailed on to acclaim, and death, in the South Pacific. He was barely twenty years old at the time he made the first British survey of the region, including this river. The charts were still essentially the ones he made. I tried to picture him, in his eighteenth-century sailors' clothes, painstakingly swinging a lead line every few yards as he leaned over the side of a dory charting the reefs and shoals.

"God, look at the depths," said Farley. "Thirty fathoms right to the shore! Our anchor chain wouldn't even reach bottom. And look at how many of the headlands are called 'Blow-me-down.' Good places to stay clear of. I think I see one safe mooring over in the western arm, though God help us if we get a wind from the north."

The cove, when we found it, was spectacular. We were surrounded on three sides by a deep evergreen forest that rose almost straight up the side of a steep cliff. Far above us we could see a fresh-water stream, the seemingly weightless drops splattering and sparkling as they fell down to the sea. North of us a landscape of glacier-worn rocks marched into the distance, and below us the water was so clear we could see right to the bottom about twenty feet down.

Once we were moored I lay idly on the afterdeck, staring into this subsurface world. Regiments of nameless little fishes swam busily by, oblivious to my observations. Starfish oozed along. Scallops slapped their shells and flipped along the bottom like subterranean flying saucers. As I watched transfixed, I imagined that someday I might write about the life of the creatures under the sea.

"Hey, look up there!" my husband's voice summoned me.

A bald eagle had just made a precarious landing on a skeletal spruce tree. In a minute there was a second one. The two eagles sat together, their amber eyes glowering into the woods around them, as uninterested in our presence as if we had been mere starfish. During the week we were in that cove, we saw at least a dozen of these stately birds, birds that the outport people called by their medieval name of "greep." They were not hunted because they were considered to be unpalatable scavengers.

We towed a small fibreglass dinghy, upon which we optimistically conferred the status of a lifeboat. Its real use was for trips ashore once the schooner was safely moored. We rowed across the western arm to a brook where we fished for trout, finding them so plentiful that even indifferent fishermen like ourselves could catch our dinner in half an hour. We picked wild blueberries, which we ate with canned milk and sugar. Later we even found wild peas—vetch, once the friend of sailors suffering from scurvy. It took me over an hour to pick enough of these tiny wild peas to constitute a serving for two people, but I didn't mind. That week I had lots of time.

Another day we caught squid, those small octopus-like creatures that swam near the shoreline and could be scooped up by hand. Though they were tough as rubber bands when they were boiled, we ate them too. Considering all the resources that the Rosey River people had, it was puzzling why they should be the objects of pity and scorn along the coast.

One day we decided to climb to the top of the cliff that loomed above our little hideaway. It was our intention to find the source of the waterfall. We climbed, with considerable difficulty, for nearly two hours, up over the vertical rocks and slippery boulders, clinging to feeble little spruce trees as we went. When we reached the crest of this isthmus which divided the inland waterway from the sea, we could once again see the Atlantic Ocean stretching into infinity to the south of us. We were ecstatic—the way Cortes must have felt—sure that we were standing in a place where no men, and certainly no women, had ever stood before. We may well have been the first. Then we started to consider our trip back down, and wondered what would happen if one of us fell and broke a leg amid the jagged crevices of this landscape that was more suited to eagles than it was to people. We climbed down with much more caution than when we had climbed up. And we never did find the source of the waterfall.

In the evenings there wasn't much we could do. We had packed a few books—our "Desert Island" library—books we felt we could read over and over in the event we were cast adrift somewhere, like Robinson Crusoe. As well as studying the field guide to *The Birds of Eastern North America*, Farley was slowly working his way through Tolstoy's *Anna Karenina*. I was reading *The Prince*, by Machiavelli.

The only other evening entertainment was to listen to the radio—whenever we could hear anything. The hills diminished the signal. Every afternoon at five we strained to hear the familiar voice of Harry Brown of CBN in St. John's reading the daily marine weather forecast. "And now the weather for mariners and ships at sea . . ." came a distant, static-ridden voice, followed by a military band playing a tune known as "The Feller from Fortune."

The weather office advised us, with depressing frequency, that out on the coast "moderate to strong winds" would be blowing from the southwest, and that "visibility will be reduced to three miles, lowering to near zero in patches of mist and fog." Which meant that if we left our idyllic cove and the shelter of the canyons, the fog would be so thick we wouldn't be able to see our hands in front of our faces. Marine weather forecasts usually erred on the side of optimism. So we would decide to stay where we were, happily justifying another day of idle seclusion. For nine days we did not see another person.

Occasionally we could catch a barely audible play on the radio, or else a program of classical music—fragments that reminded us of that segment of the world from which we felt so languorously removed. It was my salvation all the same—CBC radio. It brought me just enough of the outside world, and I could always turn it off when I had had enough. I've often wondered if the Canadian Broadcasting Corporation knows, or cares, about all those distant, unknown corners of its domain where its unique programs are heard.

If the signal didn't fade, we usually listened to the ten o'clock news. After that we took turns reading to each other from what must be the funniest boating story in the English language—*Three Men in a Boat*, by Jerome K. Jerome. Written in 1889, it was just as funny seventy years later.

"Someday," I said to Farley as I blew out the lamp, "you'll have to write a funny book about this boat and all the crazy things that have happened to us in it. It's unbelievable, really. Think of the story possibilities."

"Mmmmm, mmmmm," he muttered sleepily. "One of these days I might just do that."

Sixteen

WE SAILED BACK TO DOG COVE on a calm, late-summer day, arriving just in time to see a little parade of people—the older women dressed in black—heading for a funeral. John Quayle had died at the age of ninety-one, which was not exactly a surprise since he had been in failing health for many months. It wasn't until we started unloading that we got the more shocking news that the Pointings' house had burned to the ground.

We went to look at the still-smouldering remains of what, five days earlier, had housed eleven people. Rosie and Garland had not been home when the fire started. Neither had Edith, their eldest, nor Harold, the next eldest. The younger children had been left in the care of twelve-year-old Maizie, along with the old grandmother, who was totally blind and partly deaf. The fire had started when Frankie, aged six, had carried a coal-oil lamp upstairs, and then had accidentally knocked it over, setting fire to the bedclothes. When I heard this, I had second thoughts about the merits of picturesque lamplight. Frankie didn't know what to do about his burning bedclothes, so he started to cry. No one paid any attention. Some child was always wailing about something in that house. All the other children, including the three-week-old baby, were asleep in other rooms. Luckily, old Mrs. Pointing could smell smoke. She called Maizie in from outdoors to find out what was going on. Screaming and yelling, Maizie got everyone, including the baby and the grandmother, out into the night. Only the family dog, a fine old water-dog bitch whose puppies had been sold

217

from door to door and who had contributed her fair share to the family income, was suffocated.

"'Twas some lucky they all got out," said Dorothy, who was just back from her great-grandfather's funeral. "Bigger fire than ever I see'd on Guy Fawkes Night."

I made a mental note to order a couple of extra fire extinguishers. There was no fire-fighting equipment in Baleena. The council had often discussed the matter, but the expense of buying pumping equipment, coupled with the great difficulty of moving it hastily over the bumpy roads, pathways and foot bridges, always left the matter unresolved.

"Where are the Pointings going to live now?" I asked.

"They bides down to Manuel Tibbo's," Dorothy told me. Manuel Tibbo was Rosie's brother and had a family almost as large as his sister's.

"I hear'd they's packed in there like a can of mackerel," Ruth Quayle told me with a supercilious air.

"How ever will they manage?" I wondered out loud as I shivered in a breeze that told us summer was over.

"Got 'nother house," said five-year-old Leroy, who was relishing the disaster and all the attendant excitement.

"Really? Where?" I asked in surprise. There were so few vacant houses in the entire community that I couldn't imagine where it was.

"Ghost house I calls it," said Dorothy, condemning the place. "Nobody lived in it fer a dog's age. 'Longside the fish plant is where it's to. Right grey it is. Niver had no paint."

It was a house I'd seen out of the corner of my eye many times—a long-abandoned shanty located pungently downwind from the fish meal division of the plant. The prospect of anyone living there was appalling.

"Good riddance to 'em," said Melita Quayle when I was at the shop later in the day. "I'm glad they're gone. A hard crowd."

Melita, usually a charitable woman, wasted no sympathy on the Pointings. In truth, their departure was not lamented by any of the industrious Quayles. The Pointings had contributed little to the general well-being of our corner of the world. Despite that, I missed them. Their children had become part of the pattern of things. It had taken a long time for any of them to offer me a smile or a wave, but we had gradually established a rapport that was warmer than a nodding acquaintanceship. I had harboured the hope that someday they might regard me as a friend.

A few days later. two young men came to our door and announced that they were collecting money for the Garland Pointing family. We gave them twenty dollars, hoping that would be neither ostentatious nor parsimonious. We didn't quite know our financial obligation in this situation. Everywhere else I had lived, insurance policies had usually recompensed people for the unexpected setbacks in their lives. The only families in Baleena who carried fire insurance were people like ourselves—outsiders, who had long since dispensed with any illusion that friends or neighbours might put us back on our feet.

"We done all right so far," one of the men told us. "Near three hundred and forty dollars we got now. House cost three hundred altogither. So's we got money over fer 'ile for the stove what was given. They got chairs given, and beds. And coats fer the youngsters . . ."

"Only three hundred for the house?" I asked, incredulous.

"Yes, missus. B'longed to Harvey Spencer's poor father that been dead and gone twenty years."

"Right old, that's fer sure," said the young man.

"Wind goes through her like a basket," added the other one.

"If Garland put 'ees back to it and rigged her out 'fore the first nor'easter, could be snug," said the first one. Then they exchanged glances which said what neither of them would say on this mission of charity. No one expected much from Garland. They had the evidence of his whole life on which to base their judgement. Still, they hadn't abandoned him when disaster struck. He and Rosie and the children belonged here, for better or worse, and therefore they had to be looked after.

Dan Quayle Junior came over to deliver our flour, wearing his "flour jacket," an old coat he kept especially for this job. A fine, white film had settled into the fibre over several years of carrying sacks of flour on his shoulder. Flour was only sold in quantities of fifty or a hundred pounds, and Dan delivered it on foot to his customers, who all lived beyond roads and motor vehicles.

He sat down heavily on our daybed for a few minutes of relaxation. School had begun again and the older children were only available to help him after four o'clock. Melita was pregnant for the fifth time and so she, too, could only be of limited help in the shop. As well, she suffered from "hapsies," Dan explained to us, and she was supposed to lie down a lot. I didn't like to ask just what sort of affliction hapsies was. Years later I discovered that what he had been talking about was abscesses.

We mused over the misfortunes of the Pointings, a subject which would be in every conversation that season.

"Hard luck, fer sure. But that house weren't fittin'. I seen into it different times when I took over a sack of flour. They niver let no strangers in. I'll wager you niver seen inside of it. 'Twas why they niver got no 'lectricity. Didn't want no one come pokin' around, seein' how they lived," Dan added smugly. "And that house they got now, they'll beat it down before long. That Garland . . ." Dan shook his head in disapproval, "he owed me hundred and fifty dollars. But I wrote it off. Told 'im night of the fire, 'Forget it, start over.'"

A hundred and fifty dollars was a lot for him to dismiss, but even Dan Junior couldn't abandon the Pointings. His profits were slim and his expenses mounting. With all four children in school, the cost of books and scribblers added to the load. There were the school taxes as well. To support public education, a tax was levied on each school-age child for each term of the school year. The school tax was not included in the municipal tax, which was why it was so low. This was a curious system which penalized large families, an ironic injustice, I thought, in a land where large families were the rule. Even if they weren't desired, information about birth control was harder to find than rubies. Farley and I, with no children and an income double that of Dan's, paid no school taxes at all.

"They're after us to git uniforms fer all the youngsters," Dan told us. "I can't afford no special outfits fer my crowd. They'll go to school in whatever clothes they got."

"Who says they have to have uniforms?" I asked.

"Mrs. Drake. Mrs. Billings besides. That crowd that runs things, runs that new club they got goin'—'School and Home' they calls it. They're sayin' 'twill save us money to put our youngsters into uniforms. I can't see it myself."

I couldn't see it either, but I knew how Barbara Drake would reason. In her mind one sensible outfit for school would be more economical than an assortment of dresses, sweaters and skirts. Perhaps it hadn't crossed her mind that most families handed on clothes from one child to another until they collapsed.

"A blue gimp and a white blouse for girls, and white shirts and dark pants fer boys. All done up like they was goin' to a weddin'," Dan snorted.

He left and I started making sandwiches for our lunch. "It's unfair." I complained. "I'm sure Dan and Melita didn't really want that fifth child. The others are finally off to school now. They just don't know how to prevent it happening."

"How do you know?" Farley retorted. "This might be the one who'll look after them in their old age."

"It doesn't work out like that nowadays. People move around. Move away . . ."

"Sometimes they do. But old attitudes don't change in a hurry."

"You know what I could do? I could set myself up as an Information Centre. I could get some books and pamphlets to hand out. Let the word get around that Mrs. Mowat knows how to prevent pregnancies. I doubt if anyone here does know a thing about it. They think it's got something to do with the phases of the moon and the tide. Honestly, Iris told me that."

"Listen, you do a thing like that and you'd be far less popular than the Pointing family ever was. Besides, people here feel sorry for us because we have no children."

"I guess you're right," I said after thinking it over. "They'd probably take up a collection to buy me a one-way ticket on the next steamer."

"Bloody right. Leave well enough alone."

I did leave well enough alone. Interfering in someone else's family is a poor risk to take at best. Maybe Dan and Melita were thrilled at the thought of having a new baby in the house once again. Perhaps I was the only one who pondered the cost, the abscesses on the legs, the frozen diapers on the winter clothesline.

By the middle of October cold rain drummed against the windows with dismal frequency. The Drake family were still in Massachusetts and so the activity that normally revolved around them was in abeyance. Doug and Marjorie McEachern were spending six weeks in Ottawa while Doug was on a training course. Iris Finley had been vaguely unwell for several weeks and wasn't seeing much of her friends. With little to distract us, we immersed ourselves in our work.

Even Dorothy Quayle, still our faithful friend, came to see us less often. In grade nine by then, she had homework every night, and since her mother was pregnant, she was needed more than ever in the shop and house.

Ruth Quayle, who had just turned fifteen, had left school and gone to work in the plant, as all her sisters had done before her. I used to see Ruth hurrying into the wind, her coat buttoned over her white smock and cap, as she rushed home for dinner. She wore lipstick and her dark hair jounced with the curls of a home permanent. Dorothy and Ruth were still the best of friends. On Sundays they ambled around together, visiting here and there, giggling at times, and then solemnly exchanging the cataclysmic confidences of adolescent girls everywhere.

It had been two years since Farley started writing a book about the first Europeans to cross the Atlantic Ocean and reach North America—the Vikings. From all the sagas he had read and the navigational charts he had studied, he concluded that these first Europeans to reach this continent had landed in Labrador and Newfoundland. It was a theory which needed long and detailed documentation, evidence to refute those chauvinistic American scholars who insisted that the Vikings had bypassed the entire landmass of northeastern North America and sailed blithely on to the salubrious climate of Massachusetts.

I had been drawing the maps for this book, delineating the journeys and landings to try and make this complex story more comprehensible. It was a monumental piece of work for both of us, and it was an advantage in some ways that the weather was so dismal and we had few visitors. It kept us at our work during those dark weeks that preceded the welcome brightness of the first snowfall.

"Youse like a scoff of country meat?" asked Noah Joseph, who, along with his wife, Minnie, appeared at our door in a dark coat on a frosty evening. Grinning mischievously, he dropped a heavy bundle on our kitchen floor. In the fall anyone carrying a suspiciously bulky packsack on his back, or in his dory, did his best to conceal himself. It was illegal to hunt moose without a provincial licence—something that very few outport men were able to get. They were expensive and reserved for "sportsmen" who came from somewhere else. Moose meat served us well: moose stew, moose steaks, ground moose, curried moose and, the ne plus ultra —mooseburgers. It was every bit as versatile as beef.

Noah always insisted that he didn't want any money for the meat he brought around, that it was a gift. Yet we knew that ultimately a fair price or exchange would be agreed upon. Often it would be a couple of bottles of rum—something considerably harder to find in Baleena than a moose. Business matters of this kind were subtle, quiet-spoken exchanges between men, and were usually conducted while a visit of an appropriate length was taking place.

Noah and Minnie sat down in front of the fire from our Franklin stove. An open fire inside the house was another oddity of people from away. Most Baleena families had a modern space heater—a device which was far more efficient and far less work.

Minnie was full of talk that night about their new freezer—the household appliance that was drastically changing the nature of food distribution everywhere. It was going to make Noah Joseph's life as a hunter considerably easier. Before he got the freezer, he had stored his winter supply of meat in a snowdrift behind his house—a risky business since unexpected thaws might expose his cache for all the world to see.

We talked for some time about the freezer and enumerated all those things like bread and fish and berries, as well as meat, that could be stored in it for many months. When everything that could be said on the subject had been said, Noah fell silent. It wasn't like him to be sombre when he went out visiting. We sensed that something was on his mind, and it was only after several attempts on Farley's part that he unburdened himself.

Having been Freeman Drake's "guide" for many years, he had come to think of himself as more than just an employee of the plant. In his way he believed he was Mr. Drake's friend—his adviser about important things like where the best salmon fishing was or where to look for turrs. Having shared so many expeditions with them, he felt close to the whole family—Mrs. Drake and the children too.

But during recent months there was once again a groundswell of discontent among the plant workers, and Freeman was becoming gruff with everyone, even Noah. "Feels like I was just a paid hand," Noah explained sadly. When Freeman had departed for Boston, he hadn't said goodbye to Noah, nor discussed any future gunning expeditions, as he had usually done in the past.

So Noah's pride was hurt. He had already told Minnie that he was thinking of quitting his job.

To me his grievance did not seem such a serious matter. Having come from a city where working for wages was the only way I knew how to survive, the bad humour of one's bosses was something we generally had to endure. We didn't like it, but we got used to it, like a thorn in the sole of a shoe. We limped along. Noah wasn't going to do that.

"My dear, Noah been that unhappy I told him we'd go on dole 'fore he'd go on workin' fer Mr. Drake," said Minnie supportively.

"We won't be takin' dole and that's fer sure. But I won't be takin' this aggravation neither," said Noah.

Noah was as resilient as a lacrosse ball and he would figure out a way to survive even if it meant giving up his new freezer. He could always sell "country meat" if it came to that; though if the Mountie caught you doing it, you might well go off to jail. One thing he did know was that whatever he had to do, he would stay in Baleena where he belonged. He would never again go away looking for work.

Noah had only been away from the coast once in his life. At the beginning of the Second World War, when the United States Navy was building a base at Argentia, hundreds of men and boys, most of them either too old or too young to join the British forces, flocked to the base looking for work. Noah was fifteen years old in the winter of 1942 when he boarded a steamer, seeking the chance to work for cash instead of for credit.

Noah's upbringing had been far from luxurious, but nothing in his background had seemed to him as harsh and inhuman as the conditions encountered in Argentia. There the men worked outdoors ten hours a day, seven days a week, all through the winter. They slept in overcrowded bunkhouses that were often without heat. They lined up outdoors for breakfast in the pitch dark of six o'clock in the morning. After huddling for half an hour against the wind and the cold, they pushed their way into the cookhouse to engage in an insane scramble to grab a mug and a plate and a spoon. There was never enough cutlery and there was never enough food either. The men shoved to reach the counter to get hard biscuits, bread, molasses and tea—to sustain them until the midday meal. Dinner and supper were depressingly alike—baloney and beans. Noah had figured out how to eat these without a knife or fork. He held his hand in front of him and showed us how you could slide all the beans onto the slice of baloney, then fold it over like a sandwich. That way you could get it down in a hurry and try to fill up on bread and jam, if there was any left on the table.

After three months of concentration-camp conditions, Noah quit the job and came home. His first experience with the industrial world was also his last. At fifteen, he already knew that life in Baleena was preferable to the kind of life people lived in places like Argentia. Poor he would always be, but at least he would be in a place he belonged. He would never shiver in a lineup for baloney again—not even if the fish plant closed forever, a possibility the seemed to accept.

"One of these times," he prophesied, his eyes narrowing, "if Mr. Drake gits too high and mighty, the people could pile in together and wash right over him like a spring tide. Leave him high and dry as a beached whale. 'Twill be a dark day if we comes to it, but all the same I can sniff it in the wind."

Seventeen

IRIS FINLEY was the sole registered nurse at the hospital when, one day, a nurse's aide found her on the floor of her sitting room. She had apparently been unconscious for several hours. Dr. Billings admitted her to the one private room in the hospital, and once she regained consciousness he began a long series of tests. Until the results were conclusive he prescribed total rest. I went to visit her one evening a few days after her collapse.

Propped up in bed, she was without any of her usual energy and cheerfulness. She was pale but managed a wan smile as I came in. It was incongruous to see her sick in bed, a woman who spent her life caring for others. She spoke in a flat, sad voice and was vague about why she was there. She said she had been having dizzy spells. Perhaps it was heart trouble. It ran in her family. But the cardiac tests indicated nothing irregular, and heart disease was an unlikely complaint in a woman who was not yet forty.

I had brought her a couple of novels to read, but there was already a stack of books beside her bed. Victor Moss had brought them around earlier in the day. "Was that no kind of him?" she asked me with a trace of spirit in her voice. And then she was silent again. I couldn't reach her.

I tried telling her some inconsequential local news and gossip, but she seemed uninterested. In desperation I tried telling her about the research Farley and I were doing on the early Viking voyages to Newfoundland and Labrador, but that didn't bring any response either. Finally the aide came around with the nightly ginger ale and biscuits, but Iris refused them both. She had lost her appetite, she stated. When visiting hours were over, I was relieved.

At the hospital door I stopped to button my coat against the autumn gale. Just then Roger Billings emerged from his office, also donning his coat. Jane, out for a walk with one of their dogs, was outside the door waiting for him.

"Come over for a nightcap," she suggested.

"Yes, do that. Fortify yourself for the trek back home," echoed Roger.

It was easy to be seduced by the prospect of a warm fire and a drink on that cold night, particularly after the depressing visit I'd just had with Iris. I was also curious to know if Roger had diagnosed her condition.

"Mmmmmmm," he said, stroking his chin and settling into his favourite wing chair, "could be quite a number of things. We'll have to wait and see. The tests have been sent to the lab in St. John's, but they do take a dog's age coming back."

We were interrupted by one of their servant girls, who brought a message about a sick child. There was a man waiting at their kitchen door to take the doctor over to Hann's Island to have a look at him. Roger finished his drink and left.

"Those tests won't make a particle of difference," Jane said as soon as he was gone. "This whole thing's been going on far too long. It's time someone called a halt."

Unsure of what she was talking about but not wanting to pry, I only looked concerned and let her go on talking.

"In the long run it won't do anyone any good. And it will look very bad in the eyes of the community, although they may know all about it already. A poor example, I would say. It's quite clear Iris is the one who has to be on her way. Obviously they can't let Victor go."

"Iris leaving?"

"The sooner the better. Perhaps it's only a harmless little flirtation, but what if she and Victor decide to do some foolhardy thing—run off somewhere together? What sort of mess would that leave everyone in?"

I was stunned. I didn't believe that anything other than a chummy sort of friendship existed between Iris and Victor. Iris was a friend to almost everyone. And in a less overt way, so was Victor. But Jane's revelation did help explain a few things—in particular the enduring nostalgia Iris had for Jersey Island. It was easy to imagine a love affair developing when she was the district nurse there. I somehow hadn't made the connection that once Victor had been transferred to the plant in Baleena, it had only been a couple of months before Iris also made the move. But it still didn't explain why Iris was in the hospital looking like death warmed over.

"Poor Iris, she must be very upset," I sighed. "Very, very upset," I added, fishing for more details, "to contemplate leaving here."

"Upset. Of course. All we need to do is look at what took place this week."

"This week?"

"This overdose."

"Overdose?" I repeated quietly, nearly speechless.

"You might guess she'd look for some melodramatic solution," Jane continued. "One more reason she should be working somewhere else. Roger had no choice but to let the Department of Health know."

"About the overdose?"

"That too, of course. And about this . . . this grand passion for Victor. Freeman found it necessary to speak with Roger about it months ago. After all, Victor is very valuable. Good managers don't turn up every day. If men of that age get the idea they're in love, well, their judgement isn't always what it ought to be. Something had to be done. But we needn't worry about Iris. There are jobs aplenty for nurses. She should be in a bigger hospital anyway, with more supervision."

"But she was always such a worker . . . I mean, all those years . . ."

"Yes, yes. She's a worker. And she'll find work somewhere else. Jolly good thing Roger got to her when he did. Another hour or two . . ."

I had to get out of that house. I gulped my drink and got to my feet, protesting that I'd better be getting home in case the wind got any stronger.

All the way home I thought about the sad plight of Iris and Victor. If they loved each other, how many people knew about it? Would Glynnis know? Probably not. She had contact with so few people. They were all lonely— Victor, Glynnis and Iris.

I couldn't believe that Iris had really wanted to die. She had always been so full of vitality. And it wasn't going to be easy to start her life all over again far away from everyone she cared about.

A week later Iris was discharged as a patient and she moved back upstairs to her old room in the staff quarters. She resumed work on a temporary basis because the Department of Health couldn't find anyone to replace her immediately. They had given her notice of dismissal on the grounds of "stress" due to ten years in isolated postings. However, they had promised that she would be highly recommended to one of the hospitals in St. John's. But she hated St. John's—the source of all those stuck-up nurses who had never stayed in Baleena for more than a few grudging weeks. To have to work alongside them in the city was the last thing she wanted to do.

At first Iris spent a lot of time staring out of the window, but eventually her spirits seemed to pick up. For one thing, Christmas was coming, and she decided she would finish knitting the four sweaters she had begun for the four Drake daughters—the same design for each, but in different colours. And as soon as Freeman and Barbara and their retinue returned for the winter, Iris gravitated back to the fold. She had been longing for the return of their lively household with its children and dogs and visitors and parties.

Like all harassed mothers during the month of December, Barbara had plenty of things the loyal Iris could do. One of them was to take charge of a three-month-old puppy who was temporarily being housed in an equipment shed near the plant wharf. The dog, an English setter, was a surprise Christmas gift to Freeman—a mate for his prized dog, Hunter. Iris loved dogs as much as she loved children, and taking the puppy for an evening walk was no hardship for her. It was good for her to get out on her own. She had already given the dog the temporary name of Queenie, after the dog she had had as a child. Several times she arrived at our house with the impish puppy tugging on a leash. Queenie dozed by the fire, and Iris talked about herself.

In one breath she told us she was going back to Scotland, that her mother was growing old and needed her. And in the next, that she was going to work among the Eskimos. She didn't mention Victor Moss, except for including both Victor and Glynnis among the roster of her friends. She now clung to her friends with the persistence of someone waging a campaign, and perhaps she was. Several times she hinted that her grateful patients might be getting up a petition to send to the province to insist that she be reinstated in her job.

Reverend Matthew Way spent some time trying to persuade her that life in St. John's could be very fulfilling. There were all sorts of activities there for single people (he didn't say lonely people). There were recreation centres where people could take part in sports and games, and there were evening courses at Memorial University in any subject that you cared to name. But it was all cold comfort. She couldn't bear to go.

Farley and I abandoned the typewriter and the drawing board a few days before Christmas. Our work still wasn't finished, but we couldn't carry on with such solitary tasks at this sociable time of the year. We relaxed and enjoyed it. I did some baking—fruit cake and cookies—while Farley hiked into the woods along with Doug McEachern to bring home a Christmas tree. There must have been a million spruce trees to choose from, but it was still a challenge to find one that was symmetrical, one that didn't have all the branches missing on the side that faced the wind.

Every year on December 24 Freeman Drake sent a case of liquor to the plant office. By then the draggers were tied up at the wharf, and the plant was shut down. As the men and women came by for their final pay packets of the year, they were invited into the small building that housed the filing cabinets and typewriters, and there they were offered "a drop of Christmas cheer." The women rarely stayed to take part in this unceremonious ceremony, but most of the men happily downed their small "drop" under the eye of the management. Victor Moss was assigned the job of bartender, carefully pouring out the rum, keeping score to see that no one got more than two. Meanwhile, Freeman and Barbara shook hands with each worker and wished him or her a merry Christmas.

"Good for morale," was the way Freeman put it. "Our people like to know that we appreciate them."

Obi Kendal didn't stay for a Christmas drink. He collected his wages and then joined Effie to shop for some gifts. It wasn't until he was paying for them that he found the note in his wage envelope. It read: "Commencing December 24th your employment with Baleena Fish Products is terminated."

He didn't show it to Effie. Not then. He suddenly realized that he should have bought more modest gifts, though. He clenched his teeth in quiet rage. Now what was he to do? Go back to the Great Lakes—be away from home eight months of the year? Maybe he should move his family away to some place in Ontario where there was work. But how would that be for Effie? She was shy with strangers. She would be lonely in one of those big places. She wasn't like those mainland women who went out to work somewhere and came home to give their husbands a meal of store bread and baloney. How would his children grow up in one of those cities—confined in a little yard like a flock of hens, never knowing their grandparents or their uncles, or the names of their neighbours.

He decided then and there that he would stay. He could live on his Unemployment Insurance for a few months.

That would give him time, lots of time now, to talk to people, to persuade them that they weren't totally beholden to the plant, as so many of them believed. He had the whole winter ahead of him.

He put his arm around Effie, and with their heads bent against the wind they walked home in the last glimmer of December twilight.

Eighteen

IN JANUARY, THE MONTH WHEN WHALES could be seen just off shore, the pond between the church and the school froze to Formica smoothness. Iris was often out there lacing up the skates of one of the Drakes' little daughters who, like most Baleena children that winter, were learning to skate. We waved at each other as I struggled by en route to my art class, laden with cumbersome things like net floats and Chianti bottles and pottery bowls for my students to draw.

By then I was enjoying my classes. I had finally taught my students to measure with their eyes, not their rulers. A few of them showed real promise. One girl and one boy, in particular, could draw almost as well as I could once I had weaned them away from their geometrical methods. A handful of others came close to them in ability, then there were the inevitable one or two who simply couldn't draw a line which resembled anything anyone could identify.

"How high is the rim of the bowl compared to the height of the bottle?" I asked. "How wide is the bowl compared to the basket behind it? How much of the table cloth can you see?" These were the words of my instructors at the Ontario College of Art and they miraculously came back to me when I needed them.

Originally I had been bewildered by my students' reluctance to ask questions or to ask for help, but I had come to understand that this was a matter of style, not a lack of interest. They did not leap to their feet to ask questions, nor did they jump up to answer them. In school, as at home, they took care not to humiliate one another with a display of superior knowledge. I was never quite sure whether this was because it wouldn't have been tolerated—a punch in the nose after school perhaps—or whether it was simply the way they lived their lives. Whatever the reason, the dubious merits of the competitive spirit, which had been so strongly empha-sized in my own schooling, were blessedly lacking here.

At least they had been until that winter. It was unusually cold and, with so much ice everywhere, Reverend Matthew Way decided it was a heaven-sent opportunity to teach the local boys to play hockey. Canada's "national" game was virtually unknown among most outport children, who, in that innocent era before television, had not watched other people assaulting each other hour after hour. Matthew had gone to a lot of trouble to round up enough pairs of skates, and had sent away to Cornerbrook for hockey sticks and pucks.

Nothing stands still, I had to remind myself, but I had mixed feelings about the introduction of competitive team sports to people who had been getting along nicely without them. Though I've heard a lot of rationalizations, I've yet to grasp what positive result comes from one group of people pitting themselves against another group for the express purpose of "winning." Winning what? The perverse satisfaction of humiliating someone else? It was the absence of the competitive spirit which kept my art students from speaking up in class in vainglorious demonstrations. They kept their triumphs to themselves, as well as their failures.

Matthew Way, our proponent of organized Christianity, had probably never questioned the virtues of athletic competition, and by the end of the winter he had organized a hockey team in Jersey Island as well as Baleena. By the following winter there were scheduled hockey matches between the teams of these two neighbouring outports.

He had not been so successful, however, with the young men of Rosey River. Not one person there owned a pair of skates, nor was there a patch of level ground that could have been used for even a small hockey rink. They seemed to like it that way. The "River" people remained obstinately uncompetitive, not only with the rest of the coast but with the rest of the world.

The absence of the competitive spirit also prevailed among the merchants of Baleena. Obtaining art supplies was a perennial difficulty for our class. The school had no budget for these so we could only use materials that the students could afford to buy themselves. Early in the school year I had asked Hann Brothers, the largest merchant of school supplies, to order several dozen drawing pencils. Since they had by then already sent their fall order, they waited to send in the pencil order in January after stock-taking. And then, as they explained unapologetically, somehow the January order hadn't been sent away until February. By March there still wasn't any sign of the drawing pencils. I gave up in frustration. I knew that none of the other shopkeepers would have moved any faster. Instead, I rummaged through my own art supplies and found enough tag ends of drawing pencils to supply the class.

Only once was one of my lessons a total failure. I had asked the class to design a cover for a record album. The fictitious title I gave them was "The Folk Songs of _____," leaving the nationality unstated so they could exercise some free choice. I recommended that they go to the library and look through books or magazines for pictures of whatever country they fancied.

Not one of them came to the next class with any reference material. Searching for that kind of information beyond the range of school textbooks was something with which they were totally unfamiliar. I would have been smarter, I realized later, to have brought the magazines and books to the classroom with me and introduced the research procedure there.

Although I had no qualifications to do it, I wished I could have taught them English composition too. The last remnants of an oral culture were still alive in Baleena then, while almost everywhere else in Canada the avalanche of television shows, recorded music and movies was radically altering the perceptions of most children. Some outport children, as well as adults, still composed their own songs and stories, narratives that were intended to be listened to by their families and friends.

I do believe that there are aptitudes which abound in some races of people more than others. Just as there are disproportionate numbers of Italians who can sing, Russians who can dance and Dutchmen who can paint, so it is that there are a large number of Newfoundlanders who can adroitly string words together in poetry and song. But any encouragement of these skills was totally missing from their school curriculum. It may have been just as well. The gloomy atmosphere of the classroom might have destroyed the gift.

When the news came that Doug and Marjorie McEachern were going to be transferred, I was crestfallen. I would soon be without my closest friends, since Iris would have to leave before long. The McEacherns were going to Grand Falls, where Doug would be joining a six-man police unit. It was a pulp and paper town, a company town in the interior of the province, a two-day journey from Baleena. It was connected to the rest of the province by a road, a railroad and television. There was a curling rink, a movie theatre and dances on Saturday night at the Legion. But it was miles from the sea—far from the long walks on the beach that the four of us had enjoyed so much; far from the abundance of lobsters and fresh fish.

For a policeman it also meant a distinct change of pace as he re-entered the orbit of traffic violations and a working day spent inside a car. Doug stoically accepted the news of his transfer, inevitable after his three-year posting here. Going where you were sent was part of the commitment he had made when he joined the Force. Marjorie had had to accept that too, though she was far from enthusiastic about making the move.

"Jolly well time," said Jane Billings when she heard the news. She had regarded Doug as a policeman who didn't make enough arrests. She far preferred his predecessor, a young man who made a practice of lurking whenever a wedding took place so that he could ferret out the source of the elusive "alky" that spread through the outport like twitchgrass on festive occasions.

The departure of the Mountie's wife (or the wife of any official who had come from "away") meant a farewell party given by the women.

"Surprise, my dear," Nellie Dollimount almost whispered to me over the telephone. "She's not to know so's we all got togither. We'll call her and ask her round like 'twas some other reason."

241

"I won't tell her a thing," I promised.

The Dollimount house, painted robin's egg blue, stood close by the government wharf. It was an ideal location for Billy, who, as the wharfinger. had to meet ships at all hours of the day or night. Nellie took pride in her house, which was resplendent with the newest furnishings that the mail-order catalogues had to offer. Billy was a federal civil servant, after all, and his salary was well above most of the other families in Baleena. They had more money to spend on the frills of life than we did in those days.

Nellie directed me to the bedroom where damp coats were piled over a turquoise-blue bedspread. A Kewpie doll, wearing a hand-crocheted ball gown, presided over the room. I combed my hair, refreshed my lipstick and then followed Nellie down the hall.

The living room was packed with women. There was the postmaster's wife, Mrs. Hoddinott, and Mrs. Stuckless and Mrs. Northcotte, women I knew from the library board. And Thelma Way, the clergyman's wife, along with the wives of the fishery officer, the plant accountant and the school principal. Iris Finley was there, as well as her replacement, Joan Noseworthy, who had recently arrived from St. John's.

Strangely enough, Iris was the one who tried to spark some light-hearted commentary as we sat silently in a circle around the living room. Nobody responded beyond a few strained smiles. Although I had talked with some of the women at library meetings, once we were removed from that preordained setting, they seemed to have nothing to say to me. Nor to each other.

I found it painful to sit there in silence. A lifetime habit of filling the void with small talk was so ingrained that I felt

I somehow had to be mildly entertaining to other people. But in that situation my effort at conversation was producing no reaction. I dropped some casual remarks— how surprised Marjorie was going to be, how sorry I was to see her leave, how wet the spring had been, how late the steamer had been last week. But no one picked up the conversational ball. I felt like an actor with a frozen audience. Apart from Iris, I was the only one there who felt the need to act. However, we did listen to an endless recitation from Mrs. Pardy, who told us every word her two-year-old son had said before she left the house that evening. But when she finished, no one seemed to have anything to add.

It was after nine when Nellie went to phone Marjorie and ask her to come over on the pretext of wanting her advice about making draperies. When she returned to the sitting room, she was all of a twitter. Marjorie had declined the invitation! Doug was out with the patrol boat looking for a man who had been reported missing. Marjorie felt she should stay by the police radio in case some new information arrived.

This news should have been the death knell of the party, but it brought it to life instead.

"Who's gone missing?" asked Thelma Way.

"Tsk. 'Tis Elias," Nellie grumbled.

"Hmmmph," snorted Mrs. Stuckless.

"Pitiful," clucked Mrs. Northcotte.

"Foolishness," said Mrs. Hoddinott.

"Foolishness sendin' after him right now," echoed Nellie.

I was surprised by the chorus of unsympathetic remarks regarding the disappearance of the unfortunate Elias, but at least something had brought these women to life. Elias Baxter, I soon learned from the conversation, was well known for going off in his dory gunning for birds and not getting back by nightfall. He always neglected to take along enough fuel for his old engine and he was renowned for getting lost. Twenty-eight years old, he was unmarried and still lived with his mother, and from the way they talked about him it was clear they regarded him as simple-minded and irresponsible, a nuisance rather than a menace. It appeared that he was inadvertently going to spoil our surprise party.

Iris finally rose to the occasion and said we couldn't sit there all night. We decided that a group of us would walk around to the detachment and tell Marjorie openly that we were having a party in her honour and to find someone else to listen to the radio. I was the first to go, and we did indeed persuade a genuinely surprised Marjorie to return to the party with us.

By then it was nearly eleven o'clock and I expected the evening lunch to be served, but I was wrong. Card tables appeared as if from nowhere and the women formed groups of fours.

I must explain that I do not, nay cannot, play cards. Just as there are people who cannot carry a tune, I do not have that portion of the brain which remembers numbers and symbols and can select them as required. So, having suffered through the mute constraint of the first half of the party, the second half proved to be even worse. Instead of passive endurance, I was now being called on to do something I simply couldn't do.

I was alone with my handicap. Evidently the only people in Newfoundland who didn't play cards were those who had a fundamentalist religious prohibition against it.

From the beginning it was obvious to the women that I was an incompetent blunderer. I even had difficulty holding thirteen cards in my hands. Whenever I tried to sort them out, I dropped some in my lap and the others could see what I had been dealt. Although they patiently explained the rules of the game to me, I still couldn't make an intelligent choice. When my turn came to shuffle and deal, my shame was complete. I'm sure Mr. Hoddinott could have sorted the entire week's mail more quickly than I could deal four hands of cards.

The women played with lightning dexterity, their practised hands skimming over the cards, rejecting some, rearranging others. Nellie, who had stayed out of the game in order to assemble the refreshments, continuously peered over my shoulder and selected the correct cards for me, to hurry the game along. I was humiliated and bored and felt close to tears.

When it was finally over, prizes were awarded. There was a first prize, a second prize and a dummy prize. Yes, I got the dummy prize—a glass ashtray which read "Souvenir of Baleena, Newfoundland."

When the food was served I found I had made a social blunder. Everyone except Marjorie had baked something for the party. Nellie hadn't mentioned this when she invited me. It was, like the card game, just one more thing that everyone knew. Everyone except me.

Iris left the party early, pleading a headache. Everyone else stayed until after two in the morning. We all departed together and walked along the road in a tight cluster. When we arrived at the point where the road forked, I said a cheery good night to the other women and headed for Dog Cove.

"Blessed Lord, you're not walkin' out the road all be yer ownself?" asked Mrs. Northcotte.

"You got nobody to go wit' ya, my dear girl?" asked Mrs. Stuckless.

There was a chorus of protest against my walking a mere mile or so alone at night. Mrs. Hoddinott offered to wake up her brother who lived nearby and get him to take me home in his truck. Mrs. Stuckless suggested I stay the night at her house. They were appalled when I insisted that I liked to walk and wasn't afraid of the dark.

Thus, fearless as a snake charmer, I set off along the road. A half-moon illuminated the pockmarked surface of the road. There were no lights in any of the houses, and for once the windows had no eyes. The square houses and their shadows formed a checkerboard of grey, black and purple. A sleeping dog on a doorstep opened one eye and observed me, but didn't bother to bark. Beyond the houses the sea was still and black. A bright pathway of moonlight led to the horizon. It was all so incredibly beautiful. Like no other place on earth.

Nineteen

I WASN'T ASKED TO ANY MORE card parties. Perhaps they wrote me off as being a bit dim—in the same camp as Elias, who was found safe and sound the following day, drifting in his dory in the middle of a barasway.

However, I was beginning to feel more at home among the women of Dog Cove. They had come to accept my presence in their midst—an oddity, like some bird who had flown off course. I would never be one of them, but at least they were no longer intimidated by our differences.

In the spring Melita and Dan Quayle Junior's fifth child was born. It had been six years since there was a baby in their family. There was a flurry of visitors as soon as Melita and the baby came home from the hospital. They named the baby Daniel (Danny) after both his father and his grandfather.

Grandfathers, fathers and uncles were often honoured by having a baby named after them. Jackie, their first son, had been named for his great-grandfather (the deceased John Quayle, who was thereafter known as *poor* grandfather John). Leroy, their next boy, had been named after Melita's father. But only boys were expected to live up to the merits of some relative. In Baleena, girls' names came from other sources—some whim, like the beauty of a flower, the rarity of a jewel or the glamour of a movie star.

Lizzie Quayle, the new baby's grandmother, moved busily back and forth between her house and her son's house every day. Through all her life there had never been a time when she hadn't been tending to the needs of children. I could only marvel at her endurance, a woman of fifty-three who still had seven daughters and one son at home, which was only half of the family she had raised. As a young bride, Lizzie knew what was expected of her: Be fruitful and multiply. It was a legacy from the days when nameless diseases took the lives of so many children, childbirth took the lives of many women, and the sea took so many men and boys. I used to wonder if she ever agonized over those sixteen pregnancies and deliveries and all the hazards that she had survived.

Would she had preferred a life like mine with its interminable schooling, the shifting locations and the impossible goals that my parents and teachers had set? And a late marriage, with no children? I'm sure she wouldn't have traded places with me for all the world.

Lizzie and Dan Senior's sixteen children did them proud. Hard-working, thrifty people, they had grasped life's realities at an early age. Only one of them didn't quite fit the family mould, and that was Charlie. He looked much like the others—a shorter, slightly heavier version of his older brother, Dan Junior. He lived in a small, shabby house at the other end of Dog Cove, a house whose salmon-pink paint was peeling like a sunburn. He was the rebellious Quayle, the only member of that family to have taken part in the abortive strike in 1958. Since then, Charlie had been unable to find a steady job in Baleena.

Because his father was foreman of the packing room at the fish plant and a town councillor as well, Charlie's radical activities kept the two of them at arm's length. For a year or more Charlie and Blanche and their two children had existed on welfare, a situation that was not discussed. Whenever his parents, brothers or sisters stopped by, they sidestepped any talk of wages or plant politics. They discussed the weather, family births, illnesses or deaths.

The Quayles were not fishermen. As a young man, Dan Senior had gone to sea as a crew member on various ships, and it wasn't until he was in his forties that he found steady work at the plant and stayed ashore. So none of his four sons had ever mastered the knack of dory fishing—a skill that is usually passed on from father to son.

Ezra Rose, on the other hand, had fished for sixty years and both his sons learned to fish with him, but they had moved away early in their lives and never returned. Ezra knew where the fish were, he often bragged—he could smell them! But he was in his mid-seventies and he also knew that he was too old to fish alone, that he needed a younger man in the dory with him. I suspect he understood the aimlessness of Charlie Quayle's life; and that was how Charlie—in his thirties and long past the usual age of apprenticeship—learned the craft from an old master.

Once Ezra had slapped the annual coat of dory buff on his dory the two of them fished nearly every day And for the first time in years, Charlie felt good about his life and optimistic about his future. He was able to tell the welfare officer that he no longer needed the dole.

Charlie's best buddy was Obi Kendal. Their wives, Effie and Blanche, were sisters, and often the four of them passed an evening in each other's kitchen. While the women chatted about their children, the men discussed the situation at the plant and talked about the day when the workers there would get a better deal. Eventually, the two of them resolved to try and bring a union in. No one else understood so well how much it was needed. No one else would take the risk.

One night they arrived unannounced at our house.

"P'r'aps we could get your help, sir," they asked Farley. "We wants to get a line on a union what would come in here from away."

"Damn well time," said Farley. "It's the only thing that will ever break the stranglehold the plant has on this place. Downright feudal, if you ask me. Look, I don't know much about unions, but I can find out. Leave it with me and I'll do what I can," Farley concluded, picking up the challenge.

Our friendship with the Drakes had fallen into a no-man's land of unresolved differences. We rarely got together socially anymore, but we couldn't avoid seeing them within the confines of that closed community. We often encountered one or another of them along the road, in the shops or the post office, or at meetings of the library board. We were learning what the Baleena people already knew about social amity. We had to maintain a measure of accord even with those people who did not share our views.

The next westbound coast boat carried several letters of inquiry to food workers' unions. But it was the season when ice filled the Cabot Straits and the ferry from Newfoundland to Nova Scotia sometimes took several days to make the crossing. Mail bags destined for our coast waited on the wharf at North Sydney for an additional week. Apart from the telegraph and the still-unreliable telephone system, we were inaccessible to the rest of the world.

We waited and waited but when the reply arrived, none of the unions sounded interested in having so small a jewel in its crown as the fish plant workers of Baleena in distant

Newfoundland. It would be uneconomical, they explained, to send a man there to organize the workers.

"Damn it, there has to be a way to get someone to come here," Farley told Obi in frustration. "You fellows can't launch the thing on your own."

"Over in Canada they don't know we're here 'tall," Obi conceded.

"We're not going to give up. Times are changing. People here are changing too," Farley said encouragingly.

"Well, bye, I been tellin' the facts of it all winter long, and with some of our people it's harder than catchin' mackerel in a cod trap," said Charlie. "Still and all, there's a nice few that's ready to sign on, could we get a skipper to man the wheelhouse."

Twenty

WHEN WE DID ENCOUNTER Freeman or Barbara that season, the only safe topic of conversation was the anguish of our mutual friend, Iris Finley.

"I simply don't understand her," Barbara said one night when a group of us had volunteered to paste envelopes in the back of library books. "She's had all kinds of job offers. There was one from the Indian Health Service in Saskatchewan, and another good one from some place in Manitoba. And of course there's a public health job in St. John's any time she wants it. She just won't make up her mind. Won't come to a decision."

Mrs. Stuckless and Mrs. Hoddinott listened in attentive silence. It was generally understood by the community that Iris was being "transferred" by the Department of Health but that she didn't want to go.

"We've done everything we can for her. And she's no closer to accepting the situation," Barbara continued crisply. "We even told her she could take Queenie along when she leaves—she's so attached to that dog. But even that doesn't help."

Though the plant workers were smouldering with discontent, one small corner of our community was improving by leaps and bounds. It was the library. All the new books that we had bought and begged had subsequently resulted in more readers. Our circulation jumped by 300 per cent in one year. And that meant that our provincial grant of money increased at the same rate. The majority of our new book borrowers were children, but that was where we had intended to concentrate our efforts anyway. Eventually, Mr. Pardy had grudgingly allowed his students to come over to the library on a scheduled basis during school hours once a month. In fact, Mr. Pardy himself had even borrowed a few books. And Iris Finley had set aside a shelf in the hospital where library books could be available for patients.

When I phoned Iris at the hospital, an aide told me she was asleep. I left a message but she didn't call back. I phoned every day for three days and finally she came to the telephone. She sounded vague and depressed. She said she would come up to see us "sometime" but wouldn't commit herself to a specific date. I tried to think of something to say that would cheer her up and I promised to drop in to see her next time I was near the hospital. But, as it happened, I didn't leave the house for a week.

Farley and I were swamped with work. The deadline for the manuscript was closing in. As well as drawing all the maps, I also had to type the final draft to make it readable. Farley is a slipshod typist at best, and his handwriting is even worse. So while dishes stood unwashed, bedclothes unchanged and the floor unswept, we worked diligently through a week of oblique spring rain which twice turned to snow.

As I worked I envisaged those unsung immigrants from Iceland and Greenland trying to survive in this new land. Cold and wet they must surely have been, but compared to the less fruitful earth of Greenland, in Newfoundland they would have found abundant game, good grazing for cattle and enough firewood to last forever. Historians and archeologists have deduced only the barest facts about the day-to-day existence of those plucky people who crossed the icy seas a thousand years ago. It had been absorbing to try to unravel the mysteries of Viking times, but we were bone weary from the effort. Farley was also disillusioned with his barbaric heroes, who had a nasty habit of slaughtering the native people of the new land, as well as each other, whenever a dispute arose. We both desperately wanted to get the manuscript off to the publisher and be done with the thing.

Throughout that week we had only one visitor, though he appeared several times. Ezra Rose always came calling in the worst weather. When the wind howled and sheets of grey rain swept over the land and the sea was too stormy for fishing, I could expect to hear his feet stomping on our doormat. When he had nothing to do but look out the window at passing dogs and small children, he headed our way. Where else could he find a house where the man was at home in the middle of the morning, a man who didn't work like other men but engaged in some foolishness, forever clicking out words on a typewriter?

Busy as we were, we would stop and take a tea break with Ezra. He didn't stay long, just long enough to tell us the news about our own world or else that other world that he heard about over the radio.

"Don't pay them to have no holderday away," he proclaimed on a blustery Monday. "Just git therselves killed." It was Easter Monday and he had been listening to the morning news, a regional radio broadcast compiled in Halifax which announced the number of people killed in highway accidents in the Atlantic provinces during the long weekend. This was puzzling news for someone who had always lived without automobiles. For Ezra, and everyone else there, a holiday was a day on which you didn't work— like Picnic Day (May 24) or Bonfire Night (Guy Fawkes Night, on November 5) or Christmas. What were the strange ways of people in distant Nova Scotia or New Brunswick that caused them so much death on holidays? He didn't associate our few lumbering trucks or even Fred Fudge's new taxi with death. Children, adults, dogs and sheep could still safely wander the bumpy roads of Baleena.

Ezra told us about the load of bricks that had arrived on a special freighter. They were for the construction of a new post office, the first such structure ever built in Baleena. In the 1960s the government was showering the nation with new post offices, a statement of the strengthening federal presence in a thousand small Canadian towns.

Later in the week Ezra dropped in again, this time complaining about the tardiness of the coast boat. Although he never travelled anywhere aboard it himself, he always made a mental note of her arrival time. The west-bound boat had been three days late. The world must be in a sorry state, he declared indignantly, when people had to wait so long for the boat. Nurse Finley would be late wherever she was going.

"Nurse Finley? Iris?"

"Yis, I seen her gettin' aboard."

"Where was she going?"

"Look t'me she was gittin' clear altogither. Suitcases and parcels all with 'er. Gone fer good I'd say."

"And she didn't even say goodbye to us," I said, surprised and sad.

"Niver sayed goodbye to I neither, though I called out to her," said Ezra,

So Iris had left unheralded, without even so much as a card party to wish her Godspeed. Doug and Marjorie, who left a week later, were hurt that she hadn't said goodbye to them. She hadn't given any of us a forwarding address. Not even the Drakes. who were away at a fisheries conference in England that week, had any idea where Iris had gone. She had not gone to work in St. John's. Roger Billings discovered that much.

There was considerable speculation as to why Iris had left so suddenly with no word of her destination, but not even the hospital janitor who helped carry all her luggage to the wharf had any idea, and if Victor Moss knew, he wasn't saying.

Two months later, in early June, Iris was dead. She died in a small town in northern Manitoba, where she had taken her own life. She had been working there as a district nurse to the native people in the region. Her body was found by a co-worker after she failed to show up for work. Death was due to a self-inflicted injection of some kind of barbiturate. A good nurse to the end, she knew exactly how much was needed to kill herself. She left a note, though none of her friends in Baleena ever knew what it said.

The community to which she had given so much seemed curiously silent. It was difficult to eulogize her passing. Barbara and Freeman talked only of the manner of her death. Roger Billings quoted some textbook statistics about suicides in general. The Drake children were not told that Iris had taken her life. They believed a virus was the cause of her death.

Victor Moss decided to go away for a while. He hadn't had a holiday in fifteen years, he said. He was going to take

Glynnis back to Wales for a visit. It seemed she had scarcely been out of the house for as many years.

In Dog Cove our neighbours responded to the news about Iris as a time of mourning for us. The usual parade of callers dwindled. Only Dorothy Quayle came over to see us, and she came alone, leaving her ebullient brother Leroy and her giggly sister Susie at home. She was still hoping to become a nurse, but she had to weigh some new evidence. Iris had been her idol. How could anyone who had achieved so much want to die?

It was a double blow for us to lose the McEacherns and Iris in the same season. We began to recognize a peculiar limitation of life in such a place as this. Though we made close friends, they didn't stay. The new nurse was totally unlike Iris. Cheerless and complaining, her main goal appeared to be to leave as soon as she could. And the new Mountie, a bachelor, proved to be just as glum. The Billings were still around, and from time to time so were the Drakes, but they were cold comfort.

The ambience was as grey and chill as the fog on the June evening we waited on the wharf for the stately old *Baccalieu*. We had decided we must get away for a time, and so were going on a holiday to the mainland—that nether region west of the ferry terminal at Port-aux-Basques which, to Newfoundlanders, is all the rest of Canada.

Twenty-One

"HEAR'D YOU WAS GOIN' AWAY, CLARA," said Minnie Joseph, who had emerged, cat-like, through the fog as we waited on the wharf.

"Just a holiday, Minnie," I said. "We'll be back in a few weeks. Going to visit our families. And some friends."

"My dear, I was wondering if you was to be handy to Toronto?"

"Yes, we will."

"Our Mary's gone off to Toronto. Left old Christmas Day. And don't I miss her. 'Twould be some nice if you'd pay her a visit. I got her address. Wrote out on this paper." She retrieved it from her pocket.

"Of course, Minnie. I'd be glad to."

By the time the ship departed, it was close to midnight. All night long the foghorn sounded mournfully. We reached Port-aux-Basques at eight in the morning, just in time to transfer to the ferry *William Carson*. The fog thinned during the six-hour voyage to Nova Scotia, and it was clear enough when we reached Sydney airport to see the Air Canada Vanguard coming in to land. This was the milk run, a tiresome flight that stopped in seven cities before finally completing its fragmented journey to Toronto in the middle of the night. But it was the only "direct" flight between the Atlantic provinces and central Canada. We disembarked weary and dishevelled but triumphant at our good fortune in having made the journey from Baleena to Toronto in only twenty-nine hours. In less favourable weather it could have taken three or four days.

It was about two o'clock in the morning as we crossed the tarmac to the nearly deserted terminal building. The heat enveloped us like a wet towel. The daytime temperature had been ninety degrees and in the still night air it hadn't cooled down much. Yes, this was southern Ontario, where peaches and grapes and tomatoes and tobacco grew, where trees reached the height of totem poles, where you didn't need a coat in summertime. And this was Toronto, where we merely gathered our luggage and walked away, never bothering to look for a familiar face in the crowd. As we were whisked away in a taxi, I wondered how a stranger could survive in this nighttime tangle of cars, highways and unfriendly human beings. We drove at forty miles an hour— slow by modern yardsticks but four times faster than I was used to moving. Again I had the sensation of travelling at breakneck speed.

As we sped along, the sight of the backyards abutting the highway rivetted my attention as they never had before. Blossoming trees, green lawns, pansies and marigolds had never seemed remarkable to me. Garden furniture, bird-baths and children's wading pools—the humdrum artifacts of city dwellers—were scattered about. It was so unlike the scene I had just left. I tried to imagine how it would appear to someone arriving in Ontario for the first time, to one of my neighbours from Dog Cove, those same people who found no novelty in the sight of fishing boats or wharves, and had been amused that I wanted to take pictures of them. What would they think of the endless reaches of split-level bungalows with their smug front lawns? Would they be enchanted by four-lane highways humming with speeding cars even in the middle of the night?

For a few weeks we became part of urban life again. We watched movies in air-conditioned theatres where the chairs had backs. We watched television. We both went to a dentist and had our teeth repaired. I bought some new clothes. I had my hair cut. I meandered through intriguing shops, by then renamed "boutiques," full of merchandise from India, Denmark and Italy—places that I thought were exotic. We ate meals in Greek and Hungarian restaurants. I observed the parade of students and shoppers ambling along Bloor Street. Toronto was no longer the dreary class-conscious matron she had been during my student days a decade before. I soaked up the city until I was satiated.

Just the same, it wasn't long before I grew bored with it all. I began to think about what was happening back at home. There were so many people there whose everyday lives had become part of mine. Did Dorothy pass her year at school? Were Ezra and Charlie catching lots of fish? Did Aunt Til plant her potato garden same as always? How were the Pointing children getting along? I yearned to see them all—dogs, children and grandmothers. I even began to miss the fog.

When I went to see Minnie Joseph's daughter, I had to travel to the west end of the city where I had never been before. A plain sad street of tired houses and grassless front yards, a street saved from desolation only by the big trees that had been growing there since the turn of the century. It was a far cry from the marigold-bordered lawns of suburbia.

Aunt Ida, the lady with whom Mary and her friend Doris lived, occupied the second floor of a narrow three-storey brick house. It had originally been designed for one family but had probably housed three or four for the previous fifty years.

I climbed a sagging stairway and traversed a dim hall. Then crossing a threshold, I was transported into an outport kitchen. Aunt Ida had managed to recreate the kind of kitchen in which she must have grown up. An electric stove held centre stage, in the manner of an outport wood range. The rest of the room revolved around it. There was a big wooden table painted blue, surrounded by four chairs. A worn congoleum mat covered the floor. Aging lace curtains, now out of fashion even in Baleena, obscured the view of an equally despairing house next door. The walls were painted canary yellow and the only adornments were two calendars—one from a Newfoundland grocery store whose proprietor was named Gosse, and another from a nearby Salvation Army citadel. One had a picture of a farm with immaculate children and tidy fences and fat cows—the same pastoral scene that Matilda Rose hung in her kitchen back home. The other calendar bore a sad-faced picture of Jesus. There was one other decoration—a faded, hand-tinted photograph of Aunt Ida's father which had been taken in a seaport in Portugal before the First World War.

Aunt Ida had done what I had done in reverse. I had gone off to live in Baleena with my books, pottery ashtrays, rattan furniture and hand-loomed place mats—even the inevitable Dundee marmalade jar full of pencils. While I was organizing my chamber music records, Aunt Ida was arranging plastic roses in a vase that bore a picture of Niagara Falls.

"Come in, my dear, sit down now," she welcomed me with a friendly smile. "Some nice you could run up and see us."

In her sixties or seventies, she was small and frail, with grey hair pulled back in a little knot. She had trouble with her feet. Everything about her bore the signs of wear, everything except her hazel eyes, which had the same twinkle as those of Ezra Rose.

Ida and I sat down by the kitchen table on wooden chairs with pressed designs on the back. Mary and Doris came into the room and lingered awkwardly in the doorway. After a time they sat down on the sagging daybed, that familiar piece of kitchen furniture. Mary smiled but didn't say anything. Neither Aunt Ida nor Mary bothered to introduce me to Doris Riggs, a Baleena girl I'd never met. All our positions were oddly reversed. Where I had so often stood uncertainly in the doorways and kitchens of Baleena, Mary and Doris waited with equal unease in a room in Toronto that was a loving replica of Newfoundland.

Mary, who was seventeen, looked a little bolder than she had back home. She wore lipstick and a red nylon blouse and purple stretchy slacks that were held taut by an elastic strap under each foot. She was a pretty girl, short and light like her father. She might have been a dancer or a gymnast if she had grown up in another place in another time. Doris, who was nineteen, was much larger. The signs were there that she would eventually be very plump. Her dimpled smile showed poor teeth and the beginnings of a double chin. Her hair was teased into a stiff, lacquered bouffant.

After my initial questions about their jobs or how they liked Toronto, they didn't have anything to say. Fortunately Aunt Ida filled the vacuum, chatting about the one place we all knew—Baleena. She talked about her father's schooner, the *Sophie and Ida*, and told us all about the time she and her sister had stowed away on board to get to Jersey Island to see her sister's boyfriend.

"Me poor father was riled, he was, to have two maids so idle as we!" She shook with laughter, while Mary and Doris looked on with indulgent smiles that bespoke their having heard the story often. Ida had nothing to say about the years since she left Baleena, but it was easy enough to see that nothing very fortunate had happened.

That day I borrowed my brother's car, an aging Morris Minor, to take the girls on a tour of the city. They were surprised that I had somehow acquired a car and impressed that I knew how to drive.

It wasn't until after I had parked in a vast lot downtown, just south of St. James' Cathedral, that Mary relaxed a little and began to tell me about the previous six months.

They had left Baleena after Christmas with one suitcase each and the money they had been able to save from their wages after a year's work in the fish plant. In stormy January it had taken them two days to reach Nova Scotia, where they had boarded the first of a series of buses that eventually got them to Toronto. They hadn't calculated that the bus trip would take three uncomfortable days and nights. It had cost them more money for food than they had reckoned. When they reached that most unwelcoming structure, the Dundas Street bus terminal in Toronto, someone helped them get a taxi. They were only able to tell the driver the name of the street on which Ida Buffet lived. They hadn't realized the importance of numbers on houses. Back home everyone knew who lived in every house. It would have been silly to affix numbers to them, as silly as giving numbers to the people themselves. The taxi driver must have been a saintly man, for he drove up and down the street asking at various houses if anyone knew of Ida Buffet. Luckily, someone did.

From that day on they had only been to two places in Toronto. Every morning they took the streetcar to the toy factory where they both worked. Then at night they rode the same streetcar back to Aunt Ida's, where they ate supper and watched television afterwards. The only other place they went to was the Salvation Army citadel which Ida attended on Sunday nights.

Their existence struck me as being so bleak that I couldn't imagine what was keeping them there. Why didn't they run, kicking and screaming, for the train or the bus to North Sydney, the ferry to Port-aux-Basques, and the coast boat to Baleena? The poorest people there had a better life. Even Rosie Pointing had more fun—forever trailing around somewhere with her kids. While I had spent my time in theatres, restaurants and art galleries amid the company of friends and family, Mary and Doris had only seen the inside of a factory and the view from the Queen Street car.

Enthusiastically I began telling them about Toronto Island, then about High Park, Riverdale Zoo, Edwards Gardens—all the places of my own girlhood expeditions— but I might as well have been describing the rivers of China. They had no idea where those places were or how to get to them. They hadn't even dared to venture into the depths of the Toronto subway.

We wandered into the venerable interior of St. James' Cathedral, a sanctuary of nineteenth-century tranquillity. It was cool inside and someone was practising a Bach prelude on the organ. It was so unlike the austere interior of St. Peter's Church back in Baleena that they both found it hard to believe that this was also an Anglican church.

After we left the church, I decided to leave the car in the parking lot and walk, in the hope that they would learn how to get around by themselves. We meandered up to the corner of Queen and Yonge and gazed at those master-pieces of the display artist's craft—the Yonge Street windows of Eaton's and Simpsons. Snooty store dummies in elegant clothes stared into the distance from their impeccable surroundings—a sight which thrilled Mary and Doris far more than the dusty interior of the cathedral.

"Jumpins, I'd like to have them pants fer meself," said Doris, admiring the pencil-slim slacks on a mannequin.

"My dear, lookit t'rug on the floor!" exclaimed Mary. "All big and soft, it is. Me mom would like to have that home. Just like in the catalogue."

Later we walked down to the Bank of Commerce building on King Street. Once the tallest in the Common-wealth, it was rapidly being upstaged by the ascending construction of the Toronto Dominion Bank next door. We took the elevator to the thirty-first floor to see the view.

"My Gawd, 'tis a wallow of wind!" Doris shouted in delight as we walked out on the terrace, her stiff hairdo lifting in the breeze.

Mary pulled her cardigan around as her long hair whipped about her face.

"Big blow comin'!" she called into the wind. The wind, that familiar force, had captured their attention more completely than did the view of the city below us.

We looked down at Toronto Island, a flat, manicured little garden of a place, and I explained that they could take a boat and go there for a visit. But I knew it would be a pallid imitation of the summer days when they had rowed a boat to Outer Island or Offer Island, as all Baleena children did. I myself loved those long-abandoned islands, where you could find bits of broken china, fanciful stove doors and rotting newel posts. Only the gulls and the larks greeted visitors there now.

Maybe I was the only one who had been entranced by the unseen presence of the ancestors on their forgotten islands. Had Mary or Doris ever been aware of them? Perhaps they would see the muddy archipelago of Toronto Island as a paradise of civilized pleasure, with its formal flower beds and fountains, threadbare grass and overflowing garbage buckets. Beautiful and tantalizing just because it was here, at the centre, in fabled Toronto.

It was painful to consider what they had left behind and what they might find here as a replacement. Toronto seemed lonelier and more remote to me that day than it ever had in the years I lived there. When I was about the same age as the girls, I had helped in a downtown community centre, a place that existed to comfort new arrivals like Mary and Doris, and lonely people like Aunt Ida. We had harboured the illusion that we were bringing something into their lives that they had lost—a sense of community. But until that day on top of the bank building, I hadn't truly understood the Toronto of the disinherited. How could they ever feel they belonged here?

We moved around the city and looked at other things— at Queen's Park with its flower beds and statues and the imposing Ontario Legislature Building. We took a ride on the subway, while I explained how to get through a turnstile, and how to jump aboard the train so that the door didn't catch your heels.

At the end of the day I drove them out to my brother's for supper—to a modest two-bedroom bungalow in East York. As we drove up Donlands Avenue, both girls noticed the lawn ornaments in front of the houses—the flamingoes and gnomes and black-faced footmen. They liked them. And they liked my brother's house. He was a technician and his wife a school teacher, and while their house was furnished comfortably, it was not what I would have described as luxurious. But it did have rugs on the floor and big upholstered chairs and framed pictures on the walls.

Late in the evening I drove them back to Aunt Ida's flat. "I'll see your families just as soon as I get back to Baleena," I promised. "Next week, for sure. They'll be glad to know how well you're getting along here."

I knew that was the message they wanted me to carry, and also the message their parents wanted to hear.

Twenty-Two

FOG—THE CURSE of the coastal summer—had shrouded us when we left in June and it shrouded us as we returned in July. This perverse weather obscured the sun during the brief season when it was at its warmest. We often saw more sunshine in the month of March.

The *Taverner*, a brand-new coast boat and the first one to be built in Canada, was packed with people. Most were tourists who came during the brief summer and occupied the best accommodation, to the discomfort of the local travellers. Eager to see the spectacular landscape, they were sometimes destined to spend the entire six days of the journey blindly enveloped in mist, listening to the throaty blare of the ship's horn. The clanging of unseen bell buoys, the screaming of invisible gulls and the great rocks looming through the murk would tell them they had arrived somewhere.

They weren't your average holiday tourists, these people who had turned their back on sunshine and comfort to make their way along this coast. They had surely undertaken a bit of research to find out about it. The Canadian National Railways did not advertise this service. Few Canadians or Americans knew very much about public transportation within the province of Newfoundland. It was just before the provincial Department of Tourism began to publicize their island as being full of quaint, friendly folk who wanted the world to come and see them in their happy state. It was before Newfoundland became, for the spiritual counterculture, Canada's Katmandu.

The coast boats provided service without frills. There was no entertainment, and no alcohol was available. Passengers travelling alone were usually required to share their cabin with two or three strangers of the same sex. The meals were copious but plain. Yet few tourists went home disappointed. They were fascinated and curious about what they saw. "What do people do here for a living? Is the weather this bad all the time? Are there doctors or hospitals? Are there schools? Really, no television at all? And what is the name again of that fish dish we had at breakfast?"

It was only a few years since I'd been asking questions like these myself. Now I was answering them, telling people from Scarsdale or Scarborough which port we would call at next and pointing out, with insider's knowledge, that if the wind stayed in the southeast we might not be calling at Grand Anse but would proceed directly to Baleena.

At supper we sat beside a young man from a city in Pennsylvania who was going to Grand Anse to spend an entire year. He was an anthropologist and was being sent there by the new Department of Anthropological and Sociological Studies at Memorial University. Grand Anse, he explained, was sufficiently isolated yet close enough to the mainstream of Canadian life for his purpose. He particularly intended to study the "Guest-Host Relationship" and "Work Patterns in the Extended Family."

"You'd better be diplomatic about finding out all this," Farley advised him.

He waved away the advice. "I plan to be perfectly open about everything I'm doing. I'm going to tell them I'm a social anthropologist, nothing more, nothing less."

"Well, people around here don't take too kindly to strangers asking a lot of nosy questions, despite your professional interest in them. And it won't be very clear to them just what an anthropologist does," Farley said.

"Believe me," he said confidently, "I know how to make the approaches. We study that in our courses."

The ship was scheduled to reach Baleena around nine in the evening and I stood on the deck in the opaque twilight, knowing minute by minute exactly where we were. The familiar note of the Seal Island bell buoy clanged in the slow ocean swell. The foghorn wailed loudly from the misty cliff high above our heads.

"Seven minutes," I said to the man leaning on the rail next to me. He was a tall, loose-limbed fellow who told me he was from California. "We'll be alongside the wharf in seven minutes," I repeated. And we were. I felt appropriately smug.

The wharf was packed with people on this Saturday evening. A few were there to board the ship or to meet incoming passengers, but most were drawn to the wharf to watch the world arrive at their doorstep.

"We must have the Queen on board," the Californian said to me when he beheld the crowd through the haze. Scores of faces stared up expectantly at the ship.

"Nothing special," I told him nonchalantly. "People just come down to see what's going on."

But, to be honest, even after five years in Newfoundland, I found the whole climactic moment of the ship's arrival as intriguing as he did. I had certainly never returned to Toronto to find such a sense of welcome. This was the kind of welcome which had been reserved for winners of the Stanley Cup. Here it was offered to anyone. Whoever you were, you didn't go unnoticed.

Dan Quayle Junior was on the wharf as always, waiting to load up his dory. His youngest brother, Aubrey, the only unmarried one, was there too, smartly dressed and carrying a suitcase.

"Headin' off fer Sudbury," Dan said of his eighteen-year-old brother and a young friend who was going along to chance it too. "All kinds of jobs when you gits there is what they say."

Among the crowd I noticed Edith and Maizie Pointing, both of them in smart new raincoats, bright lipstick and curly home permanents. They weren't going anywhere, they said, just passing the time. I stopped to talk to a couple of students who had been in my art class, and they told me that they had passed their art exam with high marks and were planning to stay in high school for an extra year so that they would graduate. I even waved a hello to our new Mountie—the solemn Corporal Fraser, who nodded in return. He looked stern, as if he were on the lookout for criminals.

We piled our luggage on top of Dan's doryload of groceries, and we all took off for Dog Cove. As ever, the cove children, the older men and all the local dogs were milling about in the dusk to see us come back. Their welcome was not overt. It was enough that they were there. They made the dory fast and carried the freight. The children vied with each other to see who would carry our bags, who would be first to tell everyone that, yes, Mr. and Mrs. Mowat were back, they had seen it for themselves. Dan had been over to our house that day to light the stove. Dorothy had carefully stacked up our accumulated mail on the kitchen counter.

"Glad you come back," she said. "Yer house was right dark while you was gone." She followed us into the kitchen, with Jackie and Susie and Leroy behind her. They watched with interest as we went through the procedure of settling in again—taking food out of the freezer to thaw, adjusting the hot-water heater and generally putting things where they belonged. After a while their father. having put the new stock in the shop for another week, came over for a visit and shooed the younger children home to bed. Only Dorothy was allowed to stay. She had brought over the typing lessons I had given her to work on while I was away.

"You missed the big carry-on," Dan said, bursting to tell us the news.

"What's been going on?"

"Wonderful big trouble down the plant last week. The whole cuttin' room walked out. Hung up their knives, cleared off altogether. Then 'twas no time 'til the packin' room had to quit besides 'count of no fillets to pack. They reckoned fifty ton of fish rotted on the plant wharf."

"This was bound to come," said Farley, taking in the news.

"Should have known they was up to something. Waited 'til Mr. Moss was gone on his holderday away and then Mr. Drake and his missus had left to go after salmon up the river. When he got word, Mr. Drake got a helicopter to fetch him back here quick. Fine quintal of fish he found when he got here. Nary a soul left workin', 'cept Gus Barnes, the watchman, lookin' out to the machinery. Mr. Drake niver suspected this was in the wind else he would have stayed home."

"So what's happened now? Are they calling it a strike?" Farley asked.

"Yes, sir, and they say they won't go back 'til they git a proper union started up, and then git more money and all them other things they gits away what they don't git here. Holerdays with pay 'n all. But you can bet your last penny that'll be slower than the Second Coming. That Freeman Drake is stubborner 'n a crackie dog. Already says how he's goin' to close the plant, move off somewhere else. I say we're in for hard times around here. That's t'truth of it. Already folks are scared to spend a dollar."

The plight of the workers, whose lot Dan Quayle Junior had shared in North Sydney, no longer roused his sympathy. His concern was that they would not be spending much money at his shop. Dan, our faithful neighbour and friend for so long, was veering into the opposite camp.

I hardly knew what to say to him. There was a squirming silence. Farley started to fidget and got up to look for his tobacco and pipe.

I turned my attention to Dorothy instead. For about a year I had been teaching her to type. She had been intrigued by the sound of our two typewriters pounding through the house every day and wanted to learn how to type too. Farley gave her his old portable on which to practise. She could only come for a lesson when she wasn't in school or minding baby Danny or the shop, which didn't leave much spare time in her life.

Farley and I both admired her work, several tidy pages of *fgf jhj ftf jyj*.

I praised her work. Considering that she had to do her typing practice in bed at night with her younger sister Susie trying to sleep beside her, her efforts deserved every encouragement.

"That's a bright girl you've got there, Dan," Farley said. "She could do anything she set her mind to—go to university, study nursing, anything at all."

Dan snorted at the mention of university. "Dorothy's the oldest," he said unemotionally. "Got to help in shop. Jackie's no good fer it, he's bashful. 'Sides, don't make no sense fer a girl to go gettin' education. What good is that when it comes to raisin' up a crowd of youngsters?"

I couldn't believe that anyone was still asking that worn-out old question, but I had to remember that for Dan it was a new question. Memorial University in St. John's had opened only a few years earlier. and prior to that, going away to study in either Canada or Britain had been a possibility only for the wealthy.

I wanted to argue with Dan that night, but I'm glad I didn't. In retrospect, he had a valid point of view. Was it really going to make Dorothy a happier or a better person to send her off to a university six hundred miles away in a city neither of her parents had ever seen? She would be an exile during her best marrying years, doomed either to spinsterhood or to marrying someone from elsewhere and turning her back on her home forever. I also had the disturbing example of Mary Joseph and Doris Riggs to consider.

I told Dorothy about my visit to Mary and Doris in their new "home." I didn't say much about the way they lived there, except that they were staying with Aunt Ida Buffet and had both found jobs. I did add that Mary missed home and talked of coming back to Baleena.

"Hmmmph. Foolishness comin' back here now," said Dan. "Plant closed down like it is. Better off stayin' where they's to. Mary's father won't be havin' no easy time of it neither. Noah niver went off to Rosey River with Mr. Drake this year."

"Well, it's an ill wind that doesn't blow somebody some good," I said to Dorothy, hoping to lighten the mood. "Summer's here and with Ruth out on strike the two of you will have time for some fun. Go off to the beach with a picnic. Or maybe row out to Offer Island. Just like old times."

Dorothy looked at the floor, then glanced sideways at her father.

"Ruth's gettin' married," she said finally. "August."

"Married?" I repeated. "Well . . . how nice. I always love a wedding. Who's the lucky man?"

"Cecil Tibbo."

The name meant nothing to me.

"I don't say you knows him. He most always went off to the Lakes. But this year he niver went. Bided home, worked down the plant for a while . . ."

Dan Quayle Junior didn't add anything. His sister Ruth had just turned sixteen. We all knew, though no one was saying so, that Ruth was pregnant. She would be a mother by Christmas, and her husband would be out of work so long as the strike continued.

I felt the jolt of the passing years at the thought of Ruth becoming a wife and mother. Her early marriage shouldn't have surprised me since most of her sisters had married in their teens. Yet it had only been a year since Dorothy and Ruth were school girls, giggling with secrets as they sat in my kitchen. It dawned on me that there was no adolescence here. The awesome transition from child to adult, which everywhere else in the western world seems to last forever, was almost non-existent.

As the weeks of an unusually drizzling summer passed, people took sides. The company they kept was carefully selected. Talk was guarded and speculation flourished among the men in the stages and the stores, and among the women in the kitchens. It was common knowledge that Obi Kendal and Charlie Quayle were the instigators, but it wasn't quite so clear who their allies were. However, it hadn't gone unnoticed that a dozen or more young men who usually went away to work on the Lakes had stayed home. They had gone to work at the plant, earning far less than they would have made if they had gone away. I still wonder what motivated them to do it. Was it the chance to get even with the merchant, to finally settle an old score?

Every day Freeman Drake was faced with the economic reality that there were fish in the sea which the fishermen were catching, but there were no workers in the plant in Baleena to process the catch. He had diverted his draggers to his closest plant at Jersey Island, but there were again rumblings of trouble there too. In mid-summer he gave all those workers a raise; five cents more an hour for the women, and seven cents for the men.

Freeman refused to speak with anyone claiming to represent a union. He denied that the union existed. He seemed bewildered that the people of Baleena could be so ungrateful after all he had done in bringing them a modern fish-processing plant in which to work, not to mention all his efforts as mayor. Wasn't he trying to turn this backward place into a modern town? All those tiresome meetings and letters and phone calls on behalf of council business, and this was the thanks he got!

Meanwhile, he and Barbara pursued their summer diversions. The whole family went riding, and the Billings frequently went with them. It was a formidable sight to see them, dressed in English riding clothes, as they clippety-clopped their way through the community. When they passed our house at Dog Cove, they didn't call out a greeting. On sunny days they played croquet on their lawn, a patch of greenery which had originally been imported, sod by sod, from Prince Edward Island. And they sped off aboard the *Sir Francis Drake* for picnics at the beach whenever the weather permitted it.

Dan Quayle Senior, who had recently supervised thirty women in the packing room, passed the summer at home in Dog Cove, where he painted his house and pondered his dilemma. His tenth daughter, Ruth, was about to be married to a young man who was known to be a union supporter. His third son, Charlie, was a principal organizer of the strike. But his oldest son, Dan Junior, was opposed to the union and the strike and he hadn't spoken a word to Charlie for months. His second son, Clarence, who ordinarily worked as a cutter at the plant, wouldn't say which side he was on. And his married daughters—Lucy, Clara, Ernestine, Annie, Robina, Alma, Dora, Eva and Muriel— were also keeping quiet about which side they or their husbands were supporting. How could they celebrate a wedding with the family so divided? Who would come? Who would bake and help clean up afterwards? Lizzie Quayle, who was about to be the mother of the bride for the tenth time, didn't know which ones to ask.

They decided they would have to forsake the parish hall and the crepe paper and the handwritten invitations. Ruth and Cecil would marry in the church, but afterwards they would return home for a small supper with the family members who chose to come. Other people in Baleena might mutter in disapproval over such parsimony, but times had changed. There had been fights outside the hall that summer whenever a crowd got together. There were now two Mounties in Baleena. and one of them was usually patrolling the weddings. If Cecil's union friends got a drop to drink and met the sons and sons-in-law who opposed the strike, there was no saying what might happen.

Dan couldn't help concluding that it would have been so much simpler if only Cecil Tibbo had gone back to the Lakes last spring. Still, he had to admit he liked the boy. He had a civil way about him. He was known to be a hard worker, and word had it that he had done all right on the Lake ships, moving up from deckhand to fourth engineer in three seasons. How could it be that he was one of those strikers?

On the day of the wedding, the fog moved off shore like a great theatre curtain, letting enough sunshine filter through so that it felt like a summer day. Ruth looked radiant, wearing the same long bridal dress that her sister Muriel had worn just a year before. Dorothy, her best friend and her niece, was her bridesmaid and wore a frothy dress of turquoise blue.

It was scarcely a small wedding. Just the Quayles and the Tibbos alone formed a sizable crowd—and that was without Dan Junior and Melita as well as two sisters, plus their husbands, who were all boycotting the wedding because of their anti-union feelings. Their numbers filled the kitchen and the parlour and spilled out into the yard. A gaggle of children wove in and out. Every inch of table space was laden with the best china plates piled high with food. Seven of the married sisters had risen to the occasion and baked the gooey squares, the fancy sandwiches and a big, baroque wedding cake. In the parlour the chesterfield was loaded with a mountain of gifts. It turned out to be the way a wedding should be, after all.

Cecil, the groom, who was nineteen, looked totally unlike the rest of the Tibbo family. He was over six feet tall with lanky arms and he had silky fair hair. The Tibbos were all squarely built people with curly hair. It was Ezra Rose—

who knew about these things—who told us that Cecil had been a "love child," an endearing phrase, I thought, for someone who had been born a fairly long time before his mother had married.

Cecil took time to chat with Farley. He didn't talk about the strike. No one did—there was an embargo on the subject for the day. Cecil talked about books and reading. He said that working the watches on an ore carrier had given him a lot of time to himself, so he had taken up reading. He had even read *The Grey Seas Under*, a book about salvage tugs that Farley had written a few years earlier. That was the last thing Farley ever expected to hear at a wedding in Baleena, in Dog Cove, where being an author cut little ice.

"Garlan'! You c'mere 'longside me," Rosie Pointing shrieked at her erring husband, who had arrived at the wedding party already three sheets to the wind.

Garland haunted every wedding and he never bothered to shave or to dress properly for the occasion, as the other men did. He paid scant attention to Rosie, now pregnant for the ninth time, as he strode from room to room like a dog tracking a rabbit. The only drink available, apart from the tea and coffee that Ruth's diligent sisters were pouring, was Cassie wine.

"Lard Jaysus, not fit to'drink!" Garland blurted after downing a tumbler full of the sickly sweet beverage. I knew how he felt. I couldn't drink it either.

Dan Quayle Senior reckoned they had seen the last of Garland and Rosie and their bedraggled children when their house burned down. But here they were, part of the family now—even if distantly—since Cecil was Rosie's nephew.

"That Garland is some idle," Dan Senior sighed.

"He's self-employed," Farley responded, "like I am."

"That's the truth of it. Never worked for anyone but his own self, and not much of that. At least he won't be starting any fights here tonight. Garland don't care a fig if the workers iver go back to the plant."

When the supper was over, Matthew and Thelma Way came back to our house. They tried to attend all the wedding suppers, but that summer they could hardly keep up with them. So many young men were staying home.

Thelma sat in the kitchen while I prepared some tea. Few people had fallen into their roles in life as happily as she had, as a clergyman's wife. She was an even-tempered woman who ran an efficient household and was the mother of four pleasant children. She taught Sunday School and had recently organized a Girls' Auxiliary—a group that taught teenagers about religion and citizenship, nutrition and handi-crafts, the values of the modern world which Thelma was trying to introduce. In the little spare time she had, she was taking a correspondence course for a university degree. She serenely believed that she was doing the right thing, and for that I envied her. But that evening she seemed depressed. She said that it must have been the weather that was getting her down, that the children had been indoors so much. She longed for the first of September, when all four of them would finally be in school.

Matthew was not his usual optimistic self either. The man who had led the people of Rosey River to build a new church, and the people of Jersey Island to build a new parish hall, and had taught the boys of Baleena and Jersey Island to play hockey, this man began to talk about where the Bishop might send him next.

"All this trouble at the plant," said Matthew, sipping his tea, "has disturbed the old ways."

"It's a revolution," Farley said, "in a tightly knit place like this."

"Yes, and it's surprising who's on which side. I get an earful when I go out calling. Old loyalties. Old fears. People still remember the days of the Renoufs and the LeDrews. Some people remember them, in retrospect anyway, as benefactors. They can remember how Mrs. LeDrew used to send soup around to people's homes when someone was sick. And a number of them think of the Drakes as being a continuation of that same . . . same . . ."

"Dynasty?" Farley interjected.

"The same tradition, if you will, of being the *source* of things. The people who made marketing arrangements, procured things from away—the sort of thing that, in the past, the ordinary people felt they didn't know how to do for themselves."

"Even though they had to live like serfs to get them?" Farley asked.

"In spite of that, they still fear the hard times coming back without the merchant being around," Matthew said.

"They're afraid of being without a doctor too," Thelma added. "Dr. Billings hasn't shown any sympathy with the strike, so they figure he's against it and won't look after them if they join the union."

"He bloody well wouldn't dare!" Farley exploded.

"I have the impression," Thelma said confidentially, "that Roger isn't totally opposed to the principle of the strike. Jane's the one who's taking a strong stand."

"His wife," Farley said with a grimace, "should have married a maharaja. Would have suited her down to the ground. Covered with rubies, riding an elephant . . ."

We burst out laughing at the notion of Jane Billings riding an elephant—not so difficult to visualize for those of us who had watched her imperiously riding one of her horses along the pathways of Baleena. Horsemanship. One-upmanship. I thought of all the statues I'd ever seen of kings and emperors sitting astride their noble steeds. Horses and men. Horses and women. Queen Elizabeth trooping the colours.

"Matthew, why the hell do you have to be neutral in this strike?" Farley asked. "You're a clergyman, for God's sake. Not a plant worker. Why aren't you preaching sermons that tell them to get together and stand up for their rights? And get after those Jersey Islanders to unite with their brothers and sisters in Baleena and go on strike too."

"Farley, my son, on the face of it it might look simple, but don't forget I'm the only clergy they've got. There's not another ordained man on the coast. I still have to marry them, bury them, console them, preach the word of God to them. If I come out on one side or the other, the rest are going to steer clear of me and the church. That's just going to break up the community all the more."

"But, dammit, they're not going to stay together anyway if this mess continues. Listen, do you realize why they had so many preachers in the CCF in the West back in the thirties? Because nobody else had the same kind of freedom or commanded the same respect. The farmers were too poor, the teachers had their school boards . . ."

"And I've got the Bishop," Matthew chuckled.

"Look, if you guys don't provide some kind of leadership, some example, then you're finished. Your credibility will be zero," Farley said.

"Well, I have some interesting news that I can almost tell you," Matthew said in a subdued voice. "Just among ourselves now. Someone is coming to lend support here, some leadership. And he is clergy. A Roman. A priest with experience in labour problems in communities like this where people have just the one means of employment and no chance to bargain. He's a Newfoundlander and just the man for the job. Almost an advantage that he's a Roman Catholic coming into this area where he's got no parochial involvement."

"Get him in here fast then," Farley said. "I tried to get a union organizer to come here once, but maybe I was too early. And even if someone had come, they might not have been welcomed at the time. Newfoundlanders never did take kindly to advice from anyone but one of their own."

"We are provincial, I suppose," Matthew said.

"It's more than that. It's a protective mechanism. Who else could understand this place? Look what a bloody mess the Brits made of it when they were running the show."

"It wasn't all bad," Matthew countered. "They did establish some worthwhile things. The cottage hospitals. The railway. The public library system . . ."

"And the dole," Farley interrupted. "That pitiful six cents a day they gave out. They bled the place for two centuries. Took and took without putting much back. Except a bowl of soup when some poor sod got sick."

"Just hang on now," Matthew said patiently. "We'll see some changes sooner than you'd think."

Twenty-Three

THAT FALL THERE WAS A RUN OF COD as big as anyone could remember. The plant was in its fourth month of the strike. The next-nearest plant at Jersey Island couldn't process this bonanza of fish even though everyone worked overtime. But Freeman still had his overhead in Baleena—loans to pay back to the banks and the province as well as the salaries of the management. And all was not well with the management either.

Victor Moss was back from his trip to Britain but he had begun hinting at an early retirement. He and Glynnis intended to open a guest house in a resort town in Wales. And George Cossar, the plant accountant, wanted a transfer to St. John's. He said that the schools there would be better for his children, but the real reason was that the tension was affecting him and his family as much as everyone else. Clearly something had to be done.

One October morning the community was electrified by the news that Baleena Fish Products would reopen—but with a new crew! The workers included the people who had moved in from Wilfred's Harbour three years earlier and were still insecure in their adopted home. And there were people from Rosey River and Grand Anse and beyond who had been persuaded to come to Baleena.

Thus the cutting and packing rooms were staffed again, and the conveyor belts began to move. Dan Quayle Senior went back to take charge of the packing room, but he was glad that his daughters were no longer among the young girls working there. The new workers were hated by the strikers, and Dan feared for their safety. The work moved slowly, but the *Mount Snowdon* was eventually loaded with a cargo of frozen fillets for the trip to Boston.

The strike breakers hadn't anticipated the hostility that greeted them. On windy mornings men who had their own boats discovered that the mooring lines had been cut during the night. Some found that the twine in their lobster traps had been cut to shreds and would take months to repair. If there had been cars in Baleena, I'm sure they would have been found with smashed windshields and scratched paint.

So the scab workers began to drift away, back to their poorer but more friendly outports. By November the work force had dwindled to half a dozen nervous girls and as many apprehensive men; and then Freeman decided he had had enough. He could survive without Baleena Fish Products. All his plants operated with hefty subsidies anyway, in a region so desperate for work that there was no end to the financial help that the province would give to an entrepreneur who provided jobs. What did he stand to lose if he closed this plant? His real assets, after all, were the fishing draggers and the refrigerator ship, and they were conveniently mobile.

Still, it meant abandoning the home that Barbara had taken such pains to furnish and decorate. The stables would be a loss, especially to the children. And it wouldn't be so convenient to use his hunting and fishing cabins without a base in Baleena. And of course he would no longer be the mayor. But his determination not to even consider negoti- ating with the workers outweighed all of this.

Barbara was the first to leave. In early December she and the four little girls, the ever-faithful Edna and the two dogs, three ponies and two horses left for Massachusetts aboard the *Mount Snowdon*. Most of their furniture was shipped as well, and that was when the rumours began to fly thick and fast. Freeman had cried wolf so many times over the years that many people didn't believe he actually would pull out. But when the furniture went, and he resigned as mayor, they knew the game was up.

On the plant bulletin board a small typed notice announced the permanent closure of Baleena Fish Products. It stated that the company would no longer attempt to operate this plant due to the uncooperative attitude of the workers.

Now there was no longer a strike. There was no longer an industry. Freeman Drake had played his ace.

It was a long, cold winter that followed. A "Committee for Action" was formed to seek another industry for Baleena. Led by Matthew Way, it had high hopes for "cottage industries"—knitting, quilting and model boat building. But, at best, these provided only poorly paid part-time work for a few of the women and the older men. They could never become an economic base for the main work force.

Most families were reduced to living on welfare that year. Obi Kendal and Charlie Quayle and their friends were generally being blamed for the hard times. Everyone worried that there would never be paid employment in Baleena again. Some of the younger men began drifting away once more to look for work on the Great Lakes and other mainland destinations. That sense of unity that had made me love Baleena was dissipating. It was replaced by a chill that had nothing to do with the weather.

On a March morning of slate-coloured skies, I glanced out of the kitchen window to catch a glimpse of a man entering our porch, a large figure in the unmistakable uniform of the RCMP. I opened the door with that sinking feeling that accompanies the knowledge that a policeman is waiting on the other side.

"Doug! Doug McEachern!" I shouted in relief. "What on earth are you doing here?"

Farley emerged from his office.

"Hello, you old bastard. What brings you back? Did they demote you? Send you back to the boondocks?"

"Jeez, no. I come in on the plane this morning."

We had heard the float plane circling at dawn and had assumed it was there for a medical emergency. But we were wrong.

"Eight of us come in."

"Eight! Eight police! What the hell's going on?"

"Haven't you heard yet—all the fracas they kicked up here last night?"

"No. What . . . ?"

"They beat down the place. Smashed the company store to hell. The stables all hacked up with axes. All the windows broke in the Drakes' house. And some smartass cut the lines on the *Sir Francis Drake* and let her drift down to the end of The Gut, down where the rocks are. What with that east wind last night—it's smashed to smithereens. You never seen anything like it. I'll bet they done—no exaggeration— a hundred thousand dollars damage. Wait 'til the press gets hold of this one. Keep an ear open for the radio news."

We were flabbergasted that all this had happened just a mile or so from our house and we hadn't heard about it. The old news-bearing network wasn't the same. Ezra Rose, who normally came over with the news of the day, was laid up with arthritis. The Dog Cove children were in school.

Noah and Minnie Joseph, who had often phoned us with the latest information, had had to give up their telephone when they couldn't pay the bill. And Dan Quayle Junior, still harbouring a grudge against the union, no longer meandered into our kitchen for a few moments' chatter. He still spoke to us, but only when we shopped in his store.

"Seems Corporal Fraser got notified in the middle of the night," Doug started to explain as he sat down on the daybed with a cup of tea. "Once he seen what was happening, he got on the radio for reinforcements. The sergeant whistled me in here with the rest, figuring as how I used to be posted here I might identify some of the suspects."

"And can you? I'm not asking you to name names or anything."

"That's the funny thing. Maybe one or two guys I would of named straight off as rowdy when they got a few drinks in 'em, but this is a whole new ball game. Guys I would never of dreamed of. One of them I used to hire every year to help me put a new coat of paint on the detachment. Now we've got him locked in the cell. At least half a dozen guys should be in custody right now, but we got no place to put 'em."

"Things have changed around here. Just the past few months. You'd hardly believe . . ." I began.

"Yeh, I got an earful already. Nothin' but trouble. Fraser's askin' to get transferred. Says he'll take the coast of Labrador even. Anything. Never gets a minute's peace here lately. Don't seem like the same place at all. Jeez. You know what Fraser was doin' just before all this ruckus started last night? He was down at the government wharf tryin' to catch a couple of little hookers in the act. The other constable—Smith—was off duty, sound asleep. Whoever engineered that big bust-up knew for sure that the law was occupied elsewhere."

"Hookers?" I asked.

"Yeh, you know. They do it for money. It's against the law." He smirked at me.

"Sure, Doug, I know what they do. I just didn't think we had . . . I mean . . . here?"

"See, there was this pair of sisters. Fraser had a hunch what they were up to but he couldn't catch them at it. So when the westbound boat got in, maybe one, one-thirty in the morning, Fraser calls the captain on the ship-to-shore. Sure enough, they're down there like always, waiting on the wharf. Hardly anyone else was, what with the wind howlin' and the rain and all. So the captain lets him know that they went on board. Naturally, Fraser hightails it down to the ship P.D.Q. The captain told him where to look."

"How did the captain know?"

"He knows. Fraser found one of them. Didn't even have the door locked. So Fraser hollers at her, 'How much did he give you?' And she says, 'A dollar.' She even showed it to him. Poor kid. Maybe she thought it was like the strike. She was supposed to get more."

"So now what happens? Does she get charged with . . . ?"

"Yup, that one. Her sister must of got tipped off. She was down the gangway and took off up the road before he got around to her. And while this is goin' on, maybe twenty or more guys are over the hill at The Gut waitin' for their chance to smash the place up."

"Doug," I said solemnly, "I know you're not allowed to tell names, but I've got a dreadful feeling I know the girls you're talking about. What's likely to happen to them?"

"Mmm. I dunno. The one Fraser caught'll probably get a year in the Girls' Detention Home in St. John's," Doug said without too much interest. "Lookit, I can't stay." He got up to put his damp coat and hat back on. "We're doing four-hour shifts, standing guard over what's left of Free Drake's property. I gotta get a couple of hours sleep before I get back at it. They dragged me outa bed four o'clock this morning. Anyways, glad I got the chance to say hi to you guys before I get shipped back. Great seein' ya again."

"Doug, tell us how Marjorie is. How's life been treating you both in Grand Falls?" I asked, realizing that we hadn't talked about anything except the local troubles.

"Marjorie is doin' just great. Matter of fact, she was planning to write to you with the big news. She's pregnant. Eight years married and it finally happened."

"Wonderful," I said.

"Sure hope they don't leave me here for long," Doug said as he regarded his mud-spattered boots. "Isn't this just my luck? The one part of police work I don't like—havin' to go in and maintain the peace when there's labour trouble. First thing I ever got when I was posted to Newfoundland— that Woods Workers' strike. And now here I'm stuck with the same darn thing again."

Twenty-Four

AFTER FREEMAN DRAKE LEFT, Jane Billings, formerly the deputy mayor, became the mayor of Baleena. But her small kingdom was not the compliant one that it had once been. She was the captain of a ship with a mutiny. Those who had supported the strike would never again accept the demeaning conditions they had once known. And those who had opposed the strike would never forgive those who had supported it.

Obi Kendal served five months in prison for vandalism. After being paroled, he came home and ran in a municipal by-election and won a seat on the town council. The departure of Victor Moss and George Cossar had left two vacancies. From the outset, Obi volunteered to work with the Committee for Action. There were still fish in the sea. There was an empty fish plant in Baleena and eventually a new operator for it would be found. Good times would come again, he reasoned.

That year Percy Hoddinott retired, just a week before the new brick post office was officially opened. He was succeeded by his son Sydney, an officious young man with neither the gregariousness nor the curiosity of his father. In the new building, which had bright fluorescent lights, a shiny tiled floor and a sign stating that no dogs were allowed, each family had a locked post office box in the vestibule. Unless you needed to buy stamps or send a money order. you could just collect your mail and go home without a word spoken to anyone.

"Makes me feel like a stranger." lamented Dorothy as she laid our mail on the kitchen counter. She was working full-time in the family shop by then, having bowed to her parents' pressure to leave school as soon as she was legally old enough. The walk to the post office to collect her father's mail, our mail and the Roses' was a welcome break from the routine.

She sat down on our daybed, discarding her head scarf and unzippering her jacket. It was June and unexpectedly mild. It had been cold for so long that we had forgotten we would feel warm again.

I glanced at the mail. Six letters (three of them bills), a couple of magazines and Eaton's summer sale catalogue, with the first eight pages full of bathing suits. They didn't sell many of those in Baleena.

Dorothy and Ruth were still good friends, though with Ruth married it wasn't exactly the same. That year Cecil had gone back to the Great Lakes, promising to build a smart new house with one of those big windows when he came back. Meanwhile, Ruth continued to live with her parents and passed her time with the baby, whose name was Wayne. Most mornings, with Wayne clutched against her hip, she wandered over to the shop for a chat with Dorothy and anyone else who might be there. While she bragged that Wayne at six months was already wearing sleepers that were big enough for a baby of eighteen months, Dorothy listened and nodded and dreamed her own dreams. She had been behind that counter for so long it felt as if she knew what all the customers were going to ask for before they opened their mouths. But she was still writing poems.

Her father muttered about the problems of staying in business with the only industry in Baleena closed. Yet with

Unemployment Insurance, Family Allowance and welfare, his business hadn't suffered all that much. Mostly it bothered him to see so many young men—healthy fellows of no more than eighteen or nineteen—taking the dole. In his youth he would have been too proud. "Them times we went to Nickersons in North Sydney, or we went cuttin' wood in Badger, or joined the army," he reminded us. "Gettin' money fer nothing when you're young and fit just leads to trouble."

It shouldn't have surprised me when Dorothy announced one foggy day that she was leaving home.

"Hired me on first of September up to Cornerbrook," she told me, pleased as punch, and showed me the letter from the hospital which had accepted her in their training program for nursing assistants. "Dad's took right on about it, he is. But I'm some happy to be going."

Leroy was beside her, looking sad.

"We'll miss you, Dorothy. And so will Leroy."

"I promise to write every week. Special letter for Leroy as well."

Leroy and I both brightened a little.

"Cornerbrook is a big place. You might find it lonesome there at first."

"Can't wait to see it," she said as if she were going to an exotic city like Venice or Baghdad. "I niver been anyplace away. I don't b'lieve I will git homesick neither," she added thoughtfully. "It's like I been homesick before I went. Don't seem like home anymore. Different than what it was. Me mom says I'm makin' it up in me head and it's foolishness, but I knows it's true all the same."

As it turned out, we left Baleena even before Dorothy did. We had long agonized over the decision, knowing that

Baleena wasn't home for us anymore either. It had turned into a town, a town riddled with all the problems of a collapsed economy and a legacy of ill will.

To make things worse, the nearby outport of Grand Anse was going to be relocated in the fall and two hundred people would be moving in. Strangers, removed from their familiar fishing grounds, only a few of them would be able to start over as inshore fishermen in Baleena. Their coming would only add to the strain that was breaking the neighbourly heart of Baleena.

The long-awaited television transmitter was under construction, and even though any hope of receiving a program was still months away, many families already had a blank-faced television set sitting in the corner of the kitchen.

A team of surveyors had arrived to determine the route for the first ten miles of a road into the barrens that would eventually reach the Trans-Canada Highway.

Whichever way we looked, we could see more and more of this divisive century moving in, moving in on people who weren't as case hardened to it as we were.

So one gorgeous day in August when a west wind had blown away the fog, we prepared to take our little schooner out to sea. We were going to leave the same way we had arrived, on our own ship. The skipper was anxious to get underway. Good weather never lasted long. We charted our course westward.

Three men in a dory were rowing out to our anchorage. Dan Quayle Senior and Dan Quayle Junior and Ezra Rose had come to say goodbye. Nobody made any speeches. They lingered beside us, the dory bobbing with the waves, as they watched Farley try to pull up the anchor. It wouldn't come. The chain was caught around something on the bottom, and neither the yanking nor probing with the boat hook would free it. Finally Farley stripped down to his undershorts and dove into the icy water, quickly prying it free from a tangle of sunken spruce tree roots. The men watched in fear and astonishment. None of them knew how to swim and they wouldn't have dared to do such a thing.

"You'll have a safe voyage, sure," said Dan Senior after Farley had put on dry clothes. "Bad beginning—good ending!"

"We'll miss yas." Ezra said unceremoniously as our boat moved slowly away from theirs. "'Tis always the bad dog ye misses the most!" And they laughed and waved as we moved out through the narrows.

I took the tiller as we headed out into a choppy ocean. Farley was unfurling the sails as I steered around the sunkers, out past the high island that was covered with bakeapples and partridge berries and waving summer grass. I headed resolutely into the sapphire sea. And then I looked back, which no one should do, to catch one last glimpse of the white house which from that day would no longer be our home. And there, on top of the ridge, were all the children, waving and waving. Dorothy with Leroy close beside, Susie holding their baby brother Danny, and Ruth with baby Wayne hugged close. And Jackie, the shy one, as ever a little apart from the others.

I waved back passionately as the tiny figures diminished to the vanishing point. Then I had to look ahead. The sea grew wilder and the salt spray blew steadily in my face, mixing with my tears.